MONEY, MARBLES and CHALK

The Wondrous World of Texas Politics

by
JIMMY BANKS

Texas Publishing Company, Inc.
Austin, Texas

Library of Congress Catalogue Card No. 70-180195

Printed by Steck-Warlick Co., Austin, Texas

To Mom and Dad
who always tried to teach us what
all politicians should realize: if
you do what you think is right,
you'll win in the long run . . .

CONTENTS

Contents

MONEY, MARBLES and CHALK

Chapter 1

SUMMERS OF DISCONTENT

So many people jammed the huge ballroom of the Austin Country Club on July 10, 1971, that waiters carrying trays of glasses filled with champagne frequently found themselves stymied and unable to move. The happy crowd chattered away at typical cocktail party speed, spicing the conversation frequently with juicy political morsels. The well-dressed guests admired a huge wedding cake and raised toasts frequently to Lan Bentsen and his new bride, Nancy Pittman, who had fallen in love the summer before while slaving over a duplicating machine in his father's campaign headquarters.

Suddenly, a murmur of excitement swept through the crowd as a tall, handsome, gray-haired man and his attractive, charming wife appeared. Almost miraculously, as if by some strange form of osmosis, everyone seemed to realize that Secretary of the Treasury and Mrs. John B. Connally had arrived. His magnetic personality permeated the atmosphere and many of the guests immediately began making their way over to greet the popular couple.

Most of them obviously didn't care whether Connally was a Republican or a Democrat, President Richard M. Nixon's chief economic spokesman or one of President Lyndon B. Johnson's closest personal friends, or whether 1972 would find him on a presidential ticket or back in private law practice at Houston. He was "John" and she was "Nellie" and the home folks were happy to see them—and the feeling was mutual.

One old friend greeted Connally and said, "I don't know whether to call you 'Mr. Secretary' or 'Governor' or—"

"It doesn't matter; I'll answer to anything," Connally interrupted, grinning.

"— or 'Mr. President,' " the friend concluded, with a laugh.

"Anything but that!" Connally shot back quickly. "I didn't mean—" The remainder of his disclaimer was submerged beneath another round of greetings. It was just as well, for nothing he might have said would have quieted the speculation that he might become Nixon's running mate in 1972.

Many of those who surged around the Connallys undoubtedly felt that they should greet the Secretary of the Treasury for business reasons. But most were reacting simply to the magical touch possessed by a very few Texans who have, during the past three or four decades, captivated the people of a state rich in history, strong in pride and much more powerful nationally than the Eastern press would ever admit.

Most "foreigners" find it difficult to understand why only a few men have dominated the Texas political scene during recent years but the answer is relatively simple. While most of them have been conservatives, all of them have had dynamic personalities; they have been the type of men who tend to dominate any gathering, to such an extent that—like Connally—when any one of them walks into a crowded room, everyone there suddenly feels his presence.

Party affiliations frequently have been minimized, mainly because Texas voters usually attach less significance to party affiliations than professional Democrats would like to believe. Texans traditionally *are* Democrats—but they also are independent enough to follow any personable, dynamic leader who seems to be talking sense.

They really like to follow their leaders—so long as they respect those leaders.

Lt. Gov. Ben Barnes was fully aware of this fact on Sunday afternoon, June 13, 1971, when a handful of his closest friends and advisers gathered in his State Capitol apartment for an emergency session.

An air of urgency dominated the meeting.

Barnes already had decided to run for governor in 1972 and had planned to make his announcement a few days later. But a *Dallas Morning News* article the day before had declared flatly that Frank Sharp, a Houston promoter enmeshed in a web of political-financial intrigue and scandal, would plead guilty on Monday to minor charges—and then testify against several prominent Texas politicians, including Gov. Preston Smith.

The *News* indicated that Smith and several others probably would be indicted quickly.

Under normal circumstances, this could only be counted as a tremendous "plus" for Barnes since he was not involved in the National Bankers Life-Sharpstown Bank scandal and had been at odds with Smith throughout most of his political career. But circumstances seldom are "normal" in Texas politics and the ever-alert Barnes was determined not to get trapped in a highly unusual situation which might make it appear that he was "jumping on a cripple."

If Smith was going to be indicted on Monday, which seemed at that time a strong possibility, Barnes wanted to be an announced candidate for governor before then.

Some of his friends suggested calling an extraordinary press conference on Sunday evening and announcing his candidacy. Barnes listened carefully to the views expressed by his staff members and closest friends, then decided to wait until Monday to make his announcement. That crucial decision turned out to be another wise one in his long string of political home runs.

Sharp did plead guilty on Monday to charges of making false entries in the books of his Sharpstown State Bank and of selling unregistered stocks. He was placed on probation for three years and fined $5,000—and then granted immunity, by U. S. District Judge John V. Singleton, on all other charges that might arise from the National Bankers Life scandal.

Sharp went straight from the courtroom to the grand jury room but further grand jury action was postponed indefinitely. That made Barnes's announcement place him in the role of challenging an incumbent governor who was still claiming innocence and threatening to run for a third term.

Barnes's decision was a dramatic one but it also was somewhat routine, in the wondrous world of Texas politics—a world in which a candidate's inflection or facial expression on a statewide telecast might well determine an election.

Lloyd M. Bentsen, Jr., obviously bone-tired from 10 months of grueling, statewide campaigning, sat silently in the conference room at Houston's Station KPRC-TV and read the script handed to him a few minutes earlier by George Christian. As Bentsen slowly turned the pages, Christian and several other key campaign aides studied the emotionless face of the candidate.

Their own faces seemed to show more strain than Bentsen's. This was Friday night, Oct. 30, 1970, and they all felt that the outcome of the U. S. Senate race in Texas might well hinge on the climactic 30-minute telecast the Democratic nominee was about to tape for election eve showings on stations throughout the state.

For weeks, the staff members had been bombarded by complaints—mostly from well-meaning friends—that Republican Congressman George Bush was whipping Bentsen badly on television, both in quality and quantity. Bush was saturating the major markets with slick announcements expertly produced by Harry Treleaven, who had gained a national reputation for his TV ads in President Richard Nixon's 1968 campaign. Practically all of Bentsen's few TV spots, by contrast, were simply segments clipped out of live television shows on which he answered questions telephoned in by viewers.

Now, the contrasting television images of the two candidates seemed quite likely to determine the course of Texas politics for a great many years. Bush and Paul W. Eggers, the Republican nominee for governor, were mounting the most determined bids in history to make Texas a genuine, 14-carat, two-party state; and most observers considered the Bentsen-Bush race a toss-up.

The anxiety of the Bentsen staff members had been intensified by a sudden change in plans. Bentsen originally had been scheduled to tape the question-and-answer program the following Sunday morning, after the benefit of a night's sleep. Instead, he had learned just a few hours earlier he would have to do it on Friday night, after a hard day's campaigning, in order to get copies of the tape to stations which had time available on Sunday night but not on Monday night.

Ordinarily, the taping session could simply have been moved up one day, to Saturday. But Bentsen's ambitious Saturday schedule called for a whirlwind, 1,200-mile trip from Houston to Amarillo to Lubbock to Waco to Houston.

None of those present were really thrilled by the idea that what was about to happen in the studio that night might decide the election. That prospect certainly did not appeal to Bentsen.

The affable, mild-mannered businessman finally put the script down, then took off the half-lensed spectacles he uses for reading and put them in his pocket.

"Okay," he muttered, with an air of resignation. "Maybe my mother will watch it. I doubt that anyone else will."

Christian, former press secretary to President Lyndon B. Johnson and the campaign's chief strategy quarterback, grinned. He understood well Bentsen's feeling that 30-minute political programs on television bore most people to death but he felt this one was necessary to sum up the campaign issues and counter President Nixon's all-out support of Bush.

A great many people other than Mrs. Lloyd M. Bentsen, Sr., apparently watched the program. And her son's aggressive, straightforward answers to questions generally drew favorable comments even from observers who had criticized many of his earlier television appearances. Bentsen was angry and upset during the taping but that apparently just made him appear more aggressive than ever.

What happened in that three-hour period at a Houston television station one night may have had a lasting impact on Texas politics—and on the nation's future. It may have been a key factor in Bentsen's 155,334-vote victory (1,226,568 to 1,071,234) over Bush which, coupled with Governor Smith's 158,675-vote defeat of Eggers, shattered a lot of highly optimistic Republican hopes. Last-minute television seemed particularly important in the Senate race because many voters apparently paid little attention to it until the last two weeks—although Bentsen and Bush spent a full six months in mortal but remarkably clean combat.

While most voters may think seriously about politics only for a few weeks every two years or so, the action that makes it possible for a single television appearance—or even for a 10-month campaign—to prove decisive is taking place constantly. It goes on 12 months a year, in "off years" as well as election years. In fact, many statewide campaigns in Texas are won or lost the year before they take place, when vital decisions are made on such important factors as timing and financing. Not necessarily, it should be noted, in that order.

Million-dollar and even multimillion-dollar campaigns frequently are necessary to win hotly-contested races in Texas, a state larger than any European country except the Soviet Union. Since most state officials in Texas serve two-year terms, they usually must devote the odd-numbered years to political strategy and the even-numbered, election years to tactical operations.

Thus, Texas politicians find themselves almost continually making major decisions on the political front—to such an extent that it sometimes seems remarkable that they find any time at all to perform their governmental duties. But attempts to provide four-year terms have been defeated repeatedly, perhaps because the system established in 1876 still furnishes such fascinating year-around entertainment.

It also causes a great deal of consternation among the politicians who make those tormenting, far-reaching, do-or-die decisions. "Exhibit A" in this regard is Barnes, a sandy-haired, handsome young political dynamo whose 1969 decision to seek reelection prompted Bentsen's decision to run against U. S. Senator Ralph W. Yarborough in the Democratic Primary. Bentsen's upset of Yarborough ranks as a classic among Texas campaigns.

Barnes and Bentsen are longtime friends. Had Barnes decided to run against Yarborough, Bentsen undoubtedly would have been helping him in 1970 instead of traveling 100,000 miles and making more than 1,000 speeches in his own behalf.

Barnes discussed candidly the possibility of his running against Yarborough one day in June, 1969, a few days after the Regular Session of the 61st Texas Legislature adjourned. He pondered questions about this as he chewed thoughtfully on bites of sirloin steak in a private dining room at the Forty Acres Club in Austin, while gazing thoughtfully at the University of Texas campus across the street.

A blazing summer sun already was beginning to scorch the landscape—but most politicians were oblivious to that as they contemplated the political blisters popping up in the wake of that tumultuous 140-day legislative session.

Barnes, who had celebrated his thirty-first birthday just two months earlier, emerged from that session with a remarkable reputation as the presiding officer of the Senate—but, for the first time in his fantastic career, with signs of tarnish beginning to encroach upon his glittering image.

He had weathered, apparently well, concentrated sniping from Governor Smith. Generally considered a "moderate conservative," Barnes had pleased the liberals who usually are at war with everyone else in Texas. He had won the respect and support of the 31-member Senate in a fashion which few men ever had done before. His candor and availability had furthered his popularity with the Capitol Press, an influential group of about three dozen Austin correspondents representing the *Associated Press, United Press International* and most of the state's major newspapers.

True, there were scattered critics who claimed that the 6-foot, 3-inch, 220-pound political phenomenon was getting "too big for his britches"—mainly because he had dared defy Governor Smith's budgetary recommendations. More and more, Barnes was becoming the target for veiled insinuations and questioning hints about his quick climb to apparent financial success, even though that rise appeared to be a slow motion affair when compared with his rocket-like political career.

Overall, the friendly, quick-thinking young man apparently had strengthened his position during his first five months as lieutenant governor. He was, both friend and foe admitted, "the hottest political property" in Texas. But he was nearing an important crossroads, with the course he chose likely to make or break not only his own political future but the careers of many others.

What most of the others did not realize was that Barnes also was having severe domestic problems. His charming and attractive wife, Martha, who had worked so hard to help him get elected to the Legislature, did not like living in the goldfish bowl of public office—and she really abhorred the idea of moving to Washington. Ultimately, this proved a major factor in Barnes's surprising decision to seek reelection. That decision was announced in November, shortly before he and his wife agreed upon an uncontested divorce.

On April 15, 1971, Mrs. Barnes married John Noble, an Austin insurance executive. On July 26, 1971, Barnes married the former Mrs. Nancy Sayers, widow of Scott P. Sayers, who had served in the Legislature and later on Connally's gubernatorial staff. Mrs. Sayers, long active in Democratic Party politics, also had been the only woman in history to serve as chairman of the Texas Employment Commission, a post she held for a little more than a year before the term to which Connally had appointed her expired.

Barnes's domestic problems had first come to light at a time when pressure was mounting steadily on him to run against Senator Yarborough, the longtime leader of Texas liberals, in 1970. Some of former President Johnson's close friends pushed that idea. They noted that

State Senator Ralph Hall, left, and Lt. Gov. Ben Barnes confer on strategy during a session of the Texas Senate—with Barnes keeping his big gavel handy.

Yarborough seemed willing to forgive any political foe who happened to be elected President of the United States but that this strange form of reverse amnesty expired simultaneously with his erstwhile foe's lease on the White House. Yarborough fought Johnson bitterly before he became President, supported him for the most part while he was in office and then turned on him again, even though Johnson pulled Yarborough's reelection bid out of the fire in 1964.

Other Barnes advisers insisted that he should run against an old adversary of his own, Governor Smith—a strong believer in the theory that to forgive, even on a temporary basis, those who trespass against you is foolish.

Some of the state's most powerful political figures who were expressing great interest in Barnes were concerned primarily with preventing Washington from trespassing against them in the future, particularly in regard to such matters as the oil depletion allowance.

When President Johnson "came home," they suddenly found themselves without a Texan in the top echelon of the federal government for the first time in nearly half a century. They felt that Barnes, already the biggest vote-getter in Texas history and president of the National Legislative Conference (an organization composed of state legislative leaders from throughout the nation) offered the brightest hope for regaining the type of top-level power which Texans wielded in Washington for so many years before Johnson's retirement made it conspicuous by its absence.

They never dreamed, at this point, that Nixon would appoint former Governor Connally as his Secretary of the Treasury, resident Democrat in the Cabinet, and chief economic spokesman.

Their arguments obviously had hit a nerve with Barnes. He pushed his chair back from the luncheon table, shared by two of his friends, that June day and chewed on a question about the advantages and disadvantages of running for the U. S. Senate.

"The U. S. Senate," he declared, "is where the action is. If a man is going to stay in politics the rest of his life, he ought to go to the Senate as early as he possibly can."

He also expressed concern over the possibility that winning reelection in 1970 might enable Yarborough to gain control of the state's Democratic Party machinery before the 1972 presidential election.

In Barnes's office at that time was a detailed report on a private poll, conducted by a highly-respected firm with an admirable batting average, on his chances for defeating either Yarborough or Smith in their 1970 bids for reelection. It showed that if the elections were being conducted in April of 1969, Barnes would have received 56.5 per cent of the votes in a race against Yarborough. It indicated he would have defeated Smith with 54 per cent of the vote, even though Smith had taken office only three months earlier in a state which traditionally gives its governors at least two 2-year terms.

"Seniority, of course, means a great deal in the U. S. Senate but if I went up there next year, I think I might be able to exert some influence in the 1972 presidential convention," said Barnes. "There might be a possibility that I could consolidate the South and the Southwest, so at least they wouldn't just ride us out of the party—which, right now, is what most of the people in national party leadership roles want to do to us.

"They're mad at Johnson," he declared, "and they're mad at the South and at the attitudes in the South. I think there's a chance, as a result, for me to really do something for my state. Texas needs political influence. We're at the lowest point, I think, in the history of our state— or at least since the turn of the century. I think I have some responsibility, simply because I have the opportunity. . . . ."

Barnes made those statements thoughtfully, then leaned back in his chair and crossed his legs. He looked solemnly for a moment at the pictures of former University of Texas football heroes covering a wall in the Club's "Lettermen's Room," almost as if he were planning to switch the conversation to football.

"Then, too," he added, "every day you stay down here on the state scene you get a scar. You make someone mad. And having to run every two years is a real disadvantage. In Washington, it's a whole new world. You have a six-year term and a U. S. Senator is kind of above the arena of day-to-day political confrontations. Up there, it wouldn't be Smith and Barnes arguing over a one-year or a two-year budget.

"It's just a different political world," he said, "and one that it's much easier to survive in."

Still, some of his best friends were urging him to run either for governor or for reelection. They felt he could win reelection easily in 1970, the governor's office in 1972 and again in 1974 and perhaps a U. S. Senate seat in 1976 (assuming Yarborough would still be there and ready to retire) without ever having a really tough race. Others felt just as strongly he should make his bid for the Senate in 1970, if for no other reason than to lift himself as quickly as possible above the vicious, frequently petty, often ludicrous but always intriguing world of Texas politics on the state level.

The path blazed to the Potomac—all the way to 1600 Pennsylvania Avenue—by earlier Texans obviously was tempting.

It was a path started by Colonel Edwin M. House of Austin, who managed Woodrow Wilson's first presidential campaign and became one of his closest advisers, playing a key role in drafting the Treaty of Versailles. It was trod by John Nance Garner of Uvalde, who once said he "gave up the second most important job in the government for one that didn't amount to a hill of beans" when he moved from Speaker of the House to Vice President. The late Senator Tom Connally, chairman of the Senate's Foreign Relations Committee during World War II and one of those who helped write the United Nations charter, exerted great influence in Washington for many years.

Then came Sam Rayburn of Bonham, who served as Speaker of the U. S. House of Representatives longer than anyone else in history and came close to becoming President himself; Dwight D. Eisenhower, a native of Denison, Texas, who won the state's undying gratitude for restoring its title to the oil-rich tidelands; and finally Johnson, who became the strongest Senate Majority Leader, the most powerful Vice President and one of the most maligned Presidents in history.

By the time President Nixon succeeded Johnson, the two-party system had advanced far enough in Texas for the state to have a highly-respected, second-term Republican Senator, John G. Tower of Wichita Falls, on the scene. Tower threw his diminutive weight and considerable influence behind Nixon long before the 1968 Republican National Convention in Miami Beach; that supposedly put him in a position to furnish Texans an entree to the White House, but Congressman Bush generally was considered to have more influence with President Nixon than did Tower. Bush's appointment as Ambassador to the United Nations, after his defeat by Bentsen, reinforced this belief.

But Texans had been spoiled to the extent that whatever influence Tower and Bush exerted was not enough. Six times during the nine presidential elections stretching from 1932 through 1964, a native Texan had been on the winning ticket: Garner in 1932 and 1936, Eisenhower in 1952 and 1956, Johnson in 1960 and 1964.

Most Texans do not realize how close they came to scoring again in 1968, when Nixon gave serious consideration to both Tower and Bush in picking his running mate. A streak of typical Texas subbornness coupled with apparent blindness on the part of Texas GOP leaders may have kept the state from producing still another vice president.

The Texas delegation to the Republican National Convention, guided by State Chairman Peter O'Donnell, Jr., of Dallas, insisted on "supporting" *both Tower and Bush* instead of lobbying solidly with the Nixon forces for one or the other. When Nixon sought the delegation's recommendation, he was told that both were "fine men." He knew that much, of course, or he would not have been asking. Still, Nixon's search for a young, articulate campaigner who might help counteract the George Wallace movement kept Tower and Bush in the running almost until the end. Eventually, the nationwide "anti-Texas" feeling proved a major factor in eliminating both.

A bitter division among Texas Democrats 24 years earlier probably kept Texas from having another President. The late Mr. Rayburn was high on President Franklin D. Roosevelt's list of prospective running mates in 1944 but was knocked off by factional feuding within the Texas Democratic Party, clearing the way for FDR's eventual selection of Senator Harry S. Truman.

"Cactus Jack" Garner, of course, might have remained in line had not he and Roosevelt split over the third-term issue. Garner retired to Uvalde in 1941, vowing never to cross the Potomac again. And he didn't.

By 1969, Barnes already was being heralded by many—including U. S. Senator Fred Harris of Oklahoma, then chairman of the National Democratic Party—as "the next President of the United States to come from the South or the Southwest." While such flattery undoubtedly pleased Barnes, it probably contributed little to resolving the struggle going on within his own mind over the next step to take on the political ladder.

There was little consolation to be found in the fact that this was a typical summer of discontent among Texas politicians. In addition to Smith's fight with Barnes and House Speaker Gus Mutscher of Brenham over the state budget and new taxes, heat was generated by a leadership battle within the Texas Republican Party, a similar clash in the top ranks of the State AFL-CIO, a visit to Houston by one of U. S. Senator George McGovern's task forces on Democratic Party reform, "emotional attacks" in Congress on the oil industry, and even by some Spanish treasure ships sunk more than 400 years earlier off Padre Island on the Texas Gulf Coast.

By the summer of '71, labor leaders were fighting among themselves again but most of these bones of contention were overshadowed by the allegations that Smith, Mutscher and other high-ranking officials (including Dr. Elmer C. Baum, chairman of the State Democratic Executive Committee) had made quick, fat profits out of loans they received to buy stock in National Bankers Life Insurance Company—at a time when Frank Sharp was anxiously trying to get a couple of banking bills passed by the Legislature.

Smith and Baum admitted that they each made $62,500 out of their deals with Sharp while his two bills were sailing through the Legislature but insisted there was nothing wrong with that, especially since Smith vetoed the bills.

Fat profits also were reaped by Mutscher (who complained that he held his stocks too long and later lost money on the deal), Representatives Tommy Shannon of Fort Worth and W. S. (Bill) Heatly of Paducah, and two Mutscher aides, Rush McGinty and F. C. Schulte.

Even distractions of scandal proportions interfere only slightly with the usual "odd-year" machinations of most Texas politicians. They are forced by the system of two-year terms and early primaries in election years to spend nearly every waking hour of every year campaigning—and the more successful ones probably even dream about political strategy.

Texans demonstrated in 1959, however, that they are willing to change the system when a real "emergency" comes along—such as running one of their U. S. Senators for the presidency. In 1959, the party primaries were moved up from the fourth Saturdays in July and August to the first Saturdays in May and June. That stretches out the major statewide campaigns to nearly a full year, from the filing deadline in early February to the general election in early November.

The change was made strictly for the benefit of Johnson, enabling him to win the Democratic nomination for reelection to the Senate—then tantamount to election—prior to the July, 1960, National Democratic Convention in Los Angeles. This strengthened considerably Johnson's position in his unsuccessful presidential nomination duel with then Senator John F. Kennedy.

Attempts to switch the primaries back to later dates, thus reducing the total campaign time for candidates faced with general election contests, have failed several times because most of the Democratic legislators in Texas never have strong Republican opponents. They like the idea of cutting off possible opposition early in February, then winding up the year's campaigning no later than early June.

This normally makes the summers much more pleasant for incumbents, minimizing political activity, but the blazing-hot summer of 1969 offered more theatrics than do most *election years* in Texas.

On the fringe of the center ring, several politicians other than his prospective opponents "sweated out" Barnes's 1970 decision as much as he did. These included State Senators Ralph Hall of Rockwall, Wayne Connally of Floresville, Charles F. Herring of Austin and Joe Christie of El Paso, all of whom nurtured ambitions to become lieutenant governor.

Hall, a lawyer, rancher and president of the Texas Aluminum Company, decided early that Barnes would run against Yarborough. As a result, he announced in June of 1969 that he intended to run for lieutenant governor as soon as Barnes sought greener pastures—and he immediately began campaigning.

With Barnes running for reelection, Hall decided on Feb. 2, 1970, the last day to file for a place on the primary ballot, that Governor Smith should not get by unopposed. When he tried to run against

Smith, his application and $1,000 filing fee were rejected by Dr. Baum on grounds he was ineligible.

Baum cited a provision of the State Constitution saying that no legislator, during the term for which he was elected, shall be eligible to hold any office created during that term or the emoluments of which have been raised during that term. The Legislature of which Hall was a member had raised the governor's annual salary from $40,000 to $55,000.

Hall and his attorneys took the matter to the Texas Supreme Court, arguing that the technicality involved was not intended to apply to elective offices and particularly not to the office of governor. They succeeded only in spotlighting another of the glaring weaknesses in the 1876 Constitution and Smith became the first governor in history to be unopposed in the Democratic Primary.

Meanwhile, Congressman Bush spent most of 1969 considering a 1970 race against Yarborough, who had defeated him in 1964, never dreaming that the Senator would be defeated in the Democratic Primary. The son of former U. S. Senator Prescott Bush of Connecticut had to weigh his near certainty of reelection and his place on the important House Ways and Means Committee against the possibility of defeat in the Senate race.

Friends of both Bush and Barnes, hoping to keep them from winding up in a race against each other, kept reminding them of how much they had in common—not only in philosophy, despite their different party affiliations, but also in dynamic, youthful images and in early success which promised enormous potential for the future.

Ironically, Bush wound up losing to Bentsen—with whom he had much more in common.

The pending decisions were upstaged when a McGovern Commission task force headed by U. S. Senator Birch Bayh of Indiana visited Houston and precipitated a "cuss fight" between two prominent Democratic Party leaders. Bayh probably was amazed at the blunt, plainspoken manner in which Frank C. Erwin, Jr., a conservative Austin lawyer and controversial chairman of the University of Texas Board of Regents, clashed with Albert Pena, a San Antonio liberal leader, in that public meeting on June 14, 1969.

The verbal skirmish began when Erwin, who had served as Democratic state chairman and national committeeman and ranked as Barnes's top political adviser, drew derisive laughter from the liberal audience.

"I've been losing public meetings like this and winning elections for years," he retorted.

"You've been *stealing* elections for years," said Pena.

"You're a liar!" Erwin snapped.

"And I say *you're* a liar," Pena shot back. "Like in 1956 at Fort Worth, when you had to call in Lyndon Johnson and Sam Rayburn to help you steal that convention!"

"I'm glad you finally admitted what you think of Lyndon Johnson," said Erwin. "You've been taking advantage of him for years."

While this exchange between two Democratic leaders may have shocked out-of-staters supposedly seeking methods for promoting party unity, the only thing surprising about it to Texas observers was that it occurred during the summer of an "off year" instead of during a typical campaign or convention. But off years in Texas politics rapidly are becoming as exciting as the main events.

During the 1969 off year, the two top officials of the Texas State AFL-CIO, President Hank S. Brown, a one-time plumber, and Secretary-Treasurer Roy Evans reached such a parting of the ways that they tangled in cut-throat competition. The showdown came at the organization's state convention at Corpus Christi in mid-July. Barnes cast a shadow even over that, since one of the main issues was Evans's unsuccessful attempt in 1968 to have the labor organization endorse State Representative Don Gladden of Fort Worth in his race against Barnes for lieutenant governor.

"The dissension, ill will, animosity and bitterness between your president and your secretary-treasurer is unbearable," Brown told the delegates in asking them to replace Evans with Jesse W. Sapp of Waco. When they refused, and elected both Evans and Brown to new two-year terms, the 49-year-old president found his $18,000-a-year job would still be bearable, after all.

But two years later, Brown retired—with a parting blast at Evans, who won the president's job, anyway.

Meanwhile, Republicans were licking their wounds from a party leadership fight which had been postponed a year in deference to the 1968 elections. The fact that Hubert Humphrey had carried Texas by a paper-thin margin over Nixon helped to fuel that fire, with dissident members of the Grand Old Party contending that new leadership on the state level was long overdue. That battle came to a climax at the Sheraton Crest Hotel in Austin on June 30, 1969.

The dissident Republicans lost—but by a margin which belied the new leaders' claim that the Texas GOP was more unified than it had been in years. William M. Steger, a 48-year-old Tyler attorney who had been the Republican nominee for governor in 1960 and for a congressional seat in 1962, nosed out Millard Neptune, a wealthy oil man and the party's nominee for state land commissioner in 1968, by a vote of 33-30. (Steger later was appointed to a federal district judgeship.) Mrs. Malcolm Milburn of Austin won the vice chairmanship by a 34-29 vote over Mrs. Betty Andujar of Fort Worth. Both Steger and Mrs.

Milburn had been backed by Senator Tower and by O'Donnell, who resigned the state chairmanship after forcing Albert Bel Fay of Houston off the national committee in order to take his place.

While the State Executive Committee meeting purportedly was drenched in harmony, blood continued to ooze beneath the closed doors behind which it was held—largely as a result of the bitter fight between Fay and O'Donnell.

That same day, Governor Smith announced that he had picked July 28 as the starting date for a special session (limited by the Constitution to 30 days) to adopt a budget, and pass the new taxes necessary to finance it, for the fiscal period beginning Sept. 1. The deadline pressure of such a delayed fiscal session produced new yelps of anguish from many legislators and from State Comptroller Robert S. Calvert, who complained that it would throw the mechanics of the state payroll into a clerical logjam.

That turned out to be the least of the problems involved. When the first special session used up its 30 days without reaching agreement, Smith called a second session immediately. It first enacted an emergency, 60-day budget but that was superseded by a $613 billion, two-year version after a $350 million state tax bill was passed. The 44-day, special session circus produced all sorts of fireworks, ranging from scuffles and shoving matches on the House floor to senators' bitter denunciations of each other and the governor.

Smith kindled the fire under the political pot when he vetoed the one-year, $2.8 billion "no tax" budget adopted by the Legislature during the regular session at the urging of Barnes and Mutscher. The Governor insisted on the traditional two-year appropriations pattern even though it required, under the State Constitution's "pay-as-you-go" provision, immediate enactment of new taxes. Barnes and Mutscher wanted to postpone the new taxes until 1970, arguing that a special session then would have a more accurate picture of the fiscal situation.

Smith staged a 30-minute, statewide telecast on June 20, 1969, to explain why he thought a one-year budget was illegal, immoral and unethical. In 1971, when the Legislature passed a $7 billion, two-year appropriations bill, he vetoed the second-year expenditures and said he would call a special session because one-year budgeting made a lot more sense.

The 1969 scene was enlivened by a buried treasure fight pitting Land Commissioner Jerry Sadler against several legislators. It set the stage for the upset of Sadler in the Democratic Primary by Robert L. Armstrong, a young Austin lawyer who had served four terms in the Texas House of Representatives.

The treasure fight involved at least three and perhaps as many as 14 Spanish galleons, loaded with gold and silver, which had been wrecked during a hurricane in 1553 while sailing from Vera Cruz to Spain. When some of the wrecks were located on state-owned submerged land—part of the famous tidelands—belonging to the Texas public schools, Sadler made a deal with an Indiana firm, Platoro, Ltd., Inc., to salvage the treasure and split it 50-50 with the State of Texas.

Early recovery operations produced a gold crucifix valued by Sadler at $100,000, about 1,000 gold and silver coins, a gold bar, cannons, guns and a wide assortment of ship furniture and equipment. But State Representatives Don Cavness of Austin and Jake Johnson of San Antonio complained bitterly that the salvaging methods were inefficient and that the State should get a larger share of the loot.

Johnson talked of trying to impeach the crusty, colorful Land Commissioner but finally had to settle for a House resolution handing Sadler a mild reprimand. The running battle did result, however, in legislative enactment during the second called session of an Antiquities Code pushed by Senator Don Kennard of Fort Worth. That Code created a seven-member commission (including the Land Commissioner) to preserve and protect state archeological resources, with specific authority to supervise and regulate sunken treasure recovery operations. It also provided that such treasure should be placed in the Texas Memorial Museum at Austin.

Barnes and Smith seemed more interested, meanwhile, in putting each other in a political museum. Ironically, Yarborough had no choice but to side with Smith, even though Barnes's views were considered more liberal than the Governor's, because the younger man obviously posed the greater threat to him.

As a result, the two veteran politicians—one a liberal and one a conservative—joined hands in an unlikely "mutual aid, non-aggression" alliance and decided they should stand together, shoulder to shoulder, at least until they could determine which way Barnes was headed.

Private clubs long have been considered an integral part of the Austin political scene and one of the favorites among politicians is the Forty Acres Club, noted for its excellent food. The fact that it is owned and operated by Jack Cox, a personable, colorful ex-legislator who ran for governor on the Democratic ticket in 1960 and on the Republican ticket in 1962, enhances its popularity with the politically-minded. Cox himself remains an important factor in the Texas GOP.

Some of the more astute Republicans tried unsuccessfully to get Cox to run for governor again in 1970 and remain convinced he could have defeated Smith. He was too wise to attempt such a race, however, without the backing of the party leadership.

Twelve blocks south of the Forty Acres Club stands the 24-story

Westgate Building, across the street from the Capitol and housing the elegant, prestigious Headliners Club on its top floor. This plush oasis offers an impressive bird's-eye-view on four sides—which is roughly how many there are in Texas politics at any given time.

On the north, the University of Texas campus sprawls over the landscape, having long ago burst far beyond the seams of its original 40 acres. On the east stands the magnificent, red granite Capitol, patterned after the one in Washington but with a taller dome (although the building is somewhat smaller) and the spacious, tree-covered grounds on which it is located. A stone's throw to the south is the 118-year-old Governor's Mansion and, beyond Town Lake in the distance, the circular Municipal Auditorium with its weird, multi-colored, domed roof. On the west, heavily-wooded hill country—with trees concealing vast residential areas—leap-frogs Lake Austin and stretches on toward the LBJ Ranch, 60 miles away.

The Headliners Club is a popular gathering place for politicians, lobbyists, educators and newspaper correspondents. It is one from which some of the politicians are inclined to think that they can see forever, perhaps because it overlooks so many political nerve centers. Within a one-block radius, in addition to the Capitol and the Governor's Mansion, stand the Texas State AFL-CIO Headquarters, the powerful Texas State Teachers Association's swanky home office building and the Texas Railroad Commission Building, housing the agency which regulates oil production.

Only a few blocks away, on the southeast, are the rapidly-diminishing downtown hotels. The Commodore Perry Building, formerly a hotel but now devoted almost exclusively to offices, shelters the Citadel and Deck and Austin Clubs, which also are popular places in which to page politicians.

Some of the most fascinating people in the world operate regularly within this small, scenic area, making decisions which shape the course of Texas history—and, judging from the record, perhaps the fate of the nation. Their decisions are supplemented and sometimes submerged or overruled by those made periodically in Houston law offices, in Dallas banks, on the LBJ Ranch and in fabulous hunting lodges on vast, remote ranches in South Texas.

Such spots have replaced the traditional smoke-filled room in Texas politics but the basic topic of conversation remains the selection and financing of winning candidates. More and more, the major decisions involve new tax prospects since the state's revenue always seems to lag behind its mushrooming growth and the ever-increasing demand for expansion of services. But even so, these discussions inevitably seem to revert to the intriguing personalities who will be fashioning the next tax increase.

Barnes entered this lofty atmosphere at the ripe old age of 22, with a force and style that shattered all existing records. He quickly elevated himself, during two terms as Speaker of the House, to the same political plane occupied by Senators Yarborough, Tower and Bentsen, Governor Smith, Congressman Bush, Attorney General Crawford C. Martin, Rancher-Banker Dolph Briscoe and such "elder statesmen" as former President Johnson and former Governors John Connally, Price Daniel and Allan Shivers.

This high political level can prove precarious in a state with a fast-growing population of more than 11,000,000, where severe growing pains accompany the rapidly-changing complexion of the electorate. By 1970, Texans suddenly found 40 per cent of the eligible voters living in four metropolitan counties—and straining at the leashes of traditional rural domination in state politics. Minority groups, supposedly unshackled by abolition of the poll tax in 1966, were being courted as never before by the Republicans—and, consequently, by the Democrats who had become accustomed to taking them for granted.

Texas remained in the curious position of a "one-party state" split among conservative Democrats, liberal Democrats, conservative Republicans and liberal Republicans. But the conservatives, regardless of how they were classified when it came to party affiliation, still held a slight edge.

True, repeal of the poll tax had added hundreds of thousands of Negroes and Mexican Americans to Texas voting lists but it did nothing to solve the perplexing problem of motivating them to go to the polls. More significant than poll tax repeal was the U. S. Supreme Court's "one man, one vote" decision, which signaled an end to the historic rural domination of a Legislature whose members now represented mostly city dwellers.

Even the belligerent independence of Texans appeared to be diminishing although many of them still are quick to note that the State has the right to divide itself into five states, with a total of 10 U. S. Senators. More and more Texans seem resigned to accepting the federal government domination they long have fought. The traditional political labels gradually seem to be fading into oblivion. Still, the conservatives who have dominated the state government for years and the liberals, who actually seem to enjoy being on the outside looking in and criticizing, periodically call new signals which renew their long-standing feud.

Many Texans seem baffled by the sudden changes but none, apparently, are more puzzled than Texas Republicans, who sometimes act as if they have decided on suicide as a cure for their own growing pains. They seem to have a propensity for snatching defeat from

The Texas Capitol is where the action is—for 140 days every two years, at least. The House of Representatives is in the wing at left, the Senate in the wing at right and the Governor's Office is right in the middle.

the jaws of victory, just when they appear to be on the verge of transforming Texas into a true two-party state. At times, their chieftains have let victory elude them simply by stopping on the one-yard line to squabble over dividing the spoils.

A more serious problem seems to be the division of the Texas GOP into two camps: those who apparently want to make membership a "by invitation only" affair, without letting just *anyone* in, and those who want to convert as many Democrats as possible into Republicans in order to win elections.

In 1962, for instance, Cox had something less than whole-hearted support from the Republican hierarchy ("he has been a Democrat, you know") but still polled 715,025 votes to Connally's 847,038. That is as close as the Republicans have come in modern history to winning the governor's office. A mute commentary on their lack of progress is the fact that, even with limited financing and running against a much more popular opponent, Cox received 46 per cent of the vote against Connally in 1962—and Eggers received 46 per cent against Smith in 1970.

A great many Democrats followed Cox into the Republican Party in 1962 but, after a few years, most drifted back into the party of their forefathers—not *because* it was the party of their forefathers, one of them explained, but simply because "we didn't like being forced to ride in the back of the bus." They felt that their past "sins" had condemned them to lives as second-class citizens when it came to Republican Party honors and even to candidacies for public office.

While such weighty, complicated political matters are being pondered in high places, the outcome of many important elections in Texas is influenced considerably on a much lower level—by people who embezzle bumper stickers to throw them away, who ring doorbells on behalf of candidates, who distribute voting machines adroitly, who send postcards to friends, who try to jam telephone lines in the opposition's campaign headquarters, who pull all sorts of espionage tricks— and yes, even steal votes.

One of the most bitter campaigns of all time, in a state noted for acrimonious campaigning, was that between Shivers and Yarborough in 1954. Both sides pulled a wide variety of tricks on the opposition, from bribing messenger boys into becoming spies to impersonating labor leaders on the telephone.

The U. S. Supreme Court had just handed down its school desegregation decision and East Texas, which has much in common with the Deep South, was up in arms. Governor Shivers did not learn of this ploy until long after it became history but some of his supporters sent a well-dressed Negro man, sporting an expensive gold watch and chain, through East Texas in a new Cadillac bearing Yarborough bumper stickers.

He would stop frequently at service stations manned by white men, order "a dollar's worth of gas" and then become rude, demanding faster service.

"Hurry up there," he would snap. "I'se working for Mister Yarborough!"

Meanwhile, the Yarborough forces took a picture of Shivers leaning down, from the flatbed truck on which he stood to make a speech in Lufkin, to shake hands with a Negro man. Realizing that this was an unpardonable sin to many segregationists in East Texas back in those dark ages of 1954, the Yarborough forces reproduced that picture in a pamphlet and spread it throughout the area.

The Shivers people promptly gathered up all of those pamphlets they could find—and redistributed them among Negro voters.

Many Texans insist that deception during campaigns is nothing new and really is insignificant when compared with the actual fraud involved in many vote counts. They contend that Johnson proved in 1948, when he won the Democratic nomination to the U. S. Senate by a mere 87 votes, that "you *can* steal first base." The Johnson defenders, on the other hand, claim that the 87-vote margin was all that was left after the other side "stole all it could."

One school of thought holds that it is better, regardless of the larceny possibilities, simply to *buy* first base—and also purchase second and third while you're at it.

Money remains not only the root of all evil but the lifeblood of campaigns in Texas, regardless of chicanery and charisma and faulty arithmetic and other factors which influence the outcome of elections. It is, as they say, "well ahead of whatever is in second place."

Thus, "getting financed" is the first step for any ambitious politician. Outsiders may be inclined to think that the most generous "fat cats"— the political equivalent of theatrical angels—are flamboyant oilmen but most are businessmen, lawyers, and contractors. Their interests lie in Washington as well as Austin but a surprisingly large percentage of those who contribute freely apparently expect nothing more than "good government" in return.

Contacting such people, and persuading them that he is just the one to provide good government, therefore ranks as a prime objective for every Texas politician. Of course, many candidates are happy to settle for contributions from anyone who will give, even if this necessitates a tacit understanding that future favors are being bought.

The ideal politician is one who can "sell" himself without "selling out." He has a knack for gaining the confidence of people, as surely as does the man selling insurance or used cars or anything else. And, as in any other line of endeavor, the rise to success often is directly proportional to the amount of influence wielded by the people who become his friends—and especially people who can open a lot of doors for the candidate.

For that reason, Christmas in 1967 proved one of the merriest and happiest in Ben Barnes's young life. He attended a dinner party with about a dozen other people at the Austin home of U. S. Circuit Judge Homer Thornberry, whose 1968 nomination to the U. S. Supreme Court by President Johnson was torpedoed by the Senate refusal to confirm the simultaneous promotion of Justice Abe Fortas to Chief Justice.

The dinner party was a gala affair. Among the guests were President and Mrs. Johnson, along with Luci and Pat Nugent; J. C. Kellam, general manager of the Johnsons' Austin radio and television stations; Donald Thomas, a longtime LBJ associate, business partner and lawyer; J. Sam Winters, a Thomas law partner and insurance lobbyist, and Frank Erwin.

Santa Claus himself could not have made Barnes any happier than President Johnson did when he called him aside, near the end of the party.

"Ben, I just want you to know," said the President of the United States, "that I'm for you—money, marbles and chalk."

Chapter 2

BIRTH OF A CAMPAIGN

A line of thunderstorms swept across the Rio Grande from Mexico into South Texas on Friday, May 16, 1969, splashing life-giving rains over the huge, arid area—larger than some countries—which comprises Dolph Briscoe's ranching domain.

Briscoe's broad smile offered ample evidence that the downpour followed many months of dry weather. But his comments made it clear that the badly-needed moisture was no more welcome than were the 27 weekend house guests who began arriving late that afternoon at his 165,000-acre Catarina Ranch.

They came to fish, to shoot at fast-running jackrabbits from moving, jeep-type vehicles and to discuss Briscoe's political future.

Briscoe's ranching enterprises cover approximately 1,000,000 acres of Southwest Texas land. A pioneer in conservation, he has converted much of the once barren, cactus-clogged and mesquite-choked land into lush pastures of knee-deep grass. He probably owns more bank stock, as well as more land, than any other individual in Texas. The telephone directory in Uvalde, his hometown, lists seven separate Dolph Briscoe ranches.

The handsome young millionaire also has a beautiful, charming wife and a happy marriage, three fine children, an unblemished reputation, great popularity and a host of honors gained while performing all sorts of volunteer civic work.

What else could he possibly want? The answer is simple: to be Governor of Texas or a U. S. Senator from Texas.

Why? Why would such a man, widely acclaimed for being unselfish, one who loves to hunt and fish and raise cattle and convert desolate land into productive acreage, be willing to subject himself to the rigors of a statewide campaign? Why would he be willing to go on, month after month, getting up at 5:30 in the morning to spend all day and half the night shaking hands and making speeches? Why would he be willing to invest several hundred thousand dollars of his own money in such a grind, just to win a two-year term in a job that would be almost that rigorous itself?

Briscoe struggled to find the explanation as he rode around his vast ranch inspecting the difference a rain makes, as he visited with old friends and new ones and as he hunted jackrabbits. He seemed completely happy while sitting on the elevated rear seat of a specially-modified Bronco Land Rover, pausing occasionally to eradicate a speedy jackrabbit with his 12-gauge shotgun while the vehicle bounced over rough roads and occasionally sloshed through a mudhole.

The vehicle itself, one of several similar ones in his hunting fleet, served as a tribute to his penchant for the unpretentious and functional. It had gunracks mounted on the roof over the front seat, in easy reach of hunters who rode on the roofless, elevated back seat. The hunters, with full visibility on all sides, had plenty of room to swing a rifle or a shotgun on a fast-moving deer, bobcat or jackrabbit.

For deer hunting, each of the vehicles has a signal light system permitting the hunter to direct the driver silently. Mounted on the dashboard are four lights—green for "go," yellow for "slow," red for "stop" and white for "reverse." Comparable buttons on the back edge of the cab's roof, at the hunter's fingertips, enable the man with the gun to call signals.

Briscoe's ranch has none of the plush "blinds" from which many Texans hunt deer. He believes the quarry—even if it is a bobcat or one of the countless jackrabbits which destroy his precious grass— is entitled to the sporting chance that comes when the hunter is moving along at 20 or 30 miles an hour on a bumpy road.

A guest riding with him on this particular rabbit hunt finally commented that Briscoe's first shot inevitably seemed to miss any jackrabbit that was sitting still but his second dropped it unerringly, after the rabbit had gained full speed.

District Judge Ross E. Doughty of Uvalde, driving the vehicle, explained.

"Dolph won't hit 'em standing still," said the Judge, a longtime friend who traveled with Briscoe throughout the 1968 campaign. "He fires a shot to get 'em moving, then hits 'em on the run."

Briscoe's polite, mild-mannered and gentlemanly sporting instincts may have hampered his remarkable 1968 bid for the governorship to some extent, especially since his late-blooming campaign was not designed as expertly as were his hunting vehicles. Some observers felt he exemplified the theory that "nice guys finish last." But his campaign slogan, "Everyone who knows Dolph Briscoe will vote for him," proved remarkably prophetic. The election results, according to his friends, merely proved that not enough people knew him.

With a better-organized, earlier-starting campaign, Briscoe might have won—despite the disdain of the political soothsayers. They erred in thinking that Governor Connally could hand down his mantle to Eugene Locke, a prominent Dallas lawyer who had served as Ambassador to Pakistan, Deputy Ambassador to South Vietnam and as Connally's campaign manager in 1962.

There are those, including Briscoe, who believe that Briscoe would

Dolph Briscoe, a millionaire rancher and banker, loves to cruise around his huge domain in his specially-designed hunting vehicles with elevated rear seats.

have won the 1968 race had Connally backed him instead of Locke. Ironically, it was at this same Catarina Ranch that Connally, during a strategy meeting in December of 1961, picked Locke to manage his first campaign—and also introduced Ben Barnes to some of his king-making friends.

Briscoe recalled that meeting as he drove around the ranch, reflecting upon the past as well as the future.

"Yes, I think I could have won in 1968 if Connally had backed me," he declared.

"Why did he back Locke instead of you?" he was asked.

"I think he felt a very strong personal obligation to Locke because Gene had been his campaign manager," said Briscoe. "Connally never misled me. He never led me to believe he was going to back me. I talked to him several times before I announced but he never gave me any encouragement or discouragement."

Connally's reticence may have been prompted by the belief that Briscoe was not known well enough and was not dynamic enough to win. The Governor had worked for months trying to find a strong opponent for Smith, with whom he had been at odds for a long time.

Connally tried unsuccessfully to get Barnes to run but the young Speaker of the House chose to run for lieutenant governor. Former Congressman Joe Kilgore, whom President Johnson forced out of the U. S. Senate race in 1964, now had a prosperous law practice flourishing in Austin and declined to run. Frank Ikard of Wichita Falls, who had moved from Congress to the highly-paid presidency of the American Petroleum Institute, also turned down the honor.

Locke wanted it, perhaps even more than Briscoe did. Not only did he have a stronger claim on Connally's friendship, as a result of that 1962 campaign, but he apparently convinced him that he had a better chance to win.

Actually, more people probably recognized Briscoe's name than Locke's at the start of the 1968 Democratic Primary race, even though the young businessman-rancher had been out of politics for 12 years.

Reared almost at the knee of John Nance Garner, Briscoe grew up in a ranching atmosphere where politics was discussed about as often as rain or the lack of it. His late father, Dolph Briscoe, Sr., who went broke twice in the ranching business before finally achieving success in it, had formed a ranching partnership with Governor Ross Sterling in 1923, the year Dolph, Jr., was born.

The younger Briscoe was an only child who did not act like one. By the time he was grown, he owned considerable wealth but remained so modest and self-effacing that it was inconspicuous. Shortly after the 1968 race, a visitor asked a prominent Uvalde citizen how much he thought Briscoe was "worth" and was told: "Down here, we never thought of trying to put a dollar mark on Dolph."

Briscoe won election to the Texas House of Representatives in 1948. He joined Senator Neveille Colson of Navasota in sponsoring the Colson-Briscoe Act, which allocated $15 million annually for new construction of farm-to-market roads in rural areas. It has been widely acclaimed as the act which "got Texas out of the mud."

Briscoe served four uncontested terms in the Legislature and retired unopposed in 1956, when he decided he could no longer devote to the job the time it demanded. But 12 years later, the soft-spoken, modest young millionaire decided he had both the time and the money to seek the Democratic nomination for governor.

Not many people were inclined to take him seriously at first. He did not announce his candidacy until January 25, 1968, and the field then already was crowded with well-known names. These included Lieutenant Governor Smith, former Attorney General Waggoner Carr and Secretary of State John L. Hill, who also hoped to win Connally's endorsement. But Connally already had given his blessing to Locke, who paid his $1,000 filing fee the same day Briscoe announced.

Don Yarborough, a Houston lawyer and perennial labor-backed candidate (not related to Ralph Yarborough, except politically) showed up a few days later to enter the race, explaining that he had spent most of the previous year in Europe writing a book. Pat O'Daniel, son of former Governor W. Lee "Pappy" O'Daniel, also entered the 1968 race in hopes his famous surname might electrify the voters the way it had in 1938, when his father swamped 12 opponents and rode into office on a wave of hillbilly music. Three unknowns—Edward L. Whittenburg, Alfonso Veloz and Johnnie Mae Hackworthe—completed the 10-candidate field.

Yarborough, Smith, Carr, Briscoe, Locke and Hill, all of whom mounted intensive, well-financed campaigns, finished the first primary race in that order. Locke's campaign probably was the most expensive, utilizing a Madison Avenue approach which featured a catchy, tuneful jingle declaring that "Eugene Locke should be Governor of Texas."

Yarborough, as he had planned and as nearly everyone expected, collected a lion's share of the liberal support to lead in the first primary with 419,003 of the 1,750,728 votes. Smith was second with 389,564, Carr third with 257,535, Briscoe a surprising fourth with 225,686, Locke fifth with 218,118, and Hill sixth with 154,908.

Carr, Briscoe, Locke and Hill all threw their support to Smith in the runoff, helping him to beat Yarborough, 771,648 to 617,063. Smith had a closer race than expected in the general election but defeated

Eggers, who started the race as a political unknown, 1,662,019 to 1,254,333.

But it was the first primary race that was uppermost in the minds of Briscoe's weekend guests since the group included backers of Smith, Locke, Hill and Carr, along with a few longtime friends of Briscoe.

Some of the first-time visitors had trouble finding the long, low, unpretentious but plush ranch house, which can sleep 100 people comfortably. Salt cedar trees screen most of it from the road, making it appear to be nothing more than a small farmhouse.

Once upon a time, it was. The new part has a corrugated metal roof over it, matching that on the original structure. But now there are nine bedrooms, seven of which are large enough to shelter four or five double beds each—without any crowding. Each bed has an elaborately carved, antique-styled headboard. In addition, a wide screened-in porch enclosed by glass jalousies runs along three sides of the house; it is furnished with comfortable chairs, sofas and coffee tables, along with about 60 steel-frame cots.

The main living area has been fashioned around the original house. Two large rooms and a smaller one, all connected by wall-to-wall openings, provide ample space for dining, entertaining and talking politics. A 19th Century bar, complete with the inevitable mirror behind it and supporting an old-fashioned cash register, occupies part of the smaller room and frequently stimulates the political discussions.

But on the nights of May 16 and 17, 1969, the discussions were sober, serious and candid. Considering the widely-divergent viewpoints represented, they ended on a surprising note of unity.

Briscoe admitted Friday afternoon, as he waited for his guests to arrive, that he did not know exactly what to expect. He did not even know all those who were coming. Some had been invited by friends of friends but all undoubtedly had been cleared by the prime mover of the meeting, Herbert C. Petry, Jr., a Carrizo Springs attorney and member of the State Highway Commission.

While driving around that afternoon, Briscoe stopped his jeep near the front gate of the ranch to greet two of his old friends, Joe La-Mantia and Scott Toothaker, both of McAllen.

"Joe used to live in Carrizo Springs and now he's in the produce business down in McAllen, as both a grower and a shipper," Briscoe explained. "Scott's an attorney down there.

"There are three people coming from Houston. I don't know them but they're friends of Herb's. Garrett Morris (a member of the Highway Commission) from Fort Worth, of course, I know—but I don't know the two he's bringing with him. Bill Clement from Longview is an old friend. He's in the cattle business, very active in the East Texas Chamber of Commerce. Ernest Powers from Carthage—he's also in the cattle business, and you'll never meet a finer guy. Lewis Bracy is from Austin, a banker, and also an old friend.

"Clint Brasher and Norment Foley are very good personal friends of mine who live in Uvalde," Briscoe continued. "They're coming out really to help with the people who want to go fishing because they know where the tanks are and they know the ranch real well."

Briscoe has a standing rule that no one goes fishing—in the 75 or 80 water reservoirs, ranging from stock tanks to small lakes—or hunting or exploring or anything else on the Catarina Ranch without someone along who knows his way around. As he continued to explain the invitation list, Briscoe was totally unaware that the wisdom of this policy was about to be demonstrated rather dramatically.

He mentioned two more old friends, Harry Provence, editor of the *Waco News-Tribune*, and George Christian.

"I have no commitment of any kind from George," Briscoe hastened to explain, "that he would help me in any way. But he is an old friend and I think very highly of him."

Many of the guests arrived early enough to go fishing late Friday afternoon. These included Dr. Ben Procter, a Texas Christian University history professor who had supported John Hill in the 1968 governor's race, and Charles (Sonny) Sowell, a Houston lawyer, real estate developer and strong Smith supporter who had played on the same University of Texas football team with Procter. Sowell and Procter managed to compete during the weekend on just about everything from eating eggs to catching fish, dividing all the honors except those for walking in shorts about four miles through antagonistic cactus at night. Procter conceded the championship in that dubious division to Sowell.

Briscoe considered thoughtfully a far different type of competition as he drove around the ranch, admiring the mud puddles in this land of rare rains.

"With everything you have going for you in private life," he was asked, "why do you want to run for governor?"

Briscoe thought that one over for a moment as he whipped the vehicle, almost automatically, through a morass of mud.

"That's a real good question," he responded. "It sounds very trite and corny, I know, to say that I'm concerned over the future of this state. But that's true. I wonder sometimes, myself, why I would get mixed up in something like a governor's race instead of just coming out here and hunting or fishing.

"You might say a fellow would have to be crazy to do that, and you *do* have to be—well, at least different, I guess, in order to do it," he declared. "After all, a candidate is subjected to a lot of things. He's fair game and it's open season on him—which is the American system.

"Why? I've thought about that a lot and tried to answer the question for myself," Briscoe continued. "I think Winston Churchill summed it up pretty well by saying something to the effect that he wanted to do everything worthwhile that he could while he was here on this earth. You just go through this life one time. I think you should try to do everything you can, serve wherever you can.

"I think we're living in very dangerous times but I also think this is always true, regardless of what time it is," he said. "There is no such thing as having a completely peaceful or settled time. But I would like to be able to contribute something to the growth and prosperity of the state, and also to the stability of the state.

"Why does a man take a job on a school board, or as president of the Texas and Southwestern Cattle Raisers Association? I don't know the answer to that, really. Maybe sometimes you get talked into it. But that can't be the whole answer because nothing, really, is forced on you—especially in politics.

"People do go out and work hard to try to get a job that, it seems like, has nothing but headaches and problems—and a lot of those problems almost without solution," said Briscoe.

Reminded that he generally was considered a liberal while serving in the Legislature but now was classified as a conservative or as a moderate, Briscoe was asked if he felt his philosophy had changed or if the traditional labels and definitions had changed.

"I would take issue with having been a liberal while I was in the Legislature," he replied quickly. "This came up during the last campaign. But during the four terms I served in the Legislature, I represented a very conservative area—and during that time, I never did have an opponent. When I decided I couldn't run again, I didn't have one. What I'm saying is that I represented a very conservative area and I did it in a way that satisfied my constituents.

"Now I was not, while I was in the Legislature, what you would call a part of the team," said Briscoe. "I tried to vote on every issue for what I thought was best for the state. Certainly, I was at cross purposes with the 'team' effort to do away with part of the farm-to-market road program.

"I would consider myself to be conservative now, very definitely," he added.

In an era when many candidates seem determined to feather their own nests, Briscoe had spent an estimated $350,000 of his own money on his 1968 campaign with no hope of recovering that investment.

"You know, politics has been expensive for me," he acknowledged, without saying just how much he had spent on his race. "It hasn't been a money-maker at all, that's for sure. Some people seem to do all right in politics but it has been very costly to me. Now, so far as business is concerned, I've been very lucky. My father was successful in the ranching business, even though he had his ups and downs. He started out with very little. He got going pretty well and then, back in the 1920s, he lost everything he'd made.

"He got going again and then lost that during the depression," said Briscoe. "His best chance came through Mister Sterling. He wanted to get into the ranching business and got together with my father through a mutual friend, Malcolm Monroe.

"Mister Sterling bought a large herd of cows and my father managed it for him, and finally they went into a partnership. They operated several ranches together and later had *this* ranch. They started in business together about 1923, the year I was born, but they went broke during the depression. Mister Sterling lost his fortune and my father lost what he had been able to accumulate."

Briscoe paused as he guided the vehicle through a swamp-like area which normally was as dry as the Sahara.

"My father was wiped out," said Briscoe, "but he kept on going in the cattle business and he came back and built a very fine ranching business. We've been fortunate enough to make it grow.

"I've never considered myself wealthy," he added, "because we have an operating business. It's not a cinch we're going to make money this year, or any year. We don't have a cinch income from investments that you know are going to pay dividends or yields from bonds to depend on. Ours is an operating business that requires considerable working capital."

Briscoe conceded that "working capital" is perhaps even more essential in a statewide political campaign than it is in a large-scale ranching operation.

"How does a person start to organize a statewide campaign—by trying to get financed?" he was asked.

Briscoe thought about that for a moment as he glanced out at a huge, beautiful pasture—one in which he obviously had invested the huge amount of money necessary for the "root-plowing" that rid it of mesquite and transformed it into a grassy wonderland.

"I don't know how the others have started out to make a statewide race," he said. "Of course, financial support is essential. But I think a good, working group of friends in each area—not just in the metropolitan areas but in each part of the metropolitan areas—is the most important thing. After all, a metropolitan area may represent as many people, and as many votes, as 60 or 70 rural counties."

"Do you think," he was asked, "that your campaign last year produced the first step in establishing a strong organization? In other words, do you think you have the basic foundation you need to build on for another race?"

"Well, we ended up with *some* help in every county," he replied. "Where we were able to spend the time and effort to develop an effective organization, the results were sure obvious. Where we had it, the results were good; and where we didn't, they were bad.

"I hope I learned some things from the last campaign, and one thing I know I learned is this: if a person is going to make a race, it's absolutely necessary for him to get ready and get started early," he said. "Otherwise, there just isn't time to cover this state and do anything like the job that needs to be done. You just run out of time. And this happened to me during the last campaign."

Briscoe's greatest campaign gimmick during that 1968 race was a telephone crusade. During the two or three weeks immediately preceding the election, households all over Texas received telephone calls from people asking votes for Briscoe. Some of the callers were volunteers and some were professionals. The volunteers were more persuasive and more effective than the paid workers, of course; although they were outnumbered by the latter, they probably did as much as anything else in enabling Briscoe to finish a surprising fourth, ahead of Eugene Locke.

Some of the grandstand quarterbacks figure this phase of Briscoe's campaign started a week or so too late—that it might have put him "over the top" had it been launched a week or two earlier.

Such elements of timing were one of the things the "fishermen" had in mind that Friday night as they settled back for a full-scale discussion of politics, after stuffing themselves on barbecue.

The gathering included Charles G. Purnell and Rob See, Jr. of Dallas; Bob Eckels, John S. Brunson and Frank G. Evans III of Houston; State Representative David Finney of Fort Worth; Fred Shield of San Antonio; Happy Shahan of Brackettville; Cecil E. Rusk and Frank Driskill of Austin, and Calvin R. Guest of Bryan.

Herb Petry opened the discussion by explaining that the meeting was designed merely to "get the thinking of people who are interested in the future of Texas" and to see if they could begin working toward a common goal. He noted that the ranch house in which this group was gathered had been the scene of "other first meetings" for highly successful Texas politicians, calling particular attention to the Connally session in 1961.

Pictures on the walls bore testimony to visits from Sam Rayburn, John Nance Garner and Johnson, as well as Connally.

Petry appointed Christian—somewhat to Christian's surprise—as

Former Vice President John Nance Garner admires two lunker bass caught at Dolph Briscoe's Catarina Ranch by Sam Rayburn. From left to right above are Garner, Rayburn, Congressman Jack Brooks and Briscoe.

moderator, asking everyone to express himself on the Texas political situation. But he stressed the idea that no one was being asked, or would be asked, to make a commitment to Briscoe that weekend.

One by one, starting with Highway Commissioner Morris, the guests rose to express their views. Most of them did so quite candidly, which seemed surprising in view of the fact that many of them had met each other for the first time only a few hours earlier.

Not surprisingly, nearly everyone agreed that Briscoe should make another race for governor. The only disagreement seemed to revolve around the timing—as to whether he should plan on running against Smith in 1970 or merely start working toward a 1972 race.

Some contended that Smith, who had been in office only four months at that point, already had alienated many people. If he continued to do so, they said, he would be extremely vulnerable one year later, in the 1970 Democratic Primary. Others stuck to the traditional viewpoint that no incumbent, first-term governor could be defeated for reelection, barring a major scandal involving him or his close associates.

Woven throughout the discussion was the ever-present threat of Barnes. Nearly everyone agreed that he was the strongest political candidate in sight but most of them were convinced that he already had decided to run against Senator Yarborough in 1970.

Some of that may have been wishful thinking, of course; and, immediately after the 1970 elections, they began hoping Barnes would run against Senator Tower in 1972.

No one in the room, either liberal or conservative, wanted to see a race between Briscoe and Barnes. One of the participants even noted that Barnes, Briscoe and Bush appeared to offer the brightest hope for Texas's future and that their philosophies were so remarkably similar that it would be a shame for any two of them to run against each other.

The consensus, which finally came into focus about midnight, seemed to be that Briscoe should begin immediately utilizing the best features of both the Smith and Barnes techniques. He should, like Barnes, begin accepting as many speaking invitations as possible and, like Smith, take advantage of any lulls in the action to go around the state shaking hands with everyone he possibly could.

He should begin building a real organization, his friends felt, with a campaign manager in every county and a captain in every precinct. He should aim at the governor's race in 1972 but be ready to volunteer in case Smith stumped his toe before the entry deadline on the 1970 race. And, most of them agreed, he should pray that Barnes would run against Yarborough.

To Briscoe, one of the more encouraging aspects of the discussion

Celebrities who helped Garner (center) celebrate his 90th birthday on Nov. 22, 1958, included (left to right) Briscoe, Harry S. Truman, Lyndon B. Johnson and Price Daniel. The cake is a replica of Garner's birthplace.

undoubtedly was the candid admission of several strong Smith backers that they were committed to the Governor for only two terms. While they refused to go along with rival contentions that Smith seemed likely to alienate enough people by 1970 to become vulnerable in a second-term bid, they made it clear that they were ready to pledge their allegiance elsewhere for 1972. They had "signed up," they said, only for two terms.

It was well after midnight when the meeting broke up. Most of the participants headed for bed but half a dozen or so sat around a poker table without playing cards, too tired to do anything but talk and yet too enthralled with the birth pangs of a gubernatorial campaign to sleep. By the time the last of them went to bed, the early morning contingent of fishermen was about ready to get up.

Jack Bean, a Fort Worth businessman who had served as Hill's Tarrant County campaign manager in 1968, went out that afternoon in a jeep driven by Petry. About the time they started back to the house, the jeep suddenly quit.

"Well, it's 20 miles back to the house," Petry quipped with a straight face. "Do you want to sign up for Dolph—or walk back?"

"I'll sign, I'll sign," panted Bean, amid gales of laughter.

As it turned out, he didn't have to sign or walk either. A bit of dirt in the gas line was blown out and the vehicle quickly became operational again.

But that night, as darkness finally settled over the ranch about 9 p.m., Briscoe became concerned over the absence of another fishing party, headed by Foley. It included Sonny Sowell and his brother, Jack R. (Buzzy) Sowell, and See. That quartet had followed Briscoe and another group for a while during the afternoon, on a 25-mile trip across the ranch to the Rio Grande.

Then, after taking a look at the international border which also serves as one of Briscoe's property lines, the Foley group headed for one of the remote little lakes noted for black bass.

Briscoe double-checked with everyone who had seen the group that afternoon and concluded that they must be stranded by jeep trouble, out where the deer and the rattlesnakes play. He began organizing a search party and Judge Doughty, who knew the ranch intimately, offered to lead it. The rescuers refueled a couple of Land Rovers, then armed themselves with flashlights and tow chains and shot guns. It was about 10 p.m. when they started to leave and were stopped suddenly by the ringing of the telephone.

Briscoe answered it and heaved a huge sigh of relief when he heard Foley's voice. They had caught 57 bass, Foley reported calmly, and started back to the house. But they hit a deep gulley and the fan blade came off and flew through the radiator of the vehicle, he said.

They had walked about four miles to the nearest telephone, at a cowboy line camp 20 miles from the ranch house.

They were exhausted and half-starved, he added, and the hike through the dark had been particularly rough on Sonny Sowell because he was wearing short pants. Almost every time a piece of brush lashed his bare legs, said Foley, Sowell felt certain a snake had scored at least a near miss.

Bean, listening to Briscoe's side of the conversation and to his brief aside that the group was all right, asked if he could speak to Sonny Sowell. It may not have seemed funny to those at the line camp but the ranch house began shaking with laughter almost the moment Bean began talking.

"Sonny," he roared, "they pulled this same stuff on me and I'll tell you this: you might as well go ahead and sign up, because they won't come and get you 'til you do!"

He paused a moment as a blast of laughter drowned out the conversation.

"Yeah," he added. "I took a whole bunch of North Texas counties and you'll probably get the whole Gulf Coast. These people down here really have a system—and you've got to admit it's damned effective!"

Chapter 3

WHAT'S A CAMELOT?

On Monday evening, January 20, 1969, several thousand persons bearing $25-a-plate tickets—and in some cases, a bit of trepidation—gathered in Austin's Municipal Auditorium for the Democratic Party Victory Dinner honoring Smith and Barnes, who were to be inaugurated the next day.

The dinner marked the start of inaugural festivities featuring country and western music, a theme chosen by the first governor ever elected from far West Texas. And, already, that had become something of a *cause célèbre* between the rival Smith and Barnes factions.

Two weeks earlier, syndicated columnists Rowland Evans and Robert Novak had published a detailed account of Smith's first "veto." They said it was applied to an invitation Barnes had issued Robert Goulet, when he met the famous vocalist in Las Vegas shortly after the general election, to sing at the inauguration.

Elated when Goulet said both he and his wife, Carol Lawrence, would be delighted to entertain and without charge, Barnes called Smith to give him what he felt was great news.

"Who," Smith reportedly responded, "is Robert Goulet?"

"When Barnes informed him Goulet had starred in the original cast of 'Camelot,' Smith replied he never heard of 'Camelot' either," said Evans and Novak. "Besides, the new governor added, he wanted country music singers at his inauguration. Miffed, Barnes had to withdraw the invitation."

Smith, whose taste runs more to "Mayberry, R.F.D.," later disputed that version of the affair but, nevertheless, invited Jimmy Dean, Glen Campbell, Buck Owens and his Buckaroos, Ray Price and Charley Pride to furnish entertainment at the inauguration, which included six balls.

Although he is a notoriously poor joke-teller, Smith made a big hit at the Victory Dinner when he referred to the Goulet incident.

"That report in the Evans and Novak column is wrong," he deadpanned. "I didn't say I had never heard of 'Camelot.' What I said was, I never heard of Evans and Novak."

A lot of the guests may not have heard that remark. As Dean put it, after curtailing his singing due to the poor acoustics, "It's a pity to spend millions of dollars on such a nice auditorium and then put in an army surplus sound system."

That arrangement, however, is no greater an enigma than Smith himself. Even in a state that produced Lyndon Baines Johnson, he ranks as one of the most puzzling, mysterious and paradoxical figures of all time.

When he showed up for the inaugural balls in his tuxedo with a polka dot tie and matching cummerbund, the Governor disclosed that he had been wearing polka dot ties exclusively since 1962—because he wanted an attention-getting trademark.

"I decided I'd run for lieutenant governor that year and I went to Governor Price Daniel for help," he recalled. "He said he couldn't help me because he would probably be a candidate again himself. 'But let me make a suggestion,' he said. 'Do something just a little bit different if you want to get elected.' "

Daniel went on, said Smith, to say that he always had worn striped ties.

"That afternoon, I went to Dallas and bought some polka dot ties," said Smith. "I don't know whether that brought me good luck or not."

Although he said he had been wearing no other kind since then, no one seems to have noticed until the polka dot cummerbund appeared. As a matter of fact, Daniel's penchant for striped ties had been unnoticed almost unanimously until Smith mentioned it.

Smith took great pride, and made much campaign hay, out of the fact that he had served six years in the House of Representatives, six years in the Senate and six years as lieutenant governor. But, shortly after taking office, he recommended a two-year package of $320 million in new revenue measures to the Legislature, then apparently forgot the matter—acting as if he did not realize that the enactment of his new tax proposals would require some gubernatorial persuasion.

He had campaigned on a program which included strong doubts that any new taxes would be necessary in 1969, although this was a foregone conclusion—recognized even then by nearly everyone else in the race, by most legislators and even by the lobbyists. But he vetoed a one-year, "no tax" budget and demanded that the Legislature levy $350 million in new taxes during a special session.

Smith was blessed with a fine sense of humor and a pathetic technique for telling jokes. Despite this combination, he insisted on throwing out quips which even Bob Hope would have had trouble pitching successfully.

One of Smith's biggest laughs came when, in all seriousness, he recommended that the Legislature in 1969 levy a $10 tax on each conviction for a moving traffic law violation. He said this would raise an estimated $38 million during a two-year period but most legislators immediately rejected the idea on grounds that dispensing justice should not be a source of state revenue and laughed it down.

Smith got the last laugh on that one. In 1971, a similar tax slipped through the Legislature almost unnoticed; it levied a $2.50 tax on each traffic fine plus a $5 tax on other misdemeanor convictions—and a $10 *tax on felony convictions.*

During his first few months in office, Smith seemed to delight in embarrassing and alienating huge groups of people—such as those in Dallas and Houston and Odessa—by reminding them pointedly and publicly that they had failed to vote for him in 1968. For a while, it seemed as though he would never forgive anyone who had voted against him. But then he appointed J. Pearce Johnson of Austin, one of Briscoe's staunchest 1968 campaign workers, to the State Parks and Wildlife Commission, and he named State Representative Randy Pendleton of Andrews, who managed Carr's gubernatorial campaign in 1968, as his personal liaison representative in Washington.

In a rare stroke of political genius, Smith held a series of receptions for each of the state's 31 senatorial districts at the Governor's Mansion shortly after he moved into it. He invited all the people from each district to come and visit at specified times in the stately mansion and the lovely gardens (which had been fashioned by Mrs. John Connally, through a massive fund-raising campaign). Most Texans had never visited the Governor's Mansion and they came in bus-loads, from throughout the state.

"Any governor has to feel he really is a great man," remarked one observer, as he looked down from the Headliners Club upon one such reception, "when he sees people lined up for two blocks waiting in line to come in and shake his hand."

But if Smith happened to know that one of those coming through the line had failed to vote for him—even in the first primary of 1968— he was more than likely to make a cutting remark about it. Some- times, it almost seemed as if he did not want anyone who had ever voted against him to vote for him in the future.

After he signed with appropriate ceremonies a bill creating a branch of The University of Texas in the Midland-Odessa area, the Republican mayor of Odessa, Jim Reese, thanked him for doing so.

"It was a privilege," Smith replied, "but if everybody had voted like you all did, I wouldn't have had that privilege."

When he went to the Dallas Press Club's Gridiron Dinner on May 10, 1969, Smith sat next to Mrs. Bob Miller, wife of the *Dallas Morning News* city editor and the club's president.

There was widespread speculation at the time that Smith planned to veto a bill establishing a branch of The University of Texas at Dallas. When Mrs. Miller asked him, probably more to make con- versation than anything else, what he planned to do about it, the

Governor replied by referring to his failure to carry Dallas County in 1968.

"I plan to give it the same consideration that the voters of Dallas gave me last year," he said.

He did—roughly. He vetoed it and demanded changes (including a switch from a four-year school to an "upper level" institution offering only junior, senior and graduate courses) which were made before he signed the second version.

Smith always distrusted the press, even though it pulled his 1962 campaign out of the fire by developing fully and factually one of the charges he made. Smith admitted in 1969 that he "had forgotten" that incident, which was largely responsible for his being elected lieutenant governor after he trailed House Speaker James A. Turman by 69,526 votes in the first primary.

The telling blow in the runoff was uncovered by Kenneth Towery, who had won a Pulitzer Prize while working on the *Cuero Record* and then was working for the *Austin American-Statesman.* Towery, who later served as Senator Tower's top assistant and then as a high-ranking executive in the U. S. Information Agency, revealed that Turman had turned in a state expense account for a one-night, lobbyist-financed junket on Chesapeake Bay.

Towery said Turman and other Texas legislators who had attended a National Legislative Conference in Philadelphia Sept. 6-8, 1961, were guests of "small loan tycoon Davis Weir of Miami" the night of Sept. 10. They cruised down Chesapeake Bay on a yacht, the *Maurine II,* and spent the night at the Great Oak Lodge and Yacht Club—at the expense of Weir and at the invitation of Sam Hanna, a former state representative then lobbying for the Pacific Finance Company, Towery reported.

Other legislators who made the trip did not list any expenses for that night on their state expense accounts, said Towery, but Turman did.

The expense account item in question amounted only to $21.50 but it probably cost Turman the election. He disappeared for three days after Towery's article appeared and his campaign headquarters spokesmen told reporters seeking comment on it that they did not know where he was.

Finally, on May 30, just three days before the runoff election, Turman called in two wire service reporters for a sort of clandestine press conference in which he merely denied any wrong-doing.

"I was paid no more for the entire trip than I actually spent personally while on business for the state," said Turman, according to the *Associated Press.* "I paid for all my wife's expenses."

Turman's three-day disappearing act was credited by many with enabling Smith to defeat him, with 551,564 votes to 500,875. Despite this episode—or perhaps because of it, and its possible future implications—Smith harbored the attitude that most newsmen should be seen and not read.

Two months after Smith's inauguration, William H. Gardner, the veteran and longtime political expert of the *Houston Post,* wrote a "profile" on him that was about 99 and 44/100 per cent complimentary. It compared him with Connally, noting that both exemplified the age-old, rags-to-riches success story but that the resemblance otherwise was quite limited.

"Connally is urbane, polished and handsome," said Gardner. "People used to say: he looks like a governor ought to look. He was a friend of one president and shot down at the side of another, a traveler to foreign lands, an inspiring political leader, a national figure, a man used to high levels and inner circles.

"Smith is of a different mold. He was a successful businessman in Lubbock—movie theaters and real estate—and has had 18 years' experience in state government but the aroma of the soil still clings to him. To use a snooty word, he is in many ways provincial, definitely not a man of the world.

"His taste in clothes is good, he has a handsome family and warm friends, but he lacks the Connally charisma," Gardner continued. "He has a good sense of humor, but most of his jokes are pretty corny. He has made thousands of speeches but has never acquired the knack of public speaking. He puts the accent on the wrong word, and drops his voice in the wrong places. He wisely avoids television when possible, for he projects poorly. Apparently he knows or cares little of the world outside Texas and he has a hard time remembering names— a deplorable lapse in a politician.

"But many of Governor Smith's seeming weaknesses are his real strengths. For one thing he is a winner, and no one can quarrel with success. He is close to the ordinary people of Texas—far closer than Connally. He speaks their language, and in the same flat Texas drawl they use."

Gardner noted that Smith insisted "we're just common folks—and that's all we've ever been and that's all we'll ever be."

"He is, to the contrary, a most uncommon man," Gardner concluded. "No run-of-the-mill politician could have achieved his successes, often against heavy odds."

Those odds included his public relations tendencies, which prompted him to say in a speech the following week that he had been unjustly accused by Gardner of "telling corny jokes." That was the only reference he made to the highly complimentary article. He may have been merely trying to be funny but if so, he demonstrated once again his weakness for corny jokes and, more importantly from the view-point of the press, his tendency to find fault with nearly everything written about him.

He seemed to feel that reporters should either be "for" or "against" him. He could not understand the columnists' criticizing him pro-fusely for a number of things which happened early in his adminis-tration—and then praising him for his move to investigate an 11.4 per cent increase, which he felt unjustified, in private passenger auto-mobile insurance rates. He could not seem to understand that most of the columnists criticized him when they felt he was wrong and praised him when they felt he was right. Admittedly, this never was a 50-50 proposition, for they generally felt he was wrong more than he was right.

Smith occasionally surprised people by flashing a bit of humor at unexpected times.

On Jan. 26, 1971, for instance, he spoke at an Austin luncheon spon-sored by the Texas Association of Life Underwriters. The Securities and Exchange Commission's investigation of the Sharpstown-National Bankers Life scandal, and Smith's role in it, was fresh on everyone's mind. And the Governor had just been released from the hospital, where he had been treated for a stomach disorder.

"You know, when I was in the hospital," he said, "the reporters sent me a get-well card. I hear the vote on sending it was 11 to nine."

One of Smith's paradoxical qualities was demonstrated by his knack for looking on the dark side of most articles written about him while searching out the silver lining in nearly everything else.

His closest friends pictured him as an incurable optimist. There certainly was nothing in his tax recommendations, in 1969 or 1971, to dispute that view; when he proposed, in 1971, a constitutional amendment to authorize issuance of $450 million in bonds to pay current state government expenses, the House buried that idea under a 125-22 vote and gales of laughter. He reportedly had been optimistic enough to think that plan actually would be adopted.

Smith had demonstrated considerable optimism in 1929 when, at the age of 17, he packed his belongings in a knapsack, left the Daw-son County farm to which his family had moved from Williamson County four years earlier, and walked 17 miles to enter high school at Lamesa. The seventh of 13 children in his family, Smith worked in a combination grocery store and service station in Lamesa to earn his way through high school.

In 1932, he persuaded Ted Tipps, a Lubbock grain and feed dealer who owned a major oil company distributorship, to lease him a ser-vice station so he could operate it to finance his studies at Texas Tech.

"I don't think I ever saw a more active college boy," Tipps recalled later. "He not only leased the station and worked his way through college but he also hired other students, helping them work their way, too."

Even so, Tipps did not know about all of Smith's activities. The future governor also picked cotton and cleaned windows in his "spare" time to get through college. As soon as he received his degree, he married Miss Ima Smith, a tall, attractive brunette whom he had met as a result of the alphabetical seating arrangement which put them side by side in class. And then he borrowed enough money to open a theater across the street from the Tech campus.

"We borrowed money from everybody," Smith recalled. "By the time we opened for business we owed a thousand dollars. Half the customers on opening night were bill collectors. Our first film was 'After Office Hours' starring Clark Gable. We couldn't pay cash for help, so we started getting Tech football players. to work for us in exchange for passes. I guess over the years we must have used more than 500 of them."

The business was on the verge of collapse when Max Schmeling came to the rescue. The film of Schmeling's kayoing Joe Louis played to a packed house for two weeks and Smith's financial worries were over—at least insofar as the theater was concerned. But that was before he entered politics.

Smith won a race for the House of Representatives in 1944 and served six years before making an unsuccessful bid for lieutenant governor in 1950, when he finished third in a field of 12. Two years later, he ran for the State Senate but lost to Senator Kilmer Corbin by 566 votes out of almost 42,000 cast. In 1956, he won election to the Senate and six years later was elected lieutenant governor.

Smith later recalled a financial crisis during that 1962 campaign as a significant turning point in his career.

"It requires a lot of money to move around the state, to write letters and buy stamps and pay office help—and we were down to about $15," he said. "That's all we had. That was in Dallas, about a month or six weeks before the election. Our campaign really hadn't begun to roll the way I had thought it would and, actually, it didn't jell until about the last two weeks.

"Well, we went on over to Tyler from Dallas and the people there said they had been able to raise a little money. They had about $1,000 for us—and that really put us back on the road, where we could move."

As lieutenant governor, Smith accepted every speaking invitation he possibly could and criss-crossed the state countless times shaking hands. Even Barnes had to admit after the 1968 campaign that

"Smith's been to my home town [DeLeon, population 2,122] more in the last year than I have."

It was during that campaign that Barnes decided to stop in one little wide place in the road where he felt no candidate for statewide office ever had visited before. He introduced himself and asked for support.

"Say, where's ol' Preston?" he was asked. "We ain't seen him for a week."

Smith felt strongly that there was no substitute—not even money—for hard work. And while he took great pride in the long hours and hard work which got him elected, he habitually referred to himself as "we."

"I don't think there's any question," he said during a 1969 interview, "but what the hard work that we did by taking ourselves into the smaller communities and meeting the people was the key to our success. We didn't do this just in the small places; we went into the larger places, too. But remember this: in the larger places, like the big metropolitan areas, most of those people came from the rural areas. Most of them have relatives back in the rural areas and, surprisingly enough, a lot of them still take those rural papers from the places where they grew up."

Smith also sent 400,000 individually-typed letters to the voters. Forty-seven thousand of those went to families named Smith and asked, "Don't you think it is about time one of us was governor?"

Smith's campaign quarterbacks wisely kept him off television as much as possible, realizing that he made a much better appearance in person than on the screen. They limited his television to short spot announcements featuring brief film clips of him in action, shaking hands with voters or presiding over the Senate. He never appeared "live" on television and he shunned all invitations to participate in question-and-answer "public service" programs.

He nurtured the rather unusual theory that television is not effective, anyway, except with people whom a candidate previously has contacted in person.

"My campaign methods will always be people-to-people and person-to-person," he declared. "Of course, I enjoy TV but I don't think TV is effective at all unless you've been in the towns, the large ones and the small ones, and you've met the people in them. When you get on the TV screen, they say, 'I know that fellow—he's been here,' and then they'll listen to you. But if they've never seen you before, they won't listen to you."

Smith also held a strong belief that hard work is directly related to timing and financing.

"Prior to entering a political contest, there are very few people interested in helping you finance it," is the way he put it. "But if you get into a race and you begin to show strength, then the financial help will come to you. Timing is important and the candidate himself has to figure that out. I think my timing when I ran for governor in 1968 was exactly right, even though many people thought I entered the race too early."

Smith announced his candidacy on August 23, 1967, while Governor Connally was in Africa on a six-week safari. At that time, there was widespread speculation that Connally would seek a fourth term (the Capitol Press members polled themselves on that question and 37 of the 38 predicted he would run again). Most people felt Connally would be unbeatable but Smith announced flatly that he was running, regardless of what Connally did. He also predicted that Connally would not seek reelection.

"I just tried to put myself in his shoes," Smith explained later, "and tried to look at it like I thought he would. If I had been the governor of this state for six years, as he had been, and I'd had every honor there was to be had by serving as governor, why would I want to run for a fourth term? Why subject myself to a hard campaign and the possibility of being defeated when I could retire without being defeated and with an outstanding record as governor? This was the manner in which I looked at it and this is what convinced me that he would not be a candidate."

Smith also made it clear that he would have stayed in the race even if Connally had decided to run again.

"We made up our minds that this was the time for me to move into the governor's race if ever I was going to move," he said. "This was a matter of timing and this was pretty well true when I ran for lieutenant governor in 1962. I was serving as a state senator and we didn't have a lieutenant governor then because Ben Ramsey had moved over to the Railroad Commission. Many of my close friends said, 'Don't run for lieutenant governor—the time's not ripe.' Well, the time had to be ripe for any person who was a formidable candidate because we had no lieutenant governor.

"When I announced for governor," he added, "I had been lieutenant governor and I considered that just a stepping stone. But I know a lot of people said, 'Well, he took a long shot—money, marbles and chalk, all or nothing.' But I suppose in any political race you'd run, it would be pretty much that way because there's no reward for second place in a political race. And it costs lots of money to run."

Raising funds nearly always is a headache for any politician. Even though money generally is needed in great quantities in any campaign, a wise politician exercises some discretion in where and how and from whom he accepts it, and on what terms. After all, no one can tell when another Billie Sol Estes affair will pop up. After the "boy wonder" of West Texas agriculture and finance went bankrupt and was convicted of fraud, some of the politicians who had accepted large contributions from him while he was considered one of the state's leading citizens wished they had never heard of him. And some of them tried to act as if they never had.

Smith reported spending a total of $1,233,077 during his hotly-contested 1968 campaign for governor. But Texas candidates are required to report officially only the funds which actually are spent by the candidate or by his state campaign headquarters. In most cases, at least that much, and sometimes a great deal more, is channeled through various committees and spent on the local, county or regional level without ever finding its way into the record books.

"In our campaign," said Smith, "our contributions came from everybody—from 50 cents to a hundred dollars. We got a few large contributions, up to $1,000—I don't recall. Some of these people were in the oil business and some were not. But strangely enough, the people that contribute the most money never request anything.

"All they want is good government," he declared. "They want an economic climate whereby they can operate their business with the least amount of red tape and bureaucracy. And they don't want to be persecuted tax-wise but they're all willing to pay their share—at least what they feel is their share. But the people that support me the most financially, I never see in this office."

"What if someone," the Governor was asked, "offers you a sizable contribution in a campaign and it's someone you don't know? Do you have to make it clear there are no strings attached if you accept it?"

"This has never been any problem with me," he declared. "We've turned down some large contributions and we've taken some large contributions. But always it's understood that the only thing we've had to offer is good government—at least, the type we believe in. . . ."

Smith felt Texas was destined to remain a one-party state on the local and state levels, although, he added, "we've always had a two-party state on the national level."

"I don't think we're going to have a two-party state on the local or state level—except that a presidential election generally will pull a few over in the governor's race and in a few top-echelon races," he contended. "But Texas is just a Democratic state and I think it's going to stay that way on a state and local basis. The people have always been Democrats and I don't look for them to change. They've always been pretty independent so far as the national ticket is concerned. But on the local level, you seldom even see anybody run as a Republican."

Smith admitted that a lot of dissension existed between liberals and conservatives in the Democratic Party.

"I think the Republicans have just as much division but theirs is not pointed out as much, nor do they carry it as far as the Democrats," he said. "In other words, when a Republican is chosen as a nominee, almost all the sides go with him; but in the Democratic Party, if you choose a conservative, a lot of times the liberals stay at home or they vote against him. I think this might have happened to Waggoner Carr."

Smith referred to the unsuccessful race Carr, his erstwhile friend from Lubbock, ran against Senator Tower in 1966—not to the one he ran against Smith in the 1968 Democratic Primary. Carr did alienate the liberals who normally vote a straight Democratic ticket and, partly as a result of that but also because of Tower's popular voting record, drew what he termed "a mandate from the people to practice law."

Just as many liberals did in *that* race, a great many conservative Democrats in Texas were inclined to "go fishing" on election day or to vote for his Republican opponent every time Senator Yarborough ran.

Smith said he and Yarborough always have been friends "although I don't agree with him politically, nor do I have the same governmental philosophy that he does." And they did not grow any closer after he became governor, Smith insisted.

Although Smith professed no knowledge of it, the two worked hand-in-hand during the 1969 Regular Session of the Legislature in an unsuccessful attempt to win Senate confirmation of former Senator Dorsey B. Hardeman's appointment to the chairmanship of the State Insurance Board. The crusty, tactless and often rude Hardeman had alienated a great many of his colleagues during his 22 years in the Senate, where he had been Lieutenant Governor Smith's right-hand man.

Early in the session, 11 of the 31 senators signed a pact agreeing to vote against Hardeman, thus denying him the two-thirds majority needed for confirmation. Until then, appointments of all former members of the Senate had been confirmed almost automatically. Since most of the 11 were liberals, Yarborough took an active role in trying to convert them. He probably was drawn into the battle more by Edward Clark, an Austin lawyer whom President Johnson had appointed Ambassador to Australia, than by Smith. Clark was a long-time business associate of Johnson's and had served as one of Yarborough's main campaign money-raisers.

But Yarborough made no headway at all in his efforts to help Hardeman. When he called Senator Oscar Mauzy of Dallas, a liberal

Smith shocked a joint session by ridiculing statements just made by Senator Tower, shown at Smith's left elbow, next to Rep. Tommy Shannon. Sen. Bill Patman is shown at far right and Lt. Gov. Barnes at far left.

and one of his old friends, he had barely put in a good word for
Hardeman when he was interrupted.

"I know," said Yarborough, "that it's none of my business but—"

"You're right, Senator," Mauzy declared politely but firmly. "It's
not."

Smith repeatedly reminded the 11 recalcitrant senators of such
things as his veto power but finally, as the session ended, admitted
defeat by withdrawing Hardeman's appointment. The fiasco left
lasting wounds and perhaps even turned what was left of Smith's
hair—a subject about which he seemed to enjoy joking—a little grayer.

"Right after I received the Democratic nomination for governor,"
Smith recalled, "we were in Dallas and my wife and I got on an
elevator in a hotel about 10 o'clock one night with our kids. There
was a tall fellow on there—I guess he was about a foot taller than
the rest of us. Obviously, he wasn't feeling too much pain. He
looked at me and he said, 'You know, you look just like Preston
Smith; but of course I know you're *not* Preston Smith because you
have more hair than he does.' I told him who I was but he wouldn't
believe me."

One of Smith's major problems was that many people found it hard
to believe him, partly because he denied such unimportant but obvious facts as his being in the theater business. He even said he had
no interest in a Lubbock real estate firm bearing his name—that a
friend of his just wanted to use his name and he granted permission.

On Jan. 16, 1968, he took an unnecessary slap at the press, during
a campaign speech in Greenville, for allegedly labeling him the "ultra
conservative candidate" in the governor's race.

"You never read in the papers or hear on the radio or television,"
he said, being careful not to miss antagonizing any of the media,
"how I carried 218 of the 254 counties in Texas in the last general
election or how I polled 81 per cent of the votes (for lieutenant governor) in the last Democratic Primary."

Smith claimed that he had never voted against a "progressive" piece
of legislation—even though he was noted, as a senator, for being
absent when many controversial issues came up. He contended that
he was a "moderate" and added that he was not concerned over the
opinions of the press since "I learned a long time ago that the voters
don't pay much attention to the press."

He may have moderated that particular view somewhat in May of
1969, after he went to Washington and expressed opposition to President Nixon's housing program.

"Smith said he is specifically opposed to the elimination of slums,"
said Leslie Carpenter in his Washington column for Texas newspapers.

Carpenter quoted Smith as saying, "Some people like to live in slums." Then, added Carpenter, Smith was asked specifically about the Nixon proposal.

"From what I know about the program, I'm opposed to it," Smith said.

"How much do you know?" a reporter inquired.

"Not very much," Smith said candidly, according to Carpenter.

On May 30, 1969, Senator Tower addressed a joint session of the Texas Legislature and, after he finished, Smith felt compelled to make a most unusual rebuttal. Tower had expressed optimism over the possibility that the federal government would some day share income tax revenue with the states, since Nixon had approved the idea.

"I have 29 cents in my pocket," Smith told the Legislature when Tower finished his speech, "and I feel that's more than we will ever get from the federal government through revenue-sharing."

On June 10, 1969, Smith challenged the validity of 41 measures passed by the regular session of the Legislature, on grounds they had not been signed in the presence of both houses by their presiding officers before adjournment. On June 19, he vetoed 37 of them—and on June 21, *he signed the other four* into law.

Before vetoing the one-year, no-tax budget in 1969, Smith signed a bill granting school teachers a 10-year schedule of pay raises, which the privately-financed Texas Research League estimated would cost the State a total of $3.9 billion. On Oct. 8, 1969, Smith astounded even his most ardent supporters by telling newsmen that the teacher pay raise scheduled to go into effect in 1971, under that bill, might have to be reconsidered and postponed to avoid higher taxes.

That statement came out, oddly enough, while the reporters were questioning him about his appointment the day before of Richard Lee Penn, husband of Smith's personal secretary for eight years, to a six-year term as the "employer" representative on the Texas Industrial Accident Board. Penn had never been an employer, having spent most of his adult life working for state agencies. But he resigned from a job with the State Building Commission on a Friday to spend the weekend as an "executive vice president" of a printing firm which published Industrial Accident reports, in order to qualify technically on Monday as an "employer."

"It was all set up so it would be legal if any questions were asked," Penn explained quite candidly. "I considered buying a service station and then selling it but that would have taken more time—and I wouldn't have been any more official."

Perhaps not. He served in the $19,000-a-year post from November, 1969, until May, 1971, when the appointment went before the Senate for confirmation. The Senate Nominations Committee asked for an official ruling and Attorney General Martin quickly held that the two-day stint at the printing firm did not qualify Penn to serve as the employers' representative on the Board. Smith then withdrew the appointment.

Such fiascoes prompted unusual speculation that Smith might not automatically be given the traditional second term. As Bo Byers put it in his Sept. 28, 1969, *Houston Chronicle* column:

"There has been increasing speculation that Smith may prove a one-term governor because of general public reaction to his insistence on a two-year, $6 billion state budget that jumped $1 billion over 1968-69 and required a $350 million tax bill. There also is discontent with Smith's administration based on a feeling of lack of direction under his leadership."

Despite rebuffs from the press, the State Senate and strangers in elevators, Smith became the first governor in history to escape opposition in a Democratic Primary. He was widely acclaimed as the luckiest politician who had ever lived—at least until the Sharpstown scandals came to light—and he seemed to enjoy being governor more than most of his predecessors had.

He treated Texas's loss of political influence in Washington about as lightly as he did his own loss of hair.

"Personally, I'm not too concerned about it," he said, long before Connally was named to the Nixon Cabinet. "Of course we miss Lyndon Johnson and Sam Rayburn and people like that up there.

"But you must remember we still have George Mahon, who is chairman of the House Appropriations Committee; we still have Bob Poage, who heads the House Agriculture Committee; we still have Wright Patman, chairman of the Banking Committee; we still have Omar Burleson—we have perhaps greater representation chairmanship-wise than almost any other state. I think Texas is in a good position, insofar as the national government is concerned."

It probably was in a better position then, at least with the Nixon Administration, than it was after Smith failed to appear at a White House dinner for the nation's governors on Feb. 23, 1971, after he had accepted an invitation to it. At first, the Governor said he did not attend because he was working on a proposal for federal financing of welfare which he planned to present the following day at the National Governors' Conference in Washington. When he returned home, he claimed he had never responded to the invitation—which, in itself, would be a *faux pas* of astronomical proportions.

Had Smith really thought the Texas influence in Washington was dead, he probably would have tried to make a joke of it on June 11, 1969, when he appeared once again at Austin's Municipal Auditorium.

This time, it was to address a convention of the Texas Funeral Directors and Embalmers Association.

"I want to thank you for asking me to be here today," he began. "It is truly an honor to be with you. Some of the wags in my office had told me that this would be a very stiff and lifeless affair but I am happy to see that it is not.

"Have you gentlemen heard about the newest and most inexpensive funeral that has been initiated in other parts of the country?" asked the Governor of Texas. "They stand the deceased on his tip-toes and drive him into the ground, one arm out-stretched holding his American Express card. . . .'"

Smith almost muffed the biggest break in his 1970 campaign against Eggers. It came when a belligerent crowd kept him from delivering a speech on the University of Houston campus. Even some of Smith's strongest critics deeply resented the Governor's being jeered off the campus of a state-supported university and not being permitted to speak.

The unruly students shouted Smith down with cries of "Free Lee Otis!" They were demanding a parole for Lee Otis Johnson, a militant Negro who had been sentenced to 30 years in prison for possession of marijuana.

But the Governor immediately told a radio interviewer: "I thought they were saying 'we want frijoles.' And you know frijoles are something they have on the menu in Mexican—uh, American restaurants. I think they're fried beans. So I asked someone, 'Why are they saying they want frijoles?' And they said, they're not saying they want frijoles, they're saying, 'Free Lee Otis.'"

As the *Dallas Times Herald* put it in a headline on the story:

SMITH DIDN'T KNOW
BEANS ABOUT CHANT

Courageous if nothing else, Smith bravely showed up in Austin's Municipal Auditorium again in February, 1971, for the annual Headliners Club stag luncheon, at which public figures are scorched unmercifully. And he was at his best in delivering a hilarious speech which had been written for him, especially attuned to the Sharpstown scandal.

"Let him who is without stock throw the first rock," the Governor began. By the time he got through poking fun at himself for about 15 minutes, Smith had the huge crowd eating out of his hand.

But many of those present felt there was a lot of truth in the response of Cactus Pryor, Austin television humorist and one of the wittiest entertainers in the country.

"Preston," he said, "I've always said you are one of the funniest governors Texas ever had."

Chapter 4

MARATHON RUNNER

A prominent participant in all the parties for the Army visitors to the SMU-Army football game in Dallas on October 13, 1967, according to Paul Crume's front-page column in the *Dallas Morning News* a few days later, was Ralph Yarborough.

"Yarborough once attended West Point," Crume noted. "He was a brilliant student there back in 1919 and 1920—except in mathematics, and his weakness in mathematics ended his career at the military academy before graduation.

"One of his old classmates of the Class of '23 greeted him at a Dallas party the other night, maybe a little patronizingly.

"'Too bad, Ralph, that you couldn't finish up,'" he remarked. 'By the way, what are you doing now?'

"'I'm United States Senator from Texas,' replied the Senator genially. 'What are *you* doing?'"

This marked one of the few times in Ralph Webster Yarborough's career that he used a soft answer to retaliate. Usually, he is about as subtle as a sledge hammer.

"You ought to take Dallas off the map," he declared in Brownwood, during his 1964 reelection campaign as he recalled the assassination of President John F. Kennedy.

A few weeks later, *Reader's Digest* published an article about an Area Redevelopment Administration project which failed at Crockett, Texas, after receiving a glowing endorsement from Yarborough. The Senator blamed that article's criticism of him on his 1964 opponent, George Bush, and Bush's father, the former Senator from Connecticut.

"Smilin' Ralph" said Bush's "multimillionaire father's Wall Street investment banking connections enable the planting of false and libelous articles about me in national magazines like the *Reader's Digest*."

Yarborough claims he has been a constant target throughout his political career for "libelous" articles, for villification by his opponents, for vile plots by governors of Texas and for telephone-tapping, which he said on July 11, 1969, had been going on for so long that he had become accustomed to it.

"All senators' phones are tapped all the time," he declared.

His own experience, he said, was most serious during his 1964 campaign, when he suspected a "triple tap" on his phone.

Yarborough became so upset during that campaign that he continued to denounce Bush even after it ended. On election night he declared: "I think my opponent ought to pack up his suitcase and go back where he came from. He carried on the vilest and most defaming campaign I have ever seen."

To Yarborough, any campaign in which he had an opponent was a vile and defaming one. President Johnson did his best to see that Yarborough escaped a campaign altogether in 1964 but when two materialized—one in the Democratic Primary and one in the general election—LBJ put his arm around Smilin' Ralph and, with a timely assist from the FBI, pulled him through.

This came as quite a shock to people who knew President Johnson well, since Yarborough had refused to ride in the same car with him on November 21, 1963, in San Antonio and Houston. While it seemed understandable that Yarborough was willing to forget that and "let bygones be by-gones" as soon as Johnson became President, many observers found it amazing that Johnson appeared willing to bury the hatchet.

They found the hatchet in the back of Joe Kilgore, then a Congressman from McAllen and a close friend of Governor Connally. After Kilgore announced he would not seek reelection and hinted he might oppose Yarborough, a high-ranking associate of President Johnson advised him that the President would "cut off" his campaign financing and also persuade the major Texas newspapers to oppose him if he ran for the Senate.

When the threats did little more than arouse Kilgore's ire, the tactics were switched. The conservative Congressman then was advised that Johnson's future as President, particularly his ability to obtain the Democratic Party's nomination in 1964, might be at stake.

Johnson had assured national labor leaders that peace and harmony would prevail that year in the Texas Democratic Party and that he could promise Yarborough's reelection. Fulfilling that promise was vitally important to Johnson, who had not gained control of the Democratic National Committee at that point.

Kilgore was told that "the national welfare" could hinge on his decision and that Johnson could do more for Texas as President than Kilgore could as a senator.

Ultimately, these appeals succeeded where the threats had failed. They tipped the scales against Kilgore's making the race—a race which, from a personal standpoint, he had never been enthusiastic about anyway.

But if Kilgore was *not* embittered by the presidential pressure which forced him out of the race, Connally *was*. The incident provoked one of the most serious of many spats between Johnson and Connally, straining their relationship almost to the breaking point.

Connally was so incensed over it that he threatened to either run for the Senate himself or to retire from politics that year.

When Connally finally decided in 1967 to retire without seeking a fourth term in 1968, Yarborough could not resist taking another swat at him. He said the Governor had seen "the handwriting on the wall" and that he had been popular "only because he was shot with President Kennedy."

That statement came while Connally was being rumored as a possible appointee to succeed Robert S. McNamara as Secretary of Defense. Yarborough said he did not think it possible that President Johnson would pick his old friend and campaign manager for such an important post.

"He knows Connally doesn't have the temperament or qualifications for the job," Yarborough told Martin Casey of the *Dallas News*. "It doesn't make sense to put in that terribly difficult job a man who is just not qualified."

Yarborough insisted that, despite his longtime political feud with Connally, he was "putting prejudice aside" and making his statements as "an informed observer on the political scene."

In the same interview, Yarborough said he had a friendly relationship with President Johnson "but he hasn't appointed anybody up here that has supported me. . . . We don't talk about those unpleasant subjects."

Johnson had barely settled down on his LBJ Ranch after leaving the White House, however, before he became one of Yarborough's favorite "unpleasant subjects." When a dozen top-ranking labor leaders gathered in Washington during the spring of 1969 to begin preliminary planning for his 1970 reelection campaign, Yarborough spent more than 30 minutes berating Johnson.

His tirade alarmed some of the labor officials so much that they telephoned Hank Brown, president of the Texas AFL-CIO, and got him to fly to Washington that night. Brown talked to Yarborough and urged him to soft-pedal his bitter criticism of the former President.

Reports of the affair quickly got back to Johnson, who confided to close friends that he was tired of getting slapped by a man to whom he had shown nothing but kindness.

It seems typically paradoxical of Yarborough that while he continued to spend 365 days of every year seeking votes, he went out of his way to antagonize people such as Johnson even after they had retired to the sidelines.

As chairman of the Senate Committee on Labor and Public Welfare, he approached the 1970 campaign in what Governor Smith described as a stronger position than ever. Yarborough even drew a broad cross-section of Democrats to a September 25, 1969, "appreciation dinner" in Dallas, long noted as an anti-Yarborough stronghold. The Senator explained his surprisingly friendly reception by declaring that "Dallas is coming more and more into the mainstream of life in Texas and the rest of the country."

Yarborough, of course, felt the mainstream encompassed most of his own views. He had decided a few weeks earlier that the Vietnam War had been a mistake from the beginning, that it should be financed "at least in part" by an excess profits tax and that the vast majority of Texans supported Senator Edward M. Kennedy strongly even after Chappaquiddick. He co-authored with Kennedy a bill to revise the draft and put it on a lottery basis but said what he really favored was a volunteer army with pay high enough to attract volunteers.

He strongly opposed the right-to-work law and President Nixon's proposal for post office reform. He favored the oil depletion allowance only on domestic production, feeling it should be repealed on overseas operations, and he worked for raising the personal income tax exemption.

In a May 6, 1969, speech in Washington, Yarborough bitterly assailed "war profiteers" and called the anti-ballistic missile system "a big boondoggle packaged in a big hornswoggle." He decried budget cuts during the Johnson administration for schools and colleges, public health and public works, saying Vietnam War costs had gone up $36 billion during that five-year period.

"Talk about student rioting," he told a meeting of the Business Executives Move for Vietnam Peace (BEM) organization, "if the people understood what had been done to them these last five years, the majority of Americans would be ready to riot."

Yarborough's turning on Johnson again seemed no more shocking than did the changes in his personality and philosophy noted by his close friends shortly after he was stung unmercifully, about 20 years earlier, by the political bug. The stings apparently carried with them an overdose of persistence, enabling him to weather four defeats in statewide races before he finally won his Senate seat with a plurality in an April 2, 1957, special election.

A few days after that election, Margaret Mayer of the *Dallas Times Herald* described Yarborough as a man whom his longtime friends knew "more as a friendly intellectual than as the politician his publicists have devised."

"The Yarborough family has gained high respect in 27 years' residence in Austin, such respect that their townsmen were amazed when the friendly lawyer became an adamant politician who refused to acknowledge defeat," wrote Miss Mayer. "They view him as a 'fanatic' and, in the less polite language that inevitably crops up in politics, as a 'crazy man.'

"A campaign lieutenant concedes some truth to their estimates of Yarborough's intense concern with politics, but he also analyzes the reasons more closely than can the casual observer.

"'He was driven by two factors,' this lieutenant says. 'One was his overwhelming desire for victory. Second was the sincere, honest belief that he was fighting for the right thing. It was such a driving force that he became completely wrapped up in it.'

"A neighbor who has lived next door to the Yarboroughs for five years agrees that the often-defeated, finally-elected Yarborough has been nothing but sincere in his desire to save the people from political machines which he feels have corrupted the state.

"'I've talked to him privately, as neighbors do out in the back yard, and I know he has the people of Texas at heart,' he says. 'The people wouldn't believe it when he told them that in his campaigns, but I know it was true.'"

Miss Mayer added that Yarborough "is not a 'dry' but drinks only rarely. He does not smoke. He is not a golfer but likes hunting and fishing—geese and ducks for hunting and the hook and line type of fishing he learned as a boy in East Texas."

It was in 1952, during the first of his three unsuccessful tries for the governor's office, that many of his old friends say they first detected a drastic change in Yarborough. He had won great respect while serving as a district judge in Austin from 1936 until 1941, winning an election after his initial appointment by the late Governor James V. Allred.

Yarborough took a brief leave of absence from the bench to run for attorney general in 1938, then left it for good in 1942 when he was commissioned as a captain in the 97th Division. He served in both Europe and the Pacific, attaining the rank of lieutenant colonel before World War II ended, and then returned to private law practice in Austin.

Many of his old friends, who felt his views had been on the moderate side, believe he was "pushed" into the extreme liberal camp by his post-war political ambitions simply because it was the liberals who were looking for someone to carry their banner. In addition, Governor Shivers's support of Eisenhower in 1952 gave Yarborough a "party loyalty" issue which became one of his favorites.

Yarborough insisted that he simply could not understand the term, "Eisenhower Democrat."

"That's like saying you're a Christian who believes in Mohammed," he quipped.

During the 1952 campaign, Yarborough shocked some of his acquaintances by stopping them on the street and asking point-blank if they were supporting him or Shivers.

"If you even tried to beat around the bush and not give a direct answer," said one, "he'd blow his top. He probably lost quite a few votes that way."

Yarborough had planned initially to seek the attorney general's office again that year. Price Daniel was leaving it to run for the U. S. Senate but Yarborough, in trying to finance his campaign, decided that Shivers already had lined up most of the contributors for his secretary of state, John Ben Shepperd.

After one trip to Houston, Yarborough was particularly discouraged—even though he had received assurance there of support from J. R. Parten, a millionaire whom Shivers had refused to reappoint to the University of Texas Board of Regents. Parten was to become one of Yarborough's strongest backers in his 1952, 1954 and 1956 races for governor and his 1957, 1958 and 1964 campaigns for the U. S. Senate.

Yarborough dropped by the Capitol Press Room one spring day after that fateful Houston trip and related his plight to a close friend, Stuart Long, operator of a news service for a number of daily newspapers and publisher of several specialized newsletters.

"If you're going to have to fight the top man," said Long, after hearing of Yarborough's financial woes, "why don't you just run against *him?*"

"You know, Bill Kittrell had that same crazy idea," Yarborough replied, mentioning a well-known political public relations consultant in Dallas.

"Three days later," Long recalled, "Ralph announced—for governor."

His announcement triggered some of the most vicious political wars the state had ever known, drawing sharp new battle lines between liberals and conservatives.

The late Allen Duckworth, who distinguished himself as political editor of the *Dallas News* for many years, noted on June 20, 1954, that Yarborough came from a family with fighting traditions.

"There was a Yarborough at Valley Forge," Duckworth wrote. "Harvey Yarborough, a grandfather, was a pioneer settler in Smith County. Grandfather Yarborough, who donated the land for Hopewell Baptist Church, later organized the first Confederate infantry company in the community and became its captain.

"Ralph Yarborough is an intense student of the Civil War. He reads every book on the subject he can find and keeps a library of Civil War books both at home and in his Austin law office. . . .

"Yarborough was the seventh in a family of eleven children.

"Before settling down to practice law, Yarborough taught in one-room schoolhouses in East Texas, worked in a student boarding house at The University of Texas, worked during vacations as a cleaner of railway coaches, in the Borger oil fields, in a Dallas lumber yard, in Oklahoma wheat fields. He spent a year in schools in France and Germany, earning expenses by working on a horse boat. . . .

"Yarborough is a morn-to-night campaigner. He meets with county organizers, addresses barbecue rallies, speaks to luncheon clubs."

Duckworth also said Yarborough claimed to be visiting towns which had been ignored by politicians for years.

"I went into a town where they said it was the first time they could remember when a candidate for governor had visited them," Yarborough was quoted. "I asked them who the last candidate was. Some of the old-timers talked it over and decided it was Sam Houston."

In 1956, as Yarborough made his third bid for the governorship, Dawson Duncan of the *Dallas News* noted that he had never quit running after his 1952 campaign.

"In this year's campaign, just as it was in 1952 and 1954, Yarborough's theme will be charges of misdeeds in the State Capitol with a promise to restore morality in the state house," said Duncan.

"The Yarborough cause will again be one of liberalism against the conservatives led by Shivers. His backers will include the liberal-loyalist Democratic faction, union members and adherents of his constant charges the Capitol needs a housecleaning to rid it of corruption."

Shivers did not seek reelection that year and U. S. Senator Daniel defeated Yarborough in a bitterly-fought runoff for the Democratic nomination, with 698,001 votes to 694,830.

That set the stage for Yarborough's victory in the 1957 special election to fill the remainder of Daniel's unexpired term—a victory achieved by his capturing 38 per cent of the vote in a race with 22 opponents.

Even after winning that election, Yarborough tried to shun an avowed "liberal" tag, contending that he always had been a Democrat and had "never attempted to give a one-word definition to my beliefs."

Yarborough's first majority victory came in his sixth statewide race on July 26, 1958, when he won a full six-year term by defeating former Senator William A. Blakley, a genial, self-made Dallas millionaire whom Shivers had appointed to succeed Daniel. Blakley did not run in the 1957 special election but became the second Texan in history to serve in both of the State's Senate seats when Daniel appointed him in 1961, after Johnson resigned to become vice president.

Blakley lost the subsequent election to Tower, despite the fact that the Legislature had enacted a "runoff" law governing special elections—replacing the "high man wins" custom—in an obvious attempt to stymie Republicans.

By mid-1969, one of Yarborough's key supporters in those early campaigns had experienced a change of heart and declared flatly that

Republican President Nixon held the key to the Senator's 1970 re-election fate, just as Democratic President Johnson did in 1964.

Fagan Dickson, a wealthy Austin lawyer who had served as Yarborough's finance director during his 1964 campaign, had moderated most of his views—except those on the Vietnam War—considerably. He thought it ironic, he said in June of 1969, that Nixon might do as much for Yarborough—unintentionally, of course—as Johnson had.

Dickson made it clear that he did not intend to take an active part in Yarborough's 1970 campaign. He indicated he was displeased with the Senator mainly because, up to that point, he had failed to denounce the Vietnam War in the same sort of terms Dickson used during his abbreviated campaign for Congress in 1968.

Dickson began running against U. S. Representative J. J. (Jake) Pickle of Austin, one of Johnson's closest friends, on a one-plank platform: "Bring Lyndon Home." He started by plastering the 10th Congressional District with billboards bearing only those three words. When Johnson announced his retirement decision on March 31, 1968, Dickson withdrew from the congressional race. He said he had been trying merely to get Johnson's attention and felt a substantial vote for him would have let the President know that many of his "home folks" felt he had painted himself into a corner and that the United States should pull out of Vietnam.

He made it clear that he had nothing personal against Johnson—or Pickle. In fact, with the obvious exception of Yarborough himself, probably no one was happier than Dickson had been when LBJ helped pull that 1964 campaign out of the fire.

"Johnson literally plucked Yarborough up and stood him beside him and elected him, in my opinion," Dickson declared. "I thought he had to do it—and he did do it. Of course, I thought Yarborough shouldn't have been thrown out at that time. He was working hard, and at that time, we didn't have the Vietnam thing so clearly before the American people.

"I didn't hear from Ralph during my little campaign," said Dickson. "I didn't solicit his support. I think the thing frightened him. He was in a box. George Meany [president of the AFL-CIO] was sitting there with LBJ on television saying Vietnam was right, endorsing it every time he appeared. Senator Yarborough was in a difficult position—and he yet has not denounced the war, although he criticizes it openly now because it takes so much money away from domestic programs he's interested in."

Dickson felt there was no doubt that Meany and other labor leaders would do everything they could for Yarborough in 1970, noting that they had given him plenty of help in the past.

"He's stronger than ever with the labor unions because he's sitting on the spot they value most highly, as chairman of the Senate Labor Committee," said Dickson. "They'll support him to the hilt. But I think a lot of his liberal groups have been disillusioned with him, mainly on Vietnam. If Nixon gets us out of Vietnam, Yarborough will be quite vulnerable. If he doesn't, George Bush—whom I think very highly of—would be wasting his money by running against him.

"Yarborough has identified himself with people who think that big money really runs things," Dickson added. "His philosophy is not really liberal but the old Populist idea—and he's good at it. Anyone who stays in office as long as he has is bound to have a lot of problems—and I don't think he has ever built an organization on the basis of rewarding his friends. As a politician, he's not good at that. He has depended on labor and people like me and people who felt in the past that he was the best under the circumstances."

Dickson recalled that, as finance chairman, he originated what he felt was one of the most helpful ideas used by Yarborough in his 1964 campaign against Bush.

"Ralph was in a bad way," said Dickson. "He didn't have any kind of identification with the business element in Texas. So I dreamed up this idea of getting a bunch of millionaires to endorse him. I enlisted the services of Ed Clark and we formed this 'Businessmen for Yarborough Committee' and listed 13 millionaires on it in the first announcement."

This turned out to be a great idea, said Dickson, even though Bush greeted it with a cutting remark that took some of the edge off it.

"A 'Businessmen for Yarborough Committee' sounds about as likely," said Bush, "as a 'Barbers for Castro Committee.' "

Yarborough did not quit running after his 1970 defeat by Bentsen. He probably broke all existing records for the number of press releases issued by a lame duck. And he kept insisting he was not through.

"I will not retire to a rocking chair to calmly watch while the institutions of Texas are debauched," he told Karen Elliott of the *Dallas Morning News* on Dec. 2, 1970. "I've had my eye on the governor's office for 30 years and on the presidency for 13 and, frankly, I could fill any of those jobs. At least I wouldn't make the colossal mistakes being made now.

"It's just like setting a row of ice cream cones in front of me," he added. "I won't know which one to choose until after I have made thorough surveys."

Yarborough didn't mention running for the presidency when he was interviewed April 12, 1971, on a weekly television and radio program, "Capital Eye," in Austin. He did not rule out a 1972 race against Senator Tower but said mail urging him to run for office again was "two or three to one in favor of a race for governor."

He said he was seriously considering such a race, especially in view of the National Bankers Life stock scandal. And he said state officials named in connection with it would profit from a thorough investigation if they were innocent.

"I've had a personal experience with this," he said. "I was one time falsely accused of having received a large sum of money from Billie Sol Estes at the time he went bankrupt and was tried in federal court.

"The FBI sat in my office for days. The Senate had a committee, headed by Sen. John McClelland, to thoroughly investigate. The House had a committee, headed by Congressman Fountain of North Carolina. They found there wasn't a word of truth in it."

Actually, the congressional committees made little, if any, investigation of the charges against their colleague. The FBI, after a great deal of political arm-twisting, finally reported that it hadn't been able to prove anything.

But there was another investigation, complete with lie detector tests and a great many affidavits, which Yarborough failed to mention. . . .

Chapter 5

THE $50,000 QUESTION

During one of his typical whirlwind campaign tours in April of 1964, Senator Yarborough addressed the Volunteer Fire Department of Brownsboro, a little town just eight miles west of his native Chandler in Henderson County. It was a gala occasion, with a homecoming air filling the school gymnasium. The Senator's hosts rolled out the red carpet for him that Saturday night and presented his wife, Opal, with a beautiful bouquet of roses.

Fred Pass of the *Dallas Morning News* arrived a few moments after the program started and listened impatiently to Yarborough's speech. When it finally ended and the crowd began thinning out, he approached the Senator and told him he had a question he wanted to ask him privately.

"Wait just a minute," said Yarborough, with a smile. "I want to shake a few more hands."

Finally, everyone had left the gym except Yarborough, U. S. District Attorney Wayne Justice of Tyler (who later became a federal judge) and Pass.

"We would like to get your comment," Pass told the Senator, "on a report we have that Billie Sol Estes gave you $50,000 in 1960—"

Yarborough exploded, according to Pass, like a bomb with a delayed fuse.

"He started walking around in a circle," Pass recalled, "and then began cussing the *Dallas News*. 'They'll do it every time,' he said. 'The damned *Dallas News* will get you out in a little place like this where there's no other press and ask you a question like that!'"

Yarborough paused and Pass asked, "Is that your comment?"

"No, wait a minute," he replied. "Let me collect my thoughts."

"He thought for a few minutes," said Pass, "pacing the floor. Then we sat down at the head table in that big, empty room—Senator Yarborough, Wayne Justice and me—and he gave me a very brief statement."

Pass immediately phoned that statement to the *Dallas News*—which was holding, at that point, an article which this reporter had written. It quoted Estes as saying he had given Yarborough $50,000 in cash on Nov. 6, 1960, at his Pecos home. The *News* held the story until it could contact Yarborough and give him a chance to comment on it.

"This is an infamous lie out of the whole cloth," Yarborough told

Pass. "I doubt that Estes even made that statement—it sounds like another dirty *Dallas News* trick."

Estes not only had made the statement to me but had signed a sworn affidavit on it. As a *Dallas News* reporter, I knew that such a statement from the fallen king of West Texas agriculture and finance, at that point, would have to be substantiated by indisputable evidence before we could print it. So when Estes told me that two other people had witnessed the transaction, I insisted on seeing them and getting sworn statements from them—with the understanding that I would not mention their names without their permission. And they didn't want their names used, at first.

My original article quoted Estes simply as saying he gave Yarborough the money "because he called me and said he needed it."

When asked if he always gave the Senator anything he asked for, Estes replied: "At that time, we were good friends. This wasn't the first time I helped him nor the last."

Estes had been convicted in 1963 of mail fraud in connection with millions of dollars in mortgages on non-existent anhydrous ammonia tanks, and was free on bond while his 15-year sentence was being appealed. A Church of Christ lay preacher, he had been a close friend of Yarborough and had served as "statewide transportation director" in his 1954 campaign for governor.

Some of Yarborough's closest advisers recommended that he shrug off Estes's accusation and declare that he had received contributions from thousands of Texans, for his campaigns and also for the National Democratic Party, but never one of that size. They suggested that he use the same approach he did in a letter to the *Washington Post* after it criticized him on May 21, 1962, for accepting other donations from Estes, including $1,000 for 10 tickets to a fund-raising dinner honoring President Kennedy.

"Neither I nor the Democratic Party," Yarborough said in that letter, "has found it possible to screen contributors with a lie detector or look in a crystal ball to see how they will turn out in the future. . . . You, or anybody else who hints that I improperly used one bit of power of my office for Mr. Estes, lies."

Yarborough admitted that Estes had contributed funds to finance his weekly radio program in 1960 and 1961, contending that the program was necessary to keep his constituents informed because he "could not depend on the newspapers."

"Of the approximately 125 daily newspapers in Texas," said his letter, "not over seven ever endorsed me for public office in one race. Of the 12 large population centers in Texas, in only one has a daily newspaper endorsed me. . . ."

Instead of following a similar tack in this instance, Yarborough attacked the *Dallas News*. He berated the paper, claiming it had "fabricated" the story although we merely reported what Estes—and two witnesses who backed him up—had said. Yarborough's vehement, outraged denials led to subsequent publication of the two witnesses' names and their statements, kicking off a summer-long furor which sometimes resembled a "Keystone Kops" comedy.

Yarborough finally admitted he had attended the Nov. 6, 1960, barbecue at Estes's plush Pecos home, two days before the general election, and said he had been given more than $900 there.

The money was delivered by W. J. (Coot) Worsham, a Pecos farmer, to "help defray Yarborough's expenses in campaigning around the state for Kennedy-Johnson," according to the April 17, 1964, issue of the *Texas Observer*, an ultra-liberal biweekly published in Austin.

"Yarborough told the *Observer*," said that article, "that $400 of the money was put up by Estes, but that Worsham got this sum from Estes. 'There wasn't one penny of it delivered to me by Billy [sic] Sol Estes,' Yarborough said."

The *Observer* added that it contacted Worsham and he said the $50,000 report was not true.

" 'He [Estes] was always a helluva big name-dropper,' and he liked to talk big about big men and big sums of money, Worsham said," according to the *Observer*.

That seemed to leave in doubt only the exact amount of money which changed hands that day—money which may have been intended as a contribution to the Kennedy-Johnson campaign. But Yarborough's continued howls of a political plot, compounded by subsequent developments ranging from murder threats to intervention by U. S. Attorney General Robert F. Kennedy and the Federal Bureau of Investigation, made Estes's claim a prime campaign issue.

Gordon McLendon, a Dallas businessman who had made a fortune in radio and theaters but never had run a political race before, opposed Yarborough and pounded the issue heavily during the Democratic Primary campaign. It remained something of an issue during the general election race, in which Bush ran against Yarborough; but the U. S. Justice Department had rescued the Senator with a brief statement on the eve of the primary election, then promptly dropped the political hot potato while claiming its investigation would continue.

Yarborough requested the "FBI investigation" but bitterly denounced Governor Connally for asking the Texas Department of Public Safety to investigate alleged threats made against the life of a key witness in the affair.

"This is a federal matter," said Yarborough. He contended that the DPS was "trying to shore up the *Dallas News* against a libel suit."

No suit was filed. The FBI never announced any final results of its investigation and Connally chose not to disclose the report of the DPS, which is revealed here for the first time.

Several of the state's major newspapers tried to "tear down" Estes's version of the Nov. 6, 1960, incident, despite the fact that Yarborough admitted receiving cash from him on that date and both of the witnesses passed lie detector tests administered by the DPS.

When Bush suggested during the general election campaign that Yarborough should take a lie detector test, the Senator retorted: "That's an insult to the Senate. But that shows how much George Bush knows about the Senate or its workings."

Also lost in the shuffle was the fact that Yarborough had admitted on May 15, 1962, having received $1,700 from Estes to finance his weekly radio program. Later, he conceded that he had received other contributions, not previously disclosed, from Estes.

Yarborough's sworn campaign expense statements, on file with the Secretary of State, showed $2,800 in contributions from Estes for four campaigns, plus $400 from the "Estes Brothers, Pecos," and $325 from J. L. Estes, Jr., one of Billie Sol's brothers.

Yarborough declared that he had received a total of "not more than $9,000 and probably not more than $7,000 from the Estes family."

Estes continually insisted that his total contributions to Yarborough over a period of years, and including his furnishing an airplane for many campaign trips, amounted to much more than the $50,000. What infuriated Estes and eventually prompted such disclosures was a report the day after his arrest on March 29, 1962, that Yarborough, when asked for comment, had replied by asking, "Billie Sol *who?*"

Records introduced in a court of inquiry held at Pecos on June 23, 1962, indicated that Estes had talked with Yarborough on the telephone for five minutes the day the Pecos promoter was arrested. Estes was in Pecos, according to the telephone company records, and Yarborough at the Ramada Inn in Dallas during that conversation.

The records, introduced by Attorney General Will Wilson, showed a total of 37 calls, all charged to Estes's phones, made to Yarborough or Yarborough aides from Sept. 26, 1960, to March 29, 1962.

In a Washington press conference on May 18, 1962, Yarborough recalled what he termed a serious movement by "substantial people" four months earlier to draft Estes for governor.

According to *United Press International,* Yarborough said he had calls from dozens of Texans during December, 1961, and January, 1962, urging him to help "draft Billie Sol." He turned them down, he said, because he did not think Estes "politically feasible" as a candidate.

"Yarborough said Texas supporters of Estes claimed the cotton and fertilizer king would 'spellbind' his way into the statehouse if given a chance," *UPI* reported. " 'When this man preaches, people can't get into the church,' Yarborough quoted one Estes supporter as saying. 'The crowds are so big people look in the windows. He's a second Billy Graham.'

"The Senator said he never discussed the possibility of the candidacy with Estes himself."

Yarborough also, during that press conference, admitted receiving several contributions from Estes. He said Estes had asked him for assistance on several occasions but had never asked him to do anything improper.

Although there probably was little or nothing Yarborough could have done for Estes after his arrest even had he tried, the one-time financial whiz kid never forgave him for "forgetting" his last name so conveniently. Estes indicated that he revealed the $50,000 donation simply because he wanted to retaliate against an erstwhile friend he felt had deserted him in his hour of need.

The two witnesses who said they saw the money change hands were James E. Fonville, who promptly lost his job as a Midland policeman for "getting involved in politics," and Earnest Keeton of Pecos, a Negro and a retired Army sergeant. Both signed several sworn statements on the incident, once doing so on a statewide telecast produced by McLendon.

Yarborough countered with a statewide telecast in which Worsham and J. B. Kirklin, also of Pecos, swore that they were with Yarborough the entire time he was in Pecos on Nov. 6, 1960, and saw no transfer of money take place. Worsham and one of his brothers, L. G. Worsham, had signed a total of $1,667,676 in mortgages on non-existent fertilizer tanks for Estes.

It was Coot Worsham who served as the "middle man" for some of the money which Yarborough admitted receiving from Estes and which he said was used to finance his weekly radio program. According to testimony in the Pecos court of inquiry, Estes gave a series of checks to Worsham and he endorsed them to Yarborough.

The campaign controversy over the alleged $50,000 gift continued to grow until it reached a climax at 2:30 p.m. on May 1, 1964, the day before the primary election. It was then that Yarborough issued the following statement:

"On April 21st, San Jacinto Day, I went to Washington, went to the Justice Department, requested that the FBI be assigned to investigate the story of the $50,000 lie. I was referred to Assistant Attorney General Herbert Miller, chief of the Criminal Division of the Attorney General's Office, and made my request to him. I was advised that they would study the matter, and received no answer that day, but some days later was advised that the FBI had decided to re-open the matter and investigate this new angle.

"Today [May 1], I phoned Assistant Attorney General Herbert Miller and asked him what progress was being made. He reported to me that Billie Sol Estes had refused to be interviewed by the FBI but that one of the two witnesses who appeared on TV with Gordon McLendon and swore that he saw me receive $50,000 admitted to the FBI that the statement was false, that he never saw Billie Sol Estes give me $50,000, that his statement was a lie.

"This was a confession to the FBI of perjury.

"This is all the information I have at this point; but, if the press wants information I refer them to Mr. Herbert Miller in Washington, D. C.

"I want Gordon McLendon to explain this perjury in his marathon telecast Saturday, and I demand that he withdraw from the race because of having based it on perjury and character assassination.

"I will discuss this further on my statewide telecast tonight at 9:30 p.m.," Yarborough's statement concluded.

In Washington, Miller told inquiring newsmen that Keeton had "recanted" but hedged when told that Yarborough said Keeton had admitted "lying."

"I don't think I used that word when I talked to the Senator," Miller told the *Houston Post*. "In effect he recanted. Basically, the Senator is right."

He refused to divulge any more details and, meanwhile, Keeton had disappeared. His mother, Mrs. Margaret Crockett of Pecos, told Mrs. Marge Carpenter, a reporter for the *Pecos Independent*, that "an officer" visited her home late Thursday night (April 30) and told her she had "a fine, brave son and there are no black marks against him" and not to worry, that "it's all over now."

Miller refused to comment on reports that Worsham and Kirklin had decided since their television appearance that they had not actually been with Yarborough the entire time he was in Pecos, after all.

Yarborough defeated McLendon in the Democratic Primary with 905,011 votes to 672,573. The FBI suddenly seemed to lose all interest in the case, despite the mysterious disappearance of Keeton—who told Fonville three days before the election that his life had been threatened.

Fonville said that in addition to losing his job, he had found two threatening notes on the windshield of his car but felt he could protect himself.

In a sworn statement given to the *Lubbock Avalanche-Journal* on May 4, 1964, Fonville said two FBI agents had questioned him on the day before the primary election, in a Pecos motel, and one of them repeatedly told him he was lying.

"He said the outcome of the election the next day would be affected," said Fonville, "and emphasized that a U. S. Senator was involved."

When he insisted that he had told the truth originally and was sticking to it, Fonville added, the agents "did not appear to care" whether he signed a statement for them or not.

Keeton, after signing a statement for the FBI saying he had been in Juarez, Mexico, on Nov. 6, 1960, left Pecos so hurriedly he failed to notify his employer that he was quitting his job.

On May 14, 1964, Keeton turned up in El Paso, driving a taxicab. In an interview with Hugh Morgan of the *El Paso Times,* Keeton said he would "stand by what I told the FBI." Morgan said Keeton refused to comment on whether he had received any threats, other than to declare that he had *not* been threatened "by the FBI." He said the FBI had been "very nice, very polite" in questioning him two days before the election.

Earlier the same day, however, Keeton had written a letter to Estes explaining that he had repudiated his original statement only because of the threats. The letter, which Keeton described and which later was shown to me with its envelope postmarked May 14 in El Paso, began, "to my dearest friend."

In his own handwriting, Keeton apologized and asked Estes's forgiveness. He said he had to change his statement or get killed and that if he had not changed it, he would "not be here to write this letter."

On May 16, I went to El Paso and interviewed Keeton, in the presence of five witnesses. They included Mr. and Mrs. Paul W. Slone, owners of an El Paso pawn shop, and Clyde N. Foust, Jr., of Clarksville, Tenn., who said he was there to promote a leather goods importing deal. Foust said he discovered Keeton, whom he had met some time earlier through Estes, a few days before while Keeton was on his way to a hotel in Juarez where he was staying. Keeton was broke and hungry and jobless, said Foust, and he and the Slones had tried to help him. Mrs. Slone arranged for the cab-driving job.

The Slones and Foust all said that Keeton had insisted, ever since they first saw him in El Paso, that he had repudiated his original statement only because he was afraid he would be killed if he did not.

Also present during that May 16 interview at the Slones' home in El Paso were Estes and Roy Lassiter, a Raymondville cafe owner and close personal friend of Estes, a longtime gumshoe for conservative politicians who had once served as a Yarborough county campaign manager in a gubernatorial race.

Keeton came into the house that morning, sat down and began describing his ordeal—an ordeal which led eventually to his asking the Department of Public Safety for protection.

U. S. Senator Ralph Yarborough (center) joins hands with W. J. (Coot) Worsham, left, and Billie Sol Estes at the now-famed Nov. 6, 1960, barbecue at Estes' home—where the Pecos promoter says he gave $50,000 to the Senator.

He said he had contacted Estes in Abilene about a week before the election because he was scared. Estes advised him, he said, to seek protection from Sheriff A. B. Nail in Pecos.

Keeton also said he had been with Estes when a man told them that he "would kill the key witness." Estes had told the man that "no one had better harm Keeton," according to both Estes and Keeton.

Later, said Keeton, he found a note on the windshield of his car which said: "Keep your big mouth shut!"

Then, on the morning of April 30, he said, he was driving down Pecan Street in Pecos when a white man stepped off the curb and flagged him down. Keeton said the man was about his height (6 feet 2), of medium build and that he appeared to have a pistol in a shoulder holster under his coat.

Keeton said the man told him: "If you stand on that statement, it will be the last statement you ever make."

There was no doubt in his mind, Keeton declared, that the man intended to kill him unless he repudiated his original statement.

That night, he continued, he went to the sheriff's office in Pecos and asked to see Sheriff Nail. He was told that Nail was out but to sit down and wait. About five minutes later, he said, two FBI agents appeared and asked him to go to a motel room with them for questioning.

Keeton said the FBI agents insisted that his original statement was false and told him he was "risking my army pension and everything else if the statement was not true." As a result, he said, he finally signed the statement saying he had been in Juarez, not Pecos, on Nov. 6, 1960.

"Why did you say Juarez?" I asked.

"Because I had to tell them something," he replied. "What would *you* have done if you thought a man was going to *kill you* if you said you was in Pecos?"

I had no quick answer for that.

"But if the sworn statement you signed originally was true and you told the FBI it wasn't," I finally reminded him, "you have confessed to a crime you didn't commit—false swearing."

"I know," said Keeton. "But I had rather go to the pen than get a bullet in the head. A man's life is the most valuable thing he has. . . .".

Admonished that the best course always is to tell the truth, Keeton was assured that the Department of Public Safety would provide any protection he needed. He replied quickly that President Kennedy had been killed despite all the protection he had.

"If a man pointed a gun at me and told me to stop breathing," he said, "I'd be dead for thirty minutes."

On May 20, Keeton signed another sworn statement reaffirming his original ones. He declared again that these statements were true and that the only reason for the story he gave the FBI "was the pressure that was put on me and the fear that I had."

"I was afraid for my life, and I am still afraid," he said in that statement.

Keeton said he was scared because he "knew too much" and because some people thought he knew even more than he did about Estes's business affairs, as a result of having worked as a servant for him. Asked if this meant he was scared of Estes, he said it did not. Did he mean, then, that he was afraid of people whom Estes might be in a position to expose?

"I'm just scared of the whole surroundings," Keeton declared.

Foust said Keeton told him, shortly after they met in El Paso, of several mysterious deaths among people who had been involved in Estes's affairs.

"He started with Henry Marshall and went down the list," said Foust.

Marshall was the U. S. Department of Agriculture official whose strange death on June 3, 1961, near Franklin (Robertson County) was ruled suicide although he had been shot five times with a bolt action rifle and had a lethal amount of carbon monoxide in his lungs. Marshall had investigated Estes's cotton allotment transfers.

Jay Harris and Kenneth May of the *Lubbock Avalanche-Journal* disclosed on May 31, 1964, that Worsham and Kirklin had changed their versions of Yarborough's Nov. 6, 1960, visit to Pecos.

"Yarborough and two men who supported his labeling the gift an 'infamous lie,' were not together 'every minute' the Senator was in Pecos on the date in question, Nov. 6, 1960, the *Avalanche-Journal* has learned," wrote Harris and May. "The FBI learned this in talking with Yarborough in Lubbock three days before the primary, but said nothing of that in commenting on the case before the balloting.

"The *Avalanche-Journal*, acting on confidential information, later learned after the election that Yarborough and Estes not only attended church together without the two men but may have had as much as an hour together before showing up at the now famous barbecue."

When Worsham was asked about that discrepancy in his television statement, said the article, he said he "had intended to make it clear he meant he had been with Yarborough every minute 'at the barbecue,' not all the time the Senator was in town."

"Although both Fonville and Worsham—and Yarborough himself—had given their respective stories to the FBI before Keeton's reported recantation was announced, the Justice Department made no mention of their revelations in its initial, fragmentary report on the case," said the *Avalanche-Journal.*

"Herbert J. Miller, head of the department's criminal division," it added, "has taken full responsibility for the partial report, which violated the department's strict rule against commenting on investigations still in progress. Miller said he did so because of 'the people's right to know.'"

J. Edgar Hoover, director of the FBI, ran a forceful disclaimer of the entire matter in a May 2, 1964, telegram to McLendon saying it was handled personally by Attorney General Robert Kennedy. Said Hoover's telegram:

"CONCERNING YOUR TELEGRAM RECEIVED THIS DATE, I HAVE AT NO TIME FURNISHED TO SENATOR YARBOROUGH ANY INFORMATION CONCERNING THIS MATTER NOR HAVE I MADE ANY STATEMENT TO THE PUBLIC RELATIVE THERE-TO. I WAS NOT CONSULTED BY YOU LAST EVENING AND CONSEQUENTLY COULD HAVE GIVEN NO ASSURANCES. THIS ENTIRE MATTER WAS HANDLED BY THE OFFICE OF THE AG OF U. S. AND IT IS SUGGESTED THAT YOU THERE-FORE DISCUSS THE MATTER WITH HIM."

Senator Tower later asked Attorney General Kennedy to explain the role of the FBI and the Justice Department in the entire affair. Miller replied, at Kennedy's request.

Referring to reports that Keeton had disappeared after receiving personal threats, Miller said "the FBI has advised they are aware of no such incident." He told Tower that the decision to make an exception to Justice Department policy and announce Keeton's "recantation" of his story while an investigation purportedly still was in progress was not quickly or easily reached.

"It was our considered judgment that the people's right to know in this unusual matter of great public concern must prevail over regular Department policy," said Miller.

He did not explain why the information which he felt the public had a "right to know" was given to a political candidate instead of being announced through normal channels.

Despite its rights, the public probably never *will* know exactly how much money changed hands—the only matter actually in dispute— at Estes's home on Nov. 6, 1960, nor whether it represented a contribution to the presidential campaign.

The FBI never did make public a full report on its investigation but one intriguing result of the probe was reflected in the subsequent actions of an El Paso agent. He resigned from the FBI, explaining to a close friend that he was ashamed of what he had been forced to do during the investigation and wanted to "atone" for his actions; he entered a theological seminary and became a minister but still refuses to discuss the $50,000 question, apparently just wanting to forget the whole thing.

The DPS investigation ordered by Governor Connally continued until late October and was handled by some of the Department's top intelligence agents—with the late Col. Homer Garrison, Jr., the highly respected Director of the DPS, taking a personal interest in it.

Although no public announcement was made on the matter, the DPS found that the FBI had lost all interest in it immediately after the election, that Estes had given the money to Yarborough and that Keeton's life had been threatened because he was an eyewitness to the transaction—but that the evidence was insufficient to support "criminal prosecution" unless witnesses could be subpoenaed and put under oath.

These findings were summarized in the following memorandum, never before published:

DEPARTMENT OF PUBLIC SAFETY
INTEROFFICE MEMORANDUM

Date   10-26-64
Division   Intelligence

TO: Homer Garrison, Jr., Director

FROM: O. N. Humphreys, Jr., Agent in Charge

SUBJECT: THREATS TO EARNEST KEETON

In compliance with Governor Connally's request and pursuant to your instructions, an investigation was made into the alleged threats to EARNEST KEETON.

After having made an extensive inquiry into this matter, the writer would like to submit the following observations:

1. Prior to the initiation of the investigation, the investigating Federal Agency was contacted and they advised that they were no longer interested in the matter and their investigation was complete.

2. Threats upon EARNEST KEETON were made (substantiated by sworn statement and polygraph examination).

3. Reason for threats: EARNEST KEETON was a witness to the transfer of a large sum of money to a high public official (substantiated by sworn statement and polygraph examination).

4. JAMES E. FONVILLE also witnessed transfer of money (substantiated by Fonville's sworn statement and polygraph examination).

5. Pressure was exerted by a Federal Agency upon both FONVILLE and KEETON in an attempt to get them to retract their original public statements (substantiated by sworn statements and polygraph examinations).

6. Findings handed down and publicized as "fact" by a Federal Agency differ greatly from the findings of this Department.

7. Based upon evidence secured by this Department, it is our opinion that such threats and transfer of money did, in fact, take place; however, there is insufficient evidence to support criminal prosecution.

It is respectfully suggested that, whereas this Department has exhausted all apparent sources of information without conclusive proof of the ultimate issues; and, whereas this Department has but limited authority to induce truthful statements of witnesses, that investigation of this matter be continued by an Agency with authority to compel attendance of witnesses and elicit testimony of witnesses under pains of perjury.

Respectfully submitted,

/s/ O. N. Humphreys, Jr.
O. N. Humphreys, Jr.
Agent In Charge
Intelligence Section
ONHJr:bwc

During the 1964 presidential campaign, U. S. Senator Barry Goldwater charged that the Billie Sol Estes affair had tainted President Johnson's administration, casting "grave reflections right across the White House itself."

"That's the most ridiculous thing I've ever heard," declared a friend of Johnson's upon hearing that accusation. "The President told me he only remembered meeting Estes one time, at a reception, and that he'd always seemed to be more a friend of Yarborough's than of anyone else. Everybody just assumed that no one could get as big as Billie Sol did in Texas without being a friend of LBJ."

That assumption seemed natural although Estes was virtually unknown by most Texans until his downfall. It was bolstered by the fact that the collapse of Estes's "house of cards" sent tremors along Pennsylvania Avenue as well as Wall Street.

One reason for that was Estes's knack for picture-hanging as well as name-dropping. On the day of his arrest, he had pictures of such notables as President Kennedy, Vice President Johnson, Senator Yarborough, Congressman J. T. (Slick) Rutherford of Odessa, Speaker

Rayburn, Adlai Stevenson and former President Harry S. Truman hanging in his office.

Most of the pictures were autographed.

The one of Yarborough was inscribed: "To a great friend, true Texan, grand American—Billie Sol Estes of Pecos with warmest appreciation." It was dated 1958.

President Kennedy had autographed his photo: "For Billie Sol Estes with appreciation and warm regards."

Johnson signed his: "To Billie Sol Estes with warm regards and best wishes."

The revelation of such inscriptions undoubtedly led to greater caution on the part of Texas politicians when it came to autographing pictures. As it turned out, the rather noncommittal inscription on the Johnson photograph was about the most tangible piece of evidence uncovered to link him with Estes.

Rumors were rampant, shortly after Estes's arrest, about his alleged business connections with LBJ and/or Lady Bird. But extensive investigation by newspaper reporters as well as federal and state investigators—including some who admittedly were hostile toward the Johnsons—failed to uncover any substantial evidence of such an association.

Estes did have occasional contacts with Cliff Carter and Walter Jenkins, both members of Johnson's staff, and he gave Carter "about 10" tickets to a $100-a-plate, Democratic fund-raising dinner in January, 1962. Also disclosed was a brief, chummy note from Carter to Estes which indicated a highly cordial relationship.

Some Johnson critics insisted that it seemed quite strange that Estes, despite all the gifts he gave and favors he sought, never did—according to the records—give Johnson anything or ask him for anything. Of all the phone calls Estes made to Washington, none apparently went to Johnson—although he did call Carter on March 28, 1962, the day before his arrest, to ask if he were being investigated. Carter said he told him he would let him know if he heard anything but did not call him back.

Some felt it significant, too, that Estes's chief defense attorney turned out to be John D. Cofer of Austin, a longtime friend of Johnson who had helped represent him in his 1948 election controversy.

There were widespread rumors that Cofer's retainer, which happened to be $50,000, came through the Austin law firm of Clark, Thomas, Harris, Denius and Winters, which handled many of the Johnsons' private business dealings. Ambassador Clark, when asked about it several years later, said he "knew nothing" about any fee for representation of Estes having gone through his firm. Cofer also denied the report.

But a well-informed source, who was in a position to know, insisted that Cofer "had never heard of Estes until he was contacted by Clark's law firm and asked to represent him."

Despite their failure to hit pay dirt on Johnson, Republicans in Congress found plenty of Kennedy administration targets for their charges of influence-peddling involving Estes. On May 14, 1962, Senator Gordon Allott, a Colorado Republican, called for the resignation of Secretary of Agriculture Orville L. Freeman and accused the White House of maintaining a "strange silence" about the Estes affair.

Senator John J. Williams, Delaware Republican, joined Allott in charging that criminal reprisals may have been taken against U. S. Department of Agriculture employees who wanted to disclose or investigate Estes's deals.

"Allott contended that the Secretary's actions in the [Estes] case have resulted in the coining of the word 'Freemanized' to mean 'whitewashed or glossed over.' He said the agency was too important to be tainted and sullied," the *Associated Press* reported.

"Williams said a woman secretary in the Department had been 'railroaded' into a mental institution (in Washington) for 'refusing to cooperate in covering up corruption' in the Department," the *AP* added. "Freeman's office promptly issued a statement disputing this and said the department regretted that the medical problems of an employee had been made into a political controversy."

The woman had been the secretary of N. Battle Hales, an Agriculture Department official who Williams said was shifted to an insignificant job and stripped of access to files because he demanded an FBI investigation of Estes's dealings.

One of the highest ranking casualties of the Estes fiasco turned out to be his newly-found friend, Congressman Rutherford, who was defeated in the 1962 election. But the collapse of Estes's financial empire also prompted the resignation of Assistant Secretary of Labor Jerry R. Holleman, who apparently was made a scapegoat for permitting Estes to finance a party his boss gave for Johnson.

Arthur Goldberg, then Secretary of Labor, decided in 1961 to give a reception for Vice President Johnson and reportedly asked Holleman to arrange financing for it. He is said to have suggested soliciting contributions of about $100 each from "about 10 of those rich Texans." Holleman, who formerly had served as president of the Texas State AFL-CIO, contacted Estes, who immediately asked how much the party would cost. Well-informed sources contend that when Holleman told him $1,000, Estes said he would be happy to pick up the entire tab and gave Holleman a check for that amount.

In the light of subsequent developments, of course, this turned out to be a rather ill-advised method of financing a party for the Vice

President of the United States. As a result, and apparently to keep Goldberg off the spot, Holleman was forced to resign—"confessing" that Estes had given *him* the $1,000 because he had been unable to make ends meet in Washington (during 1961) on his $20,000-a-year salary.

Congressman James C. (Jim) Wright of Fort Worth defended Holleman as "an honest and honorable man," saying he had seen no indication that he had allowed the gift from Estes to compromise him.

But Holleman's head was only one of many that fell.

The greatest casualty list was compiled in the Department of Agriculture. The victims there included Emery E. Jacobs, deputy administrator of the Stabilization and Conservation Service, who let Estes pick up the tab for an expensive shopping trip at Neiman-Marcus in Dallas; Dr. James T. Ralph, assistant secretary of agriculture who the FBI said had used Estes's telephone credit card for personal long distance calls, and William E. Morris, who had served as an aide to Ralph and who failed to answer questions about his association with Estes.

Morris had once suggested to Estes that Congressman H. Carl Andersen of Minnesota might be a good "Republican contact" in Congress. He took Andersen to Pecos in early 1962 for a visit with Estes, who promptly bought $4,000 worth of stock in an Andersen-owned coal mine—reportedly helping the member of the House subcommittee on agricultural appropriations out of a financial pinch.

Estes, who climbed from rags to riches before his sudden and spectacular downfall, made no secret of his theory that the creditor "acquires an interest in the prosperity of the debtor" when a debt becomes large.

"If you get into anybody far enough, you've got yourself a partner," he used to say.

That seemed to be one of Estes's guiding principles as he parlayed a $5 ewe lamb, according to his own version of the story, into the $150 million empire which finally produced his 15-year prison sentence, leaving him with assets of $20 million and debts of $40 million. Estes contended that he converted the ewe, given to him by his parents for Christmas when he was 13 years old, into a $38,000 investment in livestock, grain and land within six years. He claimed that he made his first million before he was 30 but some of his critics were more inclined to think he borrowed it.

During this process, he became known as a close friend of many politicians—all Democrats and most of them quite liberal. What he seemed to do best, however, was borrow money. His borrowing and his dealings with the federal government which helped make it possible, largely through grain storage, led to Goldwater's charges during the 1964 campaign.

"When partisan political favoritism, or payoffs and bribery, become involved in any government program," Goldwater said in a Mason City, Kansas, campaign speech, "the seeds of destruction have been planted. Incompetent or corrupt administration of a bad program can make it worse.

"It is up to the President to expose wrong-doing in government," he declared. "But the interim president, whose office dealt with Billie Sol, does not press for exposure. His power is used for different ends—and the White House has been turned into the 'whitewash' house."

Estes, in a typical pique at having become a campaign issue, told Jack Tinsley of the *Fort Worth Star-Telegram* on Oct. 24, 1964, that the Republicans were running the U. S. Department of Agriculture during the time of his greatest gains. Tinsley's article made it clear that Estes blamed Commercial Solvents Corporation for U. S. Department of Agriculture irregularities involving his multimillion-dollar grain storage and cotton allotment transactions.

Ezra Taft Benson, a Republican, was Secretary of Agriculture at the time his government-financed shenanigans began, Estes declared.

"All my dealings began in 1958 when Al Woods was president of Commercial Solvents," he told the *Star-Telegram*. "I dealt with Woods, and not the Agriculture Department."

Estes said a U. S. House of Representatives subcommittee which supposedly investigated his dealings said it found no favoritism shown him because if it had "it would have wrapped it right around their people's neck."

The *Star-Telegram* noted, however, that two Republican senators did charge favoritism in a separate report on Estes's cotton allotment manipulations, released Sept. 30, 1964. A majority of their five-man committee said the Agriculture Department displayed "disinterest and stagnation in its handling" of Estes's cotton deals.

But the two Republican members, Senators Carl T. Curtis of Nebraska and Karl E. Mundt of South Dakota, contended that the "freewheeling, gift-giving Billie Sol Estes received favoritism on the county level, state level and in the U. S. Department of Agriculture. . . ."

During his exclusive interview with the *Fort Worth Star-Telegram*, Estes apparently refused to be quoted directly on blaming Commercial Solvents for his problems but did so time and again indirectly.

"Obviously riled at Senator Barry Goldwater's attempts to saddle the White House with responsibility for his dealings, Estes stated he knew President Johnson only slightly," said the *Star-Telegram*. "He said he met Johnson 'at a Texas get-together in Washington—I shook his hand.'

" 'Really what happened was Johnson inherited what the companies did,' he continued. 'And I didn't like it because I was getting along pretty good.' "

Estes apparently got along "pretty good" even in prison, which he left on parole July 12, 1971—with a reputation as a religiously-active, model prisoner. He had served six years. After a few days of vacationing with his family at an undisclosed location, he headed for the Callahan County farm owned by his brother, Dr. John L. Estes, Jr., an Abilene dentist. The terms of his parole required him to work on that farm and prohibited him from engaging in self-employment or "any promotional activity."

Estes used to say he could "put together a hundred deals every day." He came out of prison prohibited from doing so but probably still believing in his theory that "You can shear a sheep every year— you can't skin him but once."

Chapter 6

FIRST BASE

G loom saturated Lyndon B. Johnson's top floor suite in the Stephen F. Austin Hotel one early July night in 1941 as he and a handful of close friends pondered the results of an election he felt had been "stolen" from him.

Several of his advisers urged him to contest it. As difficult as it is to overturn the results of an election, they felt that route offered the best chance he would ever have for going to the United States Senate.

At stake was the seat vacated by the death on April 9, 1941, of Senator Morris Sheppard, who had held the office since 1912. Governor W. Lee (Pappy) O'Daniel, a political phenomenon who had sailed into office on the strains of hillbilly music, announced on April 19 that the special election would be held June 28. Then, two days later, he announced that he was appointing Andrew Jackson Houston, Sam Houston's last surviving son, as the interim senator.

That created a storm of criticism, especially when it was learned that Houston would be 87 years old on June 21, that he was sick and senile and had been a lifelong Republican. But he had one great asset in addition to his illustrious name, so far as O'Daniel was concerned: the inability to run in the special election. Houston went to Washington, over the objections of his two daughters, and took the oath on June 2. He died on June 26.

Meanwhile, O'Daniel became one of the 29 candidates in the special election race. He said his platform once again would be "the Ten Commandments and the Golden Rule," which he had exploited so successfully during his 1938 campaign. He also called for "more smokestacks and businessmen, less Johnson Grass and politicians" and a $30-a-month pension for everyone over 65 years of age.

Aided by the "Light Crust Doughboys," the hillbilly band which helped him become one of the greatest flour salesmen of all time, O'Daniel exhorted crowds at rallies throughout Texas in 1938 to "Please pass the biscuits, Pappy," and to donate freely through the small flour barrels he passed among them to finance his campaign.

O'Daniel played coy about his intention to run in the special Senate race, waiting until late May to announce. Johnson, with four years in Congress behind him and with President Roosevelt's obvious blessing, had announced his candidacy on April 22—from the steps of the White House.

Alvin Wirtz, who earlier had served in the State Senate, promptly resigned as Undersecretary of the Interior to return to Texas and help quarterback Johnson's campaign. It began with the polls showing Johnson running hopelessly behind O'Daniel, the leader; Attorney General Gerald Mann, the "Little Red Arrow" of SMU football fame; and Congressman Martin Dies, Sr., of Lufkin, who had become nationally known as chairman of the House Committee on Un-American Activities.

Johnson used a private airplane, gave away cash prizes by lottery at his campaign rallies, utilized newspaper ads extensively, made many expensive radio broadcasts and covered the state with billboards showing him and Roosevelt shaking hands.

His high-spending antics led later to complaints that he had exceeded the $25,000 limit imposed by federal law on Senate campaign expenditures. He reported expenditures of $11,818 and receipts of $9,645, but there was widespread speculation that he spent about $500,000 during that campaign.

Much of the money reportedly came, at least indirectly, from Brown and Root, Inc., a Houston construction firm for which Wirtz served as legal counsel. The Brown brothers, George and Herman, had been on the verge of bankruptcy during the depression but made a remarkable comeback, which many observers believe was not merely coincidental with Johnson's political ascendancy. By 1941, they had received enough government contracts to put them on easy street and it seemed quite obvious that "good government," to them, was exemplified by Congressman Johnson.

Despite his well-financed campaign, Johnson found himself facing strong opposition not only from Governor O'Daniel and the other candidates but also from former Governor James E. Ferguson, an anti-prohibitionist. Ferguson, elected in 1914 and reelected in 1916, had been impeached in 1917.

Twenty-one charges were brought against Ferguson by the House of Representatives. The Senate found him guilty on 10, including misapplication of funds, diversion of funds and acceptance of large sums of money from a source he refused to reveal. He gained a certain measure of revenge in 1932, when he engineered the election of his wife, Miriam A. Ferguson, as governor.

It was late in the 1941 campaign when Ferguson hit upon the idea of trying to elect O'Daniel in order to promote Lieutenant Governor Coke R. Stevenson to the governorship and, in so doing, to protect the beer industry. Johnson later blamed Ferguson for his defeat and complained that the beer lobbyists put O'Daniel in the Senate to keep him from stopping the sale of beer around army posts in Texas.

"It was ironic," said one of Johnson's friends, "that he had to run against the 'wets' when he was a 'wet' and O'Daniel was a 'dry.' But that's what cost him the election. At least, it's what enabled Ferguson to *steal it* from him.

"Johnson was leading by 5,152 votes on election night with O'Daniel second, Mann third and Dies a poor fourth. When it became obvious that Dies was out of it, they started bringing in votes from the Lufkin-Beaumont area and nearly all of them went to O'Daniel.

"Ferguson later admitted to a newspaper reporter that he felt 'one dry senator in Washington might do a little harm to the beer and whiskey business in Texas but one dry wartime governor such as O'Daniel could knock it cold.' "

O'Daniel refused to concede the election even when the Texas Election Bureau estimated on June 29 that only 25,000 votes were still out, with 96 per cent counted, and predicted Johnson would win "barring a miracle." Johnson then had 167,276 votes to O'Daniel's 162,124, Mann's 134,871 and Dies's 71,275.

The *Dallas Morning News* reported on July 1 that Johnson's lead had been carved down to 701 by "corrected totals," mostly from counties in East and South Texas. By that night, the margin had been reduced to a mere 77 votes. The next day, O'Daniel was named the winner by 1,311 votes.

Johnson's closest friends were not willing to accept that decision as final the night they gathered at the Stephen F. Austin. Among those present were Wirtz, John Connally, J. J. (Jake) Pickle, later to become a congressman; Fred Basham, a campaign worker who had been district director for the National Youth Administration; County Judge Jack Cowley of Hillsboro, and Crawford Martin, then a young Hillsboro lawyer who became known later, while serving in the State Senate, as the man who knew more about state government than anyone else.

From the suite on the northwest corner of the hotel, they could see the dome of the State Capitol—then lighted no brighter than their own hopes, which flickered between dim and dark during the discussion. Some of the participants felt the election results could be challenged successfully on grounds that thousands of ballots had been "thrown out" illegally in Houston and Wichita Falls for allegedly being marked improperly.

Wirtz, however, advised against an election contest — partly, perhaps, because he did not relish the idea of a probe on campaign expenditures. According to Connally, Wirtz also felt that it would be impossible to get a "fair" contest.

"It would have taken a year or 18 months to have a contest," said Connally, "and this was the summer of 1941. Whoever won had to run again in 1942. So even if you won the contest, you might win the battle and lose the war.

"All of us felt a grave injustice had been done—there was no question about that, in the minds of any of us," he declared. "But Johnson had come out of the campaign in very good shape, he was a young man and another election would occur within a year. We felt it would be a better risk to wait until 1942 and then run it over again, in effect."

Throughout the evening, Johnson periodically would confer privately in the bedroom with two or three of the men. Finally, he called the entire group back there to announce his decision.

"If I contest it and lose," he said, as he sat on the edge of a bed, "I'm dead—and I'm not ready to have an LBJ funeral. But I'll tell you this: if I ever get in another close election, I'm not going to lose it!"

The next day, he returned to Washington—where FDR reportedly growled at him: "Next time, sit on the ballot boxes."

Johnson fully intended at that point to run in 1942 but the start of World War II postponed his "next time" until 1948. According to his critics, he did considerably more than merely "sit on the ballot boxes" then. Connally managed his campaign and admits that, as a result of the 1941 defeat, he did persuade some election judges to sit on their returns.

"I basically lost the election, I think, in 1941," said Connally, "by telling some of the election officials in South Texas to go ahead and report their returns to the Texas Election Bureau. At that point, it never dawned on me that this could do any harm. But they went ahead and gave their complete returns to the Election Bureau, and then everybody knew exactly how many votes were down there. This was a part of the country that Johnson was carrying and this enabled the other side to know exactly how many votes they needed.

"Twelve or 15 East Texas counties kept bringing in returns Monday, Tuesday and Wednesday after the election on Saturday—and some of those counties voted *over 100 per cent* of their potential voting strength," he said. "After Dies was out of it, they voted overwhelmingly for O'Daniel—and we sat there helpless.

"Well, I learned a lesson in 1941—one which, strangely enough, was used to denounce and condemn Johnson in 1948," said Connally, "because we didn't make that mistake in 1948. We just didn't give the complete returns to the Election Bureau after that election. You're not under any compulsion to do so and it obviously was going to be a very close election.

"At one time, we had 25 or 30 counties—maybe even 50—holding back reports on their complete returns," he said. "Of course, as the pressure got on more and more, it was more difficult to hold them. But we had people up all night long Saturday and Sunday nights. We had men driving 50 or 60 miles one way to get the returns and talk to the election judges. We had 25 people on the road at one time.

"We knew how many votes were out and, in the long run, our figures were better than the Election Bureau's because we knew everything it knew plus a lot it didn't know," Connally declared. "We wanted to get the figures so there couldn't be any switching. And if we were leading, we wanted the election officials to hold back and not report the returns; if we weren't leading, we let them go ahead and report them promptly. There wasn't anything illegal about it. There wasn't anything wrong about it. It was just a question of trying to find out what was happening—because we hadn't done that in 1941."

That memorable, almost unbelievable 1948 race started when O'Daniel decided not to seek reelection. It produced, among other things, a hotel room scene—in a suite at the Blackstone, in Fort Worth— strangely similar to that which had taken place at the Stephen F. Austin in 1941. But this time, the cast and the ending, as well as the setting, were different.

Johnson campaigned by helicopter during the first primary race, dropping down out of the skies to attract the attention of startled Texans. Most of them had never seen such a flying machine before and few realized that they were gazing upon a man just as unusual as the helicopter—and equally capable of going straight up.

Meanwhile, "Calculatin' Coke" Stevenson, his major opponent, seemed to be dividing his time between performing manual labor on his ranch near Junction and cruising around the state in a car driven by his personable, one-armed nephew, Bob Murphey of Nacogdoches. Murphey later became sergeant-at-arms for the Texas House of Representatives, then district attorney at Nacogdoches and one of the wittiest, most widely-sought banquet speakers in the state.

Stevenson, born of a poor family on a Kimble County ranch in 1888, was largely self-educated but became a highly-respected lawyer. He served as county judge before winning election to the Texas House of Representatives in 1928. He was elected speaker in 1933 and again in 1935, becoming the first man in history to serve two consecutive terms in that office. With O'Daniel's endorsement, he was elected lieutenant governor in 1938 and became governor in 1941 when O'Daniel beat Johnson for the Senate. He was elected governor in 1942 and 1944 but did not seek any office in 1946.

Part of Stevenson's 1948 campaign "strategy" was to buy only five gallons of gasoline at a time so he could contact more people at service stations and ask them to vote for him. While he visited with service station attendants one or two at a time, Johnson drew crowds of hundreds and even thousands by campaigning with his helicopter, which he called the "Johnson City Windmill."

Stevenson's campaign almost seemed to be running out of gas when, on June 22, the Texas Federation of Labor met in Fort Worth and launched a full-scale attack on Johnson, primarily because he had supported the Taft-Hartley Act. Passed over President Truman's veto, that Act gave the federal government injunctive rights to prohibit strikes threatening national security and strikes in support of the "closed shop"—one in which union membership was required.

Johnson immediately charged that organized labor's leaders had made a secret agreement with Stevenson which they could not get out of him. They met in a "smoke-filled hotel room in Fort Worth," he said, in an attempt to "deliver the vote of the Texas working men" to a candidate who refused to take a stand on labor issues. He challenged Stevenson repeatedly to state his views on the Taft-Hartley Act.

It was in connection with this that Johnson gave a convincing demonstration of one of his most effective talents, the power of personal persuasion, and one of his strongest strategic gimmicks, the determination to convert his enemies.

Visiting one day in the news room of the *Austin American-Statesman,* Johnson was shaking hands with newsmen assembled around the horse-shoe-shaped news desk when an apprentice printer walked up with a handful of proofs. Johnson stuck out his hand and introduced himself.

The apprentice refused to shake hands.

"I wouldn't shake hands with you for anything," he declared belligerently, "because you took the bread right out of my mouth when you voted for Taft-Hartley."

Johnson immediately turned on the charm that was to carry him to the presidency and asked the young man if he would be kind enough to have a cup of coffee and discuss the matter. The apprentice agreed and they went to a restaurant half a block down the street. When they returned some 30 minutes later, a hole undoubtedly had been knocked in Johnson's schedule but a valuable patch had been applied to a puncture in his reputation. There is no way to estimate how many votes that one printer influenced during the following 20 years that Johnson was in office but it was, no doubt, a number well worth 30 minutes of Johnson's time that day.

Like Knute Rockne, the fabled Notre Dame football coach, Johnson always believed that a man should work on his weak spots and let his strong points take care of themselves. Johnson carried that basic idea one step further and tried to convert his foes, assuming that his friends would support him, anyway.

Stevenson led Johnson in the first primary, held on July 24, 1948, with 477,077 votes to 405,617. His failure to achieve a majority necessitated a runoff on Aug. 28 and Johnson knew that if he lost that, an "LBJ funeral" would result, ready or not. He made an all-out campaign, aided by personal appearances of several movie stars and concentrating on visits to the big cities.

The bitter, viciously-contested runoff had national implications, with President Harry S. Truman's administration backing Johnson despite his disagreement with Truman on the need for civil rights legislation. Johnson, of course, long had supported Roosevelt and he supported Truman on nearly everything except civil rights. Many southern Democrats had broken away from the national party to form a States' Rights Party with Senator J. Strom Thurmond, who was to carry four states in November, as its presidential candidate. Since Stevenson was a States' Righter, Truman hoped a Johnson victory might keep Texas in the Democratic column.

At 1:30 a.m. Sunday, Aug. 29, 1948, six and one-half hours after the polls closed, Stevenson led Johnson by a mere 54 votes—and his supporters grew alarmed when they learned that one box still was unreported from Duval County, which long had been under the control of political boss George Parr.

The complete Duval County returns (Johnson 4,622, Stevenson 40) came in Sunday night, with the late box having increased Johnson's total by 427 and Stevenson's by only two. This put Johnson ahead by 693 votes, out of 980,877 cast, at midnight Sunday.

The lead continued to see-saw back and forth, with both sides charging irregularities on "corrected" totals, until the Texas Election Bureau announced on Wednesday, Sept. 1, that it had complete returns from all counties. Those unofficial returns indicated that Stevenson had won by 113 votes out of nearly one million cast.

Included were the "complete" returns from Jim Wells County, adjoining Duval County and also part of the Parr domain, showing Johnson with 1,786 votes to Stevenson's 769. But on Friday, Sept. 3, Jim Wells County filed an amended return giving Johnson 1,988 and Stevenson 770. The accompanying explanation said a re-canvass revealed 203 votes cast in Box 13 in Alice, Texas, which had not previously been counted. The notorious Box 13 gave 202 votes to Johnson and only one to Stevenson, boosting Johnson into a winning, statewide margin of 87 votes and earning him the nickname, "Landslide Lyndon."

"I was beaten by a stuffed ballot box," Stevenson angrily told reporters, "and I can prove it!"

He felt he might be able to do so before the State Democratic Executive Committee, which had to canvass the votes officially in Fort Worth on Sept. 13 and have its decision confirmed the following day by the state convention.

He came close. He prepared his case by sending Kellis Dibrell and Jim Gardner, both lawyers and former FBI agents, to investigate. Stevenson joined them himself but Parr laughed the trio out of his office when they asked to see the Duval County voting lists, insisting that he was not an election judge and had nothing to do with the election.

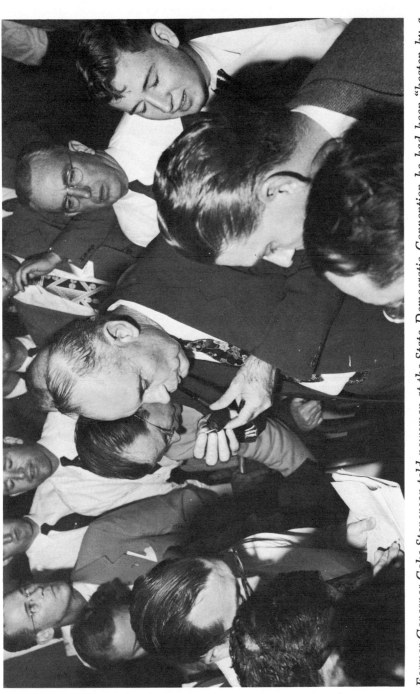

Former Governor Coke Stevenson told newsmen at the State Democratic Convention he had been "beaten by a stuffed ballot box" and would prove it. But the U. S. Supreme Court squelched his efforts to overturn LBJ's win.

The three men then went to Alice in neighboring Jim Wells County, where Harry Adams had just been elected chairman and H. L. Poole secretary of the County Democratic Executive Committee. Adams and Poole said the "amended" total reported on Sept. 3 resulted from the addition of 203 names, all in blue ink, in the same handwriting and in *alphabetical order*, to a list (that otherwise was in black ink) of people who had voted. But Adams and Poole were unable to get the list from Tom Donald, the outgoing county secretary, who also happened to be an employee of Parr's bank—and had it locked up in the bank vault.

A dramatic showdown resulted on the morning of Sept. 9. Stevenson called for Captain Frank Hamer, one of the most famous Texas Rangers of all time, to come down to Alice and help keep the peace.

That morning Stevenson, Dibrell and Gardner—all coatless, to make it plain that they were unarmed—marched toward the bank with Hamer. As they approached the front door, Hamer motioned several of Parr's armed gunmen to step aside—and they did. Donald reluctantly agreed to show the highly-suspect voting list to the investigators, letting them look at it only for a few moments and refusing to let them copy down any names.

Dibrell and Gardner were able to verify the fact that the last 203 names were in the same handwriting and in alphabetical order—a rather unusual manner for voters to show up at the polls. They were able to memorize enough names to verify later that at least three of the names on the list belonged to people who had long been dead. They also contacted two other people whose names were listed and obtained affidavits from them declaring they had not voted at all.

The Stevenson forces decided that night that they had enough evidence—and enough votes on the County Executive Committee—to have the returns from Box 13 thrown out, which would have been enough to give Stevenson a stàtewide majority. But the Johnson forces learned almost immediately of their plan to have the County Committee meet on Friday morning, Sept. 10, and managed to drop a bombshell on it.

They obtained a temporary injunction from District Judge Roy C. Archer in Austin prohibiting the County Committee from investigating the Box 13 vote. The petition charged that Stevenson, Dibrell and Gardner had entered into a conspiracy to have Box 13 thrown out on grounds of fraud and irregularities. It also claimed that the alleged conspiracy was being aided by "threats and intimidation" from Captain Hamer.

Less than an hour before the Jim Wells County Executive Committee was to meet, notices of the injunction were served on its members and the other principals. That left the entire matter up to the State

Tension covered the faces of the spectators as the State Democratic Executive Committee's canvassing committee, in Fort Worth, decided to recommend certification of LBJ's 1948 nomination to the U. S. Senate by 87 votes.

Democratic Executive Committee and the State Democratic Convention.

Charles I. Francis, a Houston lawyer whose firm was one of the most powerful in the state, and John D. Cofer argued eloquently for Johnson before the Executive Committee. Clint Small of Austin, representing Stevenson, insisted that the "ghost" voters of Box 13 should not be allowed to determine the U. S. Senate race. The meeting went on all day and well into the night. The Johnson forces found one of their strongest supporters, C. C. Gibson of Amarillo, absent and began looking for him. They found him on the beach at Galveston, vacationing, and flew him to Fort Worth. He arrived just in the nick of time—but Connally still had to go get him out of the men's room to cast the decisive vote.

With the vote on whether or not to throw out Box 13 tied at 28-28, Gibson charged into the room and told Committee Chairman Robert W. Calvert, who later became chief justice of the Texas Supreme Court: "I'm Charley Gibson from Amarillo and I vote for Lyndon!"

That gave Johnson a 29-28 vote of the State Executive Committee to include the vital Box 13 in the vote totals.

"Stevenson planned a fight on the convention floor the next day," Duckworth and Duncan recalled in a 1950 *Dallas Morning News* series on the Parr influence. "The convention was divided on the Johnson-Stevenson matter, and also over support of the presidential nominee, Harry S. Truman. The Johnson forces perfected a coalition with the Trumanites. The Trumanites won convention control and kicked out most of the anti-Truman and anti-Johnson delegates. With the Truman victory came certification of Johnson.

"Johnson appeared on the platform and was given an ovation.

"George Parr was introduced and applauded. Stevenson men didn't try to contest in the convention. They were beaten and they knew it."

But that night, some of Stevenson's closest friends met with him in the Blackstone Hotel to explore all possibilities for changing the decision. They urged him not to surrender.

"This race is not a matter of life or death for me," Stevenson finally said. "If I lost by one vote in an honest count the heavens wouldn't fall in. But about half a million Texans voted for me and they have been defrauded and robbed. The least we can do is appeal it to the federal courts."

About 4 a.m. on Sept. 15, Dibrell and C. C. Renfro, a Dallas attorney, arrived at the weekend retreat of U. S. District Judge T. Whitfield Davidson in Harrison County, on the Louisiana border. Despite the noisy protests of Davidson's dog, they woke him up. The Judge brewed some coffee and listened to the case presented by the two attorneys, then signed a temporary restraining order preventing the Texas Secretary of State from putting Johnson's name on the general election ballot. He ordered a full hearing on Stevenson's petition for Sept. 21.

At that hearing, Judge Davidson suggested that the matter be compromised by permitting the names of both Johnson and Stevenson to go on the general election ballot, thus letting the voters decide which man they wanted to be U. S. Senator. Former Gov. Dan Moody, representing Stevenson, quickly agreed to this idea. It was rejected just as quickly, on behalf of Johnson, by Cofer.

Judge Davidson declared that "there has not been one word of evidence submitted to disprove this plaintiff's claim that he has been robbed of a seat in the United States Senate."

He then appointed a special commissioner, William Robert Smith, to investigate the matter and report back to his court on Sept. 27.

Smith found a remarkable number of witnesses "vacationing" in Mexico and was unable to obtain the necessary copies of poll lists to determine just what had happened on election day—and during the week immediately following it—in Jim Wells County.

Smith's search for evidence proved fruitless. Connally went to the Texas Supreme Court seeking an order that would require the Secretary of State to print Johnson's name on the general election ballot. When he was turned down, the Johnson forces moved their fight to Washington. It was spearheaded there by Abe Fortas; 20 years later, Johnson's attempt to promote him to Chief Justice of the Supreme Court was rejected by the Senate, and then revelations of his outside income resulted in his resignation as an associate justice.

During a brief hearing in which Governor Moody represented Stevenson, Fortas and Wirtz persuaded Justice Hugo Black to dissolve Judge Davidson's order on grounds that federal courts had no jurisdiction over state elections.

That, in effect, canceled the federal court investigation and put Johnson's name on the general election ballot. In November, Johnson defeated Republican Jack Porter of Houston with 702,985 votes to 349,665.

Years later, Johnson still complained that everyone remembered that 87-vote margin although "that wasn't even the election, it was just the nomination."

"I beat Jack Porter by nearly 400,000 votes in the election," he recalled. "But they had it fixed so that Porter was in the Senate until that court order was dissolved."

The Johnson forces noted that Stevenson filed no protest over bloc voting when he carried Duval County in several previous races. These included 1944, when he received 3,310 votes there to his opponents' combined total of 17; 1942, when he collected 2,836, while five opponents totaled 77; in 1940, when it was Stevenson 3,643, with two opponents polling a total of 141, or in 1938, when he carried Duval County with 2,627 votes to Pierce F. Brooks's 198 as he won the lieutenant governor's race the first time.

Connally and other Johnson supporters contended that Johnson got Parr's support because Stevenson had broken a promise to appoint a certain man to a district attorney post in South Texas.

"There was no question," said Connally, "but what those people down there thought he had broken a promise to them. So it was revenge against Stevenson more than love for Johnson that brought them into our camp."

And what about Box 13?

"So far as I know," said Connally, "the box reported exactly what we thought it was going to report two or three days before it reported."

Johnson's friends contended vigorously that he would have won the 1948 primary race by a much larger margin had there been "a really honest count." They cited especially a Brown County case involving a dispute in a local sheriff's race, claiming it cost Johnson 400 votes when a large number of ballots was thrown out.

Connally also recalled a "mistake" which could have proved decisive.

"In one county, I think it was Eastland County, we lost 200 votes on a pure error—pure transposition error," he said. "And they all admitted it—the election judge and everybody else admitted it. But we still couldn't get it corrected."

Johnson himself felt that he had gone to the state convention with a substantial majority and that the State Democratic Executive Committee, which he once described as Stevenson's "own hand-picked jury," decided the case.

"Actually, we had a lead of about 3,000 votes when we went to the state convention," he said later, "and after they had counted out everything they could, we still had 87 votes."

Those proved to be 87 of the biggest votes in American history. And in addition to putting a future President "on first base," they produced some unforgettable stories. Perhaps the most famous is that of a little Mexican boy in Alice, whom a friend discovered one day sitting on his front steps and crying.

"What is the matter, Juan?" asked his friend.

"My father," the youngster sobbed. "He was here last Saturday and no come to see me."

"But your father has been dead for five years, Juan."

"*Si*," sobbed the little boy. "That is true. But he was here last Saturday to vote for Lyndon Johnson—and he no come to see me."

Chapter 7

WINNERS WEEPERS

People, television cameras and muggy, stifling heat packed Johnson City High School's sparkling new gymnasium on the night of May 29, 1964, as 30 graduates waited patiently to receive their diplomas and a bit of advice from the commencement speaker.

The graduation address followed a traditional pattern but it had a more convincing ring than most. It was delivered by the school's most distinguished alumnus and one of the nation's foremost examples of ascendancy from rags to riches.

A hush fell over the crowd as he began speaking.

"Forty years ago, almost to this very night, I left my high school diploma at home and I headed west to seek the fame and fortune that I knew America offered," President Johnson declared. "About 20 months later I came back—back to Johnson City—with empty hands and empty pockets. I came back because I realized that the place to really begin was the place that I had been all the time. . . ."

In customary commencement fashion, he painted a glowing picture of the future.

"That future can also be a place in which, in a thousand towns like Johnson City, a boy, young in years but deep in dreams," he said, "can hope to come forth and to take his place among the leaders of the world."

Johnson took his place among the leaders of the world with only a handful of people knowing that he had accepted the vice presidential nomination in 1960 primarily because he thought the Democratic ticket *would be defeated.* Some of his closest friends believe he would have rejected the nomination had he thought the Kennedy-Johnson ticket *would win.* This was one of those rare cases in which Johnson felt he could win by losing—and lose by winning.

His decision was one of the most shocking in modern political history.

Rayburn has been widely credited with persuading Johnson to take the vice presidential spot but the late returns indicate that it was Rayburn who had to be persuaded.

Governor Daniel and Johnson were co-chairmen of the Texas delegation at the Los Angeles convention, where Kennedy defeated Johnson for the presidential nomination.

"Something people always seem to forget," said Daniel, "when they talk about the vice presidential nomination being offered to Johnson is that, at that time, nobody in the Johnson camp thought there was any chance for John Kennedy to win the election.

"We had been selling that idea to delegations at Los Angeles and, before that, to people at the National Governors Conference in Glacier National Park," he said. "We were really selling the idea that Kennedy couldn't win, and we believed that, and certainly the day after he was nominated there wasn't any change in that opinion.

"And so it was not in a climate of figuring that Johnson had a good chance to become vice president—or even a 50-50 chance—that he accepted the nomination," Daniel recalled. "There were many in the camp that would have opposed his accepting it, a lot harder than they did, if they had thought he had a 50-50 chance of winning. You can't really understand exactly what went on in his mind, and in the minds of the people surrounding him in Los Angeles, unless you realize that most of us were convinced that Kennedy *could not win.*

"Hindsight now, after having won, might make you think Lyndon was just latching onto a winning ticket but that's not true," he declared. "At that time he was latched up to what was thought to be a losing ticket by everybody in the Johnson suite at the Biltmore."

Including Rayburn?

"Yes, sir," said Daniel. "The theory was that if he took the nomination and they lost, Johnson would be in better shape for 1964. He would have heeded the call. He would have gotten out and done his best. And he would still be Senate Majority Leader—that would not be given up. He was still going to be majority leader because Kennedy was not going to win. But by getting out and getting his name before the people, and showing his loyalty to the party although he had opposed Kennedy, Johnson would put himself in a good position to get the presidential nomination in 1964."

That was the argument used to convince Senator Robert Kerr of Oklahoma and other skeptics, according to Daniel. Connally, in corroborating this, later recalled that "Bob Kerr came into that suite like a caged lion—just furious—and so did Speaker Rayburn."

The moment Kennedy won the presidential nomination, Rayburn asked Daniel, who was sitting beside him on the convention floor, to hand him the telephone at the chairman's seat—and to help shield his end of the conversation from the newspaper and television reporters in the aisle.

Rayburn called Johnson.

"Lyndon," he said, "it could be that these people might make an approach to you to accept the vice presidential nomination. If they do, the answer is NO! *Do you understand?* Do you agree? That would be a big mistake!"

Rayburn, apparently after getting a satisfactory answer, handed the phone back to Daniel and told him, "I just wanted to be sure that there would be no moment of weakness or indecision about that. That just must not happen."

Daniel recalls that when Kennedy first offered Johnson the vice presidential nomination, Johnson suggested that Kennedy talk to Rayburn about it "because Mr. Rayburn didn't think it was the wise thing to do."

Congressman Hale Boggs of Louisiana was dispatched to sell Rayburn on the idea, but eventually Kennedy himself had to take a hand in that. Rayburn finally agreed, somewhat reluctantly, largely because the Kennedy forces appealed to him on the basis of party loyalty—his favorite subject. If there was anything he rated above Lyndon Johnson, it was the Democratic Party.

Connally had a room next door to Johnson's suite. He said Johnson phoned him early the morning after the presidential nomination was decided.

"I had just gotten up," said Connally, "and I had showered but I hadn't shaved. He told me he needed me right then, and to come on in, so I put on a shirt and some pants and went in. He said Kennedy had just called him and said he was coming down to see him in 20 or 25 minutes. He asked me what I thought he wanted.

"I said I thought he was going to offer him the vice presidential nomination," Connally recalled. "He said, 'No, I don't believe that's right—he's probably coming down to ask my judgment about who he ought to pick or to clear some people with me.' I said, 'No, he's going to offer you the vice presidency—and you'd better be prepared to face up to it.'

"He asked me what I thought he ought to tell Kennedy. I said, 'Just tell him you have to think about it. You don't have much choice. I don't think you can summarily refuse it—and you sure can't accept it immediately. You've got to talk to an awful lot of people, one way or the other. You just have to ask for time.'

"I was still there when Kennedy came to the door," said Connally. "I went into a bedroom and waited. Kennedy wasn't there over 10 or 15 minutes at the most. As soon as he left, Johnson asked me to come back in. His first words were, 'Well, you were right.'

"I said, 'That's what I was afraid of.' So then began the series of meetings. Later, John Kennedy talked to Speaker Rayburn and Speaker Rayburn came down to the suite with Bob Kerr. The Speaker was really upset when he came in. He didn't like it and he made no bones about it.

"But some of us had had a little more time to think about it," said Connally. "I had tried to think it out, as carefully as I could, and although I didn't want him to do it, we reasoned it a number of different ways. I finally tried to think about every possible contingency—and there were four sets of circumstances you had to consider. And when you boiled it all down, he really had no choice.

"If he went on the ticket and the ticket won, obviously he would be vice president of the United States. That more or less speaks for itself without going into all the arguments. Now, assume that he went on the ticket and the ticket *lost,* where would he be? Well, obviously, the Republicans would have won but at that point, he was running for both senator and vice president. He would still be senator, he would still be majority leader, he would have been a good soldier, he would have done everything he could for the party. Kennedy would be dead politically and Johnson would be the strong man of the Democratic Party. It would put him in good shape for 1964, if he wanted to go in '64. But whether or not he wanted to, he'd still be majority leader; he and Rayburn would be the spokesmen for the Democratic Party in both houses.

"Now, if he had *not* gone on the ticket, and the ticket *won,* the argument was that he would *still be* majority leader. But being majority leader with the party in power really doesn't mean a helluva lot, as Senator Everett Dirksen found out. At that point, Johnson may or may not have been a part of the council, so to speak; he would have been just a worker for the Kennedy program without a real voice in the formulation of that program. The majority leader is pretty well boxed in; he has very little running room, or else he has to be disloyal to the head of his own party, if he takes any different position. This gets to be a pretty sticky situation.

"And if Johnson had refused to go on the ticket and it won," said Connally, "he would have had to get elected majority leader again—and you can assume there wouldn't have been too good a feeling between him and Kennedy. When you refuse to go on a ticket with a man, you have to assume the fellow is not going to appreciate it very much and he's not going to think too highly of you.

"Now, assume he refused to go on the ticket and the ticket lost. He still would have been majority leader. But looking at it then, and now, Kennedy had pretty much captivated the press even then, in 1960. If Johnson had refused to go on the ticket, beyond any question somebody would have been made the scapegoat for losing the election—and it wouldn't have been Kennedy. It would have been Johnson, just as sure as the world, because he'd refused to go on the ticket. As a matter of fact, if he hadn't gone on the ticket, Kennedy in my judgment *would* have lost.

"I thought there was an awfully good chance they would lose, anyway," Connally admitted. "I thought the only chance to win was for

John B. Connally, left, and Lyndon B. Johnson appeared more jovial after the 1960 Democratic National Convention than they—and their friends—really were.

Johnson to go on the ticket but I thought that even with him on it, the odds were against the Democrats winning.

"If you analyzed all the alternatives, Johnson really didn't have much choice. Even if he went on the ticket and the ticket lost, he at least would get credit for doing all he could, for being a good soldier, stepping down and taking second place to a young senator, and doing everything he could as a party man. This would strengthen his position, both as majority leader and as a spokesman for the party. If they had lost with him on the ticket, Johnson would not have been blamed for losing. But if he had refused to be on the ticket and it lost, he *would* have been blamed for the loss.

"We didn't have anything against John Kennedy but most of us had gone through the spring, and the part of the summer that had transpired, believing that Johnson would never take the vice presidential nomination," said Connally. "And we really didn't think the ticket could win. So we were all just kind of sick at heart about the whole turn of events."

Connally admitted that he and a lot of his coworkers really felt that Johnson probably would be better off if the ticket lost than if it won.

"The thing that made it so difficult for all of us," he declared, "was that we felt like we were kind of entrapped. We were going to have to get out and do what we could to help elect the ticket and help carry the state, which we did. And we carried the state, barely."

Daniel said everyone felt the odds were heavy that Kennedy and Johnson would not win so the Texan "wasn't giving up anything."

"I think Johnson himself felt they didn't have a good chance to win, at first—that the odds were strong against that possibility," he said. "But I think Kennedy thought this would unite the party because here was the only man who had put up a fight against him running with him. And if they got elected, it would help with his legislative program.

"Bobby Kennedy came up to the suite and said the idea of putting Johnson on the ticket was meeting with opposition in several delegations, especially Michigan," Daniel recalled. "Connally talked to him and Bobby asked if Johnson would be willing to accept the National Committee chairmanship instead of the vice presidency. Connally and Rayburn told him what he could do with that—and in no uncertain terms. They said they were not too convinced it was wise for him to run for vice president so he didn't need to trade them anything. They said for him to tell his brother that if he didn't want Lyndon, if he felt that another look should be taken at the matter, just to let them know. And they said it in much stronger language than I'm using.

"That nearly upset the apple cart," said Daniel.

It probably came as close to doing that as Senator Kerr did. When Kerr first walked into the suite, Daniel said, he pointed his index finger at Johnson's forehead and said: "I'm going to shoot you right between the eyes. What is this I hear, that you might accept the vice presidential nomination?"

"Senator Johnson told him he was thinking about it," said Daniel. "He said he couldn't go into the details of it right then but to talk to some of the other men in the room that had heard about it.

"The man who took Senator Kerr into the bathroom and explained the reasoning to him was Bobby Baker. He was secretary to the Senate Democratic majority and there was no one closer to Kerr than he was, so he gave him the pitch.

"Kerr said there was no chance for the ticket to win, not a prayer. Baker told him that was right, and that was the whole idea, but that Johnson would be putting himself in the position of heeding the party call and being in position for the next go-around.

"About that time, the chairman of the Arkansas delegation, Tom Harper, came up to see me and I went out in the hall to visit with him. Governor Orval Faubus hadn't come to the convention but had told Harper to do whatever I told him to do. He wanted to know if it was all right with me for Arkansas to cast a complimentary vote for me as vice president.

"I told him to wait a few minutes," said Daniel, "and I thought they'd have somebody they could cast a serious vote for.

"By the time I got back in the room, Senator Kerr was agreeable— but, like a lot of others, he was agreeable only from the standpoint that the loss would not be too bad. So he said it was probably the thing to do.

"And I'll never forget," Daniel added, "that he also said: 'And, if they did happen to win, there would only be a heartbeat between him and the presidency.'"

Chapter 8

MEANWHILE, BACK AT THE RANCH

Within a few weeks after Lyndon Johnson surrendered the presidency and returned to the LBJ Ranch, he apparently had convinced himself that he never had intended to run for reelection in 1968. He told several people that he and Lady Bird had decided in 1964, when he accepted the Democratic nomination in Atlantic City, New Jersey, that he would not consider more than one elective term.

Some of his closest friends scoffed at that idea.

"He probably decided not to run again in 1968 on the afternoon of March 31—he announced his decision, you know, that night," said one. "But now he wants to rewrite history, to some extent. The truth of the matter is that he thought he couldn't win in 1968. He really began thinking seriously about that during the fall of 1967. He got George Christian and Connally to do some work along about December on a statement saying he wouldn't run again. They drafted one, and he worked it over until he finally was satisfied with it.

"He carried it around in his pocket for several weeks, and some of the people closest to him thought he was going to read it the night he gave his State of the Union address," said this close friend of Johnson's. "But as usual, he kept everybody guessing until the last minute."

Johnson told some of his friends, early in 1969, that he knew most people would not believe it but that he actually had been trying, off and on, to "get out of politics" since about 1946. But he found it harder to get out of politics than to get in, he insisted. He added that while he was in Congress he thought the Senate would be a little "too pompous" for him and, despite the stories about his being power-mad, he contended that he had gone about as far as he wanted to in politics then.

"He came home in 1948 to announce that he would not run for the Senate but wound up announcing he would," recalled one of his close associates. "Connally and some of us who had worked with him convinced him he couldn't just go off and leave us stranded. We talked him into it. Actually, he felt at the start he'd probably lose but that would be a way to get out. He felt it would be hard to just quit and say he'd rather make money than be in public service."

According to Johnson, his ambitions grew after he began stepping up in politics.

"Of course, he was elected party 'whip' in 1951 and minority leader in 1953—the youngest leader ever elected by either party and he was elected unanimously," his associate added. "Then he became majority leader and they said he had turned the Senate, as far as the Democrats were concerned, into a one-man show. Well, it was *his* responsibility and he sure wasn't trying to divide that with anybody."

It is not surprising that the impressions of any famous politician's friends and enemies would be diametrically opposed. What is shocking about those who try to describe Lyndon Baines Johnson is that even his friends cannot agree on a composite picture of this puzzling, paradoxical man who frequently fluctuates between humility and supreme egotism, between ebullience and boredom, between being a stern, demanding task-master and a kind, considerate friend.

Arthur Edson of the *Associated Press* described him in December, 1963, as a "complex and contradictory figure."

"But even his closest admirers confess that, at least until he moved into the White House, his impression on the public was often unflattering and politically unfortunate," wrote Edson.

" 'He's not a cornball rural hick,' one of these admirers said, thereby admitting in effect that this has been a stereotyped version of a hand-shaking, back-pummeling, hominy-and-grits champion.

"Any reporter who has traveled with Johnson, who has watched his impressive operation as Senate Democratic leader, who has read much of what he has had to say down through the years, who has talked with friend and foe, comes up with an almost bewildering supply of impressions.

"For Johnson can be domineering and understanding, harsh and gentle, joyous and moody, conniving and naive, statesmanlike and yahoo, vain and humble all within a dizzyingly short time.

"But overriding everything is this: He demands perfection, and to get it he drives himself and his staff relentlessly," said Edson.

Johnson also can be ruthless and charitable, almost simultaneously. A few years ago, a man who had known him intimately for years contended that "he doesn't want just all the money he needs; he wants all there is." But shortly after leaving the White House, with his personal wealth estimated at well over $20,000,000, Johnson announced that the millions of dollars he expected to receive from his memoirs and other literary efforts would be contributed to a scholarship fund for the Lyndon B. Johnson School of Public Service at The University of Texas.

Johnson is a thin-skinned man, who has been known to telephone newspaper reporters and wake them up at 6 a.m. to "straighten them out" on articles in which he felt they had made mistakes, either in getting the facts or in interpreting them. But he shocked most reporters, after leaving the White House, by refusing to grant any interviews or to comment on many published articles which undoubtedly contained some erroneous information about him and his activities.

His self-imposed silence, particularly in connection with President Nixon's performance as President, produced increased respect for him. But it amazed his friends.

As this writer said in the *Dallas Morning News* on July 13, 1969:

"They laughed when President Johnson said he planned to read and write and loaf after leaving the White House, without dabbling in Texas business or politics.

"But thus far, he seems to be following his announced 'game plan' to the letter. And from all indications, he is enjoying this new way of life far more than he had anticipated, despite periodic, well-concealed flashes of indignation sparked by inaccurate newspaper or magazine reports on his activities, either past or present.

"Even some of his closest friends have not seen him in months. The closest of these seem to realize that this is not due to his becoming a recluse but simply to what one of them termed the 'de-pressurization of a man who has lived in the hot glare of public scrutiny for 30 years.' "

Earlier, on Jan. 5, 1969, we had noted that Mr. Johnson, "nearing the end of his reign as one of the most powerful men in the world, recalls his early days teaching school as 'the happiest in my life.' "

"This is the latest paradox in his remarkable career—a career filled with bizarre incidents involved in one of the most fantastic 'rags-to-riches' climbs in history," said that article in the *News.*

"Mr. Johnson, who fulfilled boyhood ambitions by gaining unprecedented political power, great wealth and finally the presidency, now longs for such simple pleasures as loafing by a sun-splattered swimming pool or riding around his home on the range, watching the deer and his prize bulls at play.

"The commander-in-chief of the nation's armed forces looks forward eagerly to Jan. 20, when he will be free to cruise around his 15,000 acres of Hill Country land without being followed by an aide carrying the key to nuclear war.

"He has convinced his closest friends that his only ambitions for the future are to rest, read, write, travel, lecture, play golf and inspire young people to careers in public service."

Johnson had told a press conference on Dec. 27, 1968, that he had "no plans to take on any jobs of any nature" and stated emphatically, "We are not going to be in any business enterprises."

If some Texas politicians and some Texas businessmen took such disclaimers with a grain of salt, it is understandable. Rumors had been rife for months that he would come home and immediately begin trying to gain control of banks and perhaps a major newspaper, and that he soon would begin displaying an active interest once again in state politics—perhaps even to the point of running again for the U. S. Senate.

Johnson scoffed at such rumors.

"If I'd wanted to stay in politics, I would have stayed where I was," he said.

He also confided to friends that one of the happiest moments of his life came when Nixon completed taking the oath of office as his successor.

"It was just like someone had lifted a truck off me," he declared. "No one in that job really *wants* a second term or a third term or a fourth term—because of the awesome responsibilities. . . ."

It was a job, however, for which many observers felt he had been better trained, when he assumed it, than had any of his predecessors. His experience, his accomplishments as the Senate Democratic Leader, his reputation as an arbiter ("Come, let us reason together") and the unprecedented responsibilities which President Kennedy gave him during his service as vice president offered an impressive combination.

In addition, he had another advantage—an important one, although it arose out of tragedy. He was reminded of it by a personal friend and frequent political foe, Allan Shivers, who had become governor of Texas when Governor Beauford Jester died on July 11, 1949.

"I told Lyndon shortly after he was sworn in as President," Shivers recalled later, "that he had the same type of opportunity—much greater, of course, as President of the United States—that I had when I became governor, because neither of us had been elected to the office. That way, you're not obligated to anyone and you can do whatever you think ought to be done.

"When you get elected," Shivers added, "you necessarily feel an obligation to a lot of supporters. I don't care what anybody says about politics, *that is* politics."

Johnson obviously felt obligated, however, to win congressional approval for many of Kennedy's proposals. He did—probably far more of them, in fact, than Kennedy could have. But his declaration of a "war on poverty" had its roots in some of his own early, dismal personal experiences.

As a youngster, Johnson shined shoes in Johnson City and worked at all sorts of odd jobs. After graduating from high school, he hitch-hiked to California but soon returned to work on a Texas road gang at $1 a day. Two years later, he finally entered college—working at various jobs, ranging from janitor to part-time history teacher—to pay his expenses.

He began teaching high school at Cotulla even before graduating from Southwest Texas State College in San Marcos—and the poverty of the Mexican youngsters in his classes undoubtedly made a lasting impression on him.

Later, he became an assistant to Congressman Richard Kleberg, and then state administrator for the National Youth Administration, one of FDR's depression-fighting programs. He was first elected to Congress in 1937 but contends the family wealth—which he insists has been greatly exaggerated—was built on his wife's 1943 investment of $17,500, which she had inherited, in an Austin radio station. Without detracting from her business ability, critics believe it took a lot more than that—and especially a friendly Federal Communications Commission—to transform that station into a $20,000,000 financial empire in 20 years.

Johnson became so concerned during the 1964 campaign about criticism of his wealth that he had a detailed audit of it made public by Haskins & Sells, the New York accounting firm. That report indicated the Johnson fortune had quadrupled between Jan. 1, 1954, and July 31, 1964, but placed its total at only $3,484,098. Haskins & Sells admitted, however, that the total was based on *original cost* of the assets rather than their current *market value.* Thus, it said, the figures were "not intended to indicate the values that might be realized if the investments were sold."

Dean Burch, then the Republican National Chairman, denounced the accounting procedures as "most peculiar" and called the total "incredibly low." He declared that using the same procedures to appraise Manhattan Island would place its value at the $24 which early settlers paid the Indians for it.

"It is peculiar that the bulk of his fortune was made in areas subject to federal control," said Burch. "There is the question of whether influence was used in a government-regulated field."

Johnson retorted a short while later that he owned no interest "in government-regulated industries of any kind" and never had owned any. Furthermore, he declared, Mrs. Johnson had placed her radio and television stock "in an irrevocable trust."

That left everything, he said, entirely up to the trustees: A. W. Moursund, a Johnson City lawyer and his lifelong friend, and J. W. Bullion, a Dallas lawyer. Although the President failed to mention it, Moursund had a direct telephone line from his office to the White House throughout Johnson's administration. He also was such a frequent passenger on presidential helicopters that his name was printed on a flight report passenger form, along with those of the Johnson family, White House staff members and Secret Service agents.

Such individuals merely had to put a check mark beside their names on this manifest instead of signing.

Moursund explained his job as one of seeing to it that "the Johnsons don't know what's going on" in their private financial affairs, lest personal business be tempted to influence the President's official decisions.

Johnson never attempted, at any time during his political career, to hide his wife's broadcasting interests or those of his close friends.

But the politically-sensitive FCC, whose members are appointed by the President, claimed that "technical reasons" were solely responsible for the fact that Austin had only one commercial television station—Lady Bird's—from 1952 until 1965, while many smaller cities had two or three. Austin, based on a 1950 population of 132,459, was given one channel in the FCC allocations. Corpus Christi, which had a population of 108,287 with about one-half of its transmission area stretching over the Gulf of Mexico, was allocated three channels.

The Johnsons' station, KTBC-TV, remained the only VHF (standard) commercial station in Austin even after KHFI-TV, a UHF (short range) station, went on the air in 1965. Until KHFI-TV became a primary affiliate of NBC on Jan. 1, 1968, KTBC-TV had enjoyed the unique distinction of having first call on all three major networks.

Louis M. Kohlmeier called attention to the "Johnson luck" in a *Wall Street Journal* article on March 23, 1964:

"Unlike most businesses, a broadcasting enterprise can exist and expand only with government approval. From the very beginning and repeatedly thereafter, the fate of the Johnson family fortune has inevitably hung not only upon business acumen but also upon favorable rulings by the Federal Communications Commission. Yet FCC public records show not a single intervention by Representative, Senator, Vice President or President Johnson in quest of a favor for his wife's company.

"Quite apparently, there was no need for it. Mrs. Johnson was able to present the FCC with a record of solid business success, whenever that was relevant to government decisions. When it was not relevant, she was—as one official of the agency remarks—consistently 'lucky'. The practical effect—disregarding intent—of a long series of FCC rulings has been to create the Johnson local TV broadcasting monopoly, expand its sphere, and defend it against incursion."

If Johnson took no interest in his wife's radio-television holdings while serving as President, he certainly did in the conception, financing and construction of the Lyndon B. Johnson State Park. After all, that was his idea.

The 269-acre park, most of it separated from the LBJ Ranch at Stonewall by the Pedernales River and Ranch Road 1, quickly became a popular tourist attraction but one which provided additional privacy for the Johnsons. That seems appropriately paradoxical, considering its name, the fact that it is a "state park" controlled by the National Park Service, and its bizarre beginning.

The Johnsons' privacy results from a large animal enclosure in the park, between their ranch and the visitor facilities—which include a tourist center with appropriate exhibits, an auditorium, a swimming pool, and picnic tables. Longhorn cattle, buffalo and deer roam the "no man's land" running along Ranch Road 1 but the visitor center does offer a glimpse of the main house on the LBJ Ranch.

In fact, that prompted Lady Bird to plant a tree beneath her husband's bathroom window in order to assure privacy.

But the really crucial "privacy" involving the LBJ State Park was provided by the strange, mysterious cloak of secrecy thrown around those who contributed money to buy the land for it. By mid-1969, the federal government had allocated $669,749 and the state government $500,000 for development of the park—but the amount contributed by individuals and business firms and foundations remained secret, thus continuing to fan the flames of curiosity.

Connally had won legislative passage in 1963 of a plan to combine the Texas Game, Fish and Oyster Commission (an agency holding life-or-death authority over the multimillion dollar dredging of shell from Texas bays) with the State Parks Department. That gave him the power to appoint all three members of the new State Parks and Wildlife Commission.

He named three close friends of Johnson: Will Odom, an Austin petroleum engineer; J. M. Dellinger, a Corpus Christi contractor, and Moursund.

Almost immediately, the new three-member Commission became involved in a dredging controversy. Sportsmen contended that live oyster reefs were being damaged—a practice highly detrimental to fishing. Critics claimed that highway construction crews, unloading oyster shells used in building new roads, frequently found in their raw material enough fresh oysters for their lunch.

Although many millions of dollars are involved in dredging, that dispute was overshadowed by the 'now-you-see-it-now-you-don't' operations covering the Lyndon B. Johnson State Park.

On Nov. 17, 1964, the three Parks and Wildlife Commissioners adopted an order designating the land immediately across the road from the LBJ Ranch as the Lyndon B. Johnson State Park. They also ordered J. Weldon Watson, then the Commission's executive secretary and a highly-respected career administrator in state government, to work with the Gillespie County Commissioners Court in acquiring the land.

Six months later, this official state agency established a "private" fund to solicit contributions for buying the land and the three commissioners appointed themselves as the "private" administrators of it. . . .

Then, wearing their "private" hats, the commissioners began actively soliciting contributions for the Lyndon B. Johnson State Park. Rumors circulated that some of the firms regulated by "the Commission" and some regulated by various federal agencies were being asked to contribute.

The rumors were furthered by the commissioners' refusal to reveal the names of donors or even the total amount collected. But while insisting this was a private matter that was none of the public's business, they managed to *condemn land* for public purposes.

This aroused the curiosity of a state senator, Jim Bates, of Edinburg, who happened to be chairman of the Senate's General Investigating Committee. He quickly learned that his position entitled him to exactly no information at all on the mysterious LBJ State Park Fund.

Odom refused to furnish information Bates requested on the names of donors and the amounts contributed. The Senator termed this "blatantly contemptible of the entire Senate of this State."

Bates said he had received complaints that the "Commission was using the name and prestige of the President of the United States to 'blackjack' contributions by various individuals, firms and corporations not only in this state, but in other states, in an effort to gain credit in the eyes of the President and of the people."

"It has further been stated to me," Bates told the Senate, "that contributions were secured by the commissioners personally approaching persons, firms and corporations who were, and are directly under and controlled by the rules, regulations and supervision of the Parks and Wildlife Commission."

Two of Bates's Senate colleagues were called to Washington for consultation on his complaints but he continued his futile fight, acknowledging that "great pressures" had been applied in an effort to stop him from asking questions—which he finally did.

He did get Odom to announce that a "total" of $196,902 in contributions had been received. About the same time, an alert newspaper reporter found a $50,000 donation to the LBJ State Park Fund listed in the annual report of the Brown Foundation, Inc., headed by Johnson's old friend, George R. Brown.

Mr. and Mrs. Earl W. Sweeney decided to fight the condemnation of their 54-acre tract of land, including a valuable peach orchard, directly across the road from the LBJ Ranch house. They took the matter to court and their case was set for hearing on Jan. 23, 1967. But on Dec. 31, 1966, after that hearing had been set, the Parks and

Wildlife Commissioners suddenly turned "the Fund"—despite its original by-laws saying no one but members of the Parks and Wildlife Commission could ever serve as administrators of it—over to former Attorney General Shepperd, now a private citizen.

That knocked the props out from under the Sweeneys' court case.

Shepperd said he would make details of the private fund, which some rumors put at a total of several million dollars, available within a few days. He never "found time" to do so although a list of donors—not necessarily a complete one—finally was made public when the park was formally dedicated on Aug. 29, 1970.

Connally once admitted that the Park Fund was "the most mishandled affair" of his administration.

Johnson, of course, always disclaimed any knowledge of the financing matter. But his interest in the park was demonstrated early when he and Mrs. Johnson personally gave instructions to the bulldozer operators who came in to do the preliminary work.

It was shown further by his popping into the Visitor Center frequently—as often as four times a day—after he left the presidency. He felt the LBJ State Park was a well-justified landmark in American history which might some day become almost as popular as Mount Vernon.

Johnson's favorite recreation, even before he left office, seemed to be driving around his ranch in a Lincoln Continental convertible, idling along and watching the huge herds of deer which roamed the area. He quickly added the LBJ State Park to the itinerary for most of his guests, along with the "LBJ Birthplace" a few miles away and the "Boyhood Home" in Johnson City. And he strongly recommended visits to the magnificent LBJ Library in Austin.

Johnson is a man who likes to see his efforts rewarded by tangible monuments. As a result, even after having served as President, he was still proud to look back and proclaim that he had "built a dam a year in Texas" while he was a member of Congress. But he also recalled his Washington influence, in the House of Representatives and the Senate and even the Presidency, as being somewhat misunderstood.

He felt he had enjoyed great prestige as a senator partly just because he was casting a vote for Texas. He once said he had the feeling when he made a speech in the Senate that his colleagues were more interested because he was speaking for Texas than they were in what he had to say. And that was a situation which had existed with senators from Texas ever since Sam Houston, he believed. He was strongly convinced that Texas's influence in Washington had been due more to the state's resources, its strength and power in elections than to individuals.

"Oil has been a handicap to every Texas politician in Washington because the press is so prejudiced against the industry," he once remarked to a friend. "The oil industry has never supported me but I was regarded in Washington as a spokesman for it."

While Johnson felt his rather distant relationship with the oil industry was over-emphasized, he believed his role as head of the National Aeronautics and Space Administration—during his term as vice president—was not fully appreciated. He was convinced he had rendered a great service to the nation when he recommended to President Kennedy that the United States try to put a man on the moon before 1970.

Kennedy, of course, sent the recommendation to Congress. When Neil Armstrong, Edwin E. Aldrin, Jr., and Michael Collins successfully completed their Apollo 11 moon-landing mission on July 24, 1969, Johnson felt that another of the many decisions he had made during his long Washington career had been justified.

One of Johnson's first recollections of Washington was of Sam Rayburn sitting in a hospital chair, dozing as a cigarette dangled from his lips. Johnson then was serving as an assistant to Congressman Kleberg. Upon conquering a fever of 105, he was pleasantly surprised to wake up and find Rayburn sitting in his room; the Congressman had come to visit simply because he had been a friend of Samuel Ealy Johnson, Jr., the young man's father.

Rayburn quickly became a close friend and adviser. He also became, according to Johnson, one of the most maligned Texans in history.

"Mr. Rayburn was identified in Texas as a liberal but in Washington as a conservative," Johnson told one of his friends after leaving the presidency. "That's what happens when you call 'em like you see 'em. Mr. Rayburn was very moderate, temperate and fair; on occasion, he would be classified as highly conservative. But he was abused by the conservative press in his own state—and not given any recognition by the liberal press."

That appraisal was in line with Johnson's theory that the traditional "conservative" and "liberal" labels are not only outdated but generally "do a great injustice."

"It's unfair to put a brand on any man," he once declared.

Johnson all but disregarded even the Democratic and Republican tags in his own association with President Eisenhower.

"I was his floor leader for six years and he said I was better than anyone in his own party could have been," Johnson has told some of his close friends. "And nobody helped me more in the presidency than Eisenhower."

Despite his disdain of labels, Johnson recognized realistically that every man classifies in his own mind the people with whom he comes into contact. Although they had widely-advertised political differences, he obviously reserved a special place of honor in his own classification system for an old political foe, Shivers—who also had little use for labels.

"If I had to have a man lead me into battle," the former President said a short while after leaving the White House, "I'd be happy to have it be Allan Shivers."

Chapter 9

TWO-PARTY PUNCH

L ate on a cold, dreary February afternoon in 1969, Allan Shivers dropped by Congressman George Bush's suite in the Commodore Perry Hotel at Austin for a brief visit. The personable young Republican excused himself from several other guests in the living room and took Shivers back to the bedroom for a private, 15-minute chat.

Their discussion concerned Bush's political future. It was one of several the two men had during the year, mostly about the outlook for the 1970 U. S. Senate race. On that particular occasion, the talk centered around results of a private poll Bush had just received concerning his chances for defeating Senator Yarborough.

"A lot of the things in the poll could be classified as very favorable," Shivers said later. "But it certainly was too early to make any decision and that was my main interest—to advise George not to rush into it. I told him he probably ought to wait until the end of the year to decide."

Bush undoubtedly was impressed by the advice, since it came from one of the most masterful politicians in Texas history. Shivers had served as governor of Texas longer than anyone else, had twice led the state into the Republican presidential column, had been offered cabinet posts by two presidents and strongly considered for one by a third—and had retired without ever losing a battle at the polls.

But neither Shivers nor Bush felt, at that point, that the Democratic nominee would be anyone other than Senator Yarborough.

Shivers made no bones about his liking for Bush. Complete candor always had been one of his most widely-recognized qualities and it was one which had earned him the respect even of political foes who hated him.

"I'm very much interested in George," said Shivers. "I think he's thoroughly honest, not only morally but intellectually. He's the kind of man I'd personally like to see go far and achieve success. I'd like to see him in the United States Senate. I think he'd make a good senator to represent Texas—Republican or Democrat or what not. He probably helps more Democrats with their problems in Washington now than Republicans, by far. And he has enough money that he can afford to serve; his personal wealth is such that he doesn't need money."

Bush's political future, Shivers believed, depended largely on timing.

His greatest reservation about Bush's running in 1970 revolved around the feeling that Texas probably was not ready to be represented by two Republicans in the U. S. Senate; and yet, he felt that Bush was in an awkward position because if he did not run in 1970, he probably would have to wait six more years.

"There is more to timing in a political race than there is in a track meet," Shivers declared. "There are times when anyone could be elected—and there are times when the best man who ever ran couldn't win."

It was because he felt the best man *should* win that Shivers always favored true two-party status for Texas, even though he refused to switch to the Republican Party and lead such a movement. He felt that he should not allow anyone to drive him out of the Democratic Party—that he could do more from the inside to reshape its course than he could from the outside.

"I'll always have a great love for the Democratic Party, although I wouldn't hesitate to disagree with it or its leaders—again—at any time when I thought it was wrong," he said. "I think the voters should have a choice. That was one of Nixon's greatest mistakes in the 1960 campaign. In the first television debate, he said there was no division between him and Kennedy.

"The secret of winning is to have your own supporters enthusiastic," said Shivers. "If they have *no choice* on issues, if there really is no difference, they're not going to be enthusiastic about a campaign. You lose the enthusiasm of your own people when you join the opposition. You don't gain two per cent of your opposition by watering down your own views in an effort to make them think you're not as bad as they thought.

"One of the greatest criticisms laymen have of candidates is that they all sound alike," he noted. "A man must have certain well-defined views—but that doesn't mean he must say everything is all black or all white. And he must be enthusiastic to win a political campaign. Campaigning is the hardest work in the world and the voters' interest is proportionate to the candidate's interest.

"I think two-party government would be good for Texas. In a one-party state, you get too much into an individual popularity campaign and it frequently becomes a mud-slinging affair. In most two-party states, they deal more with issues and responsibilities. Two-party government, in the state as well as the nation, results in greater responsibility in office. The contest for authority between the two parties is really one of the bulwarks of our system of government."

Even so, Shivers admitted that his decision to support Eisenhower in 1952 was the toughest of his political career.

"It probably caused me more sleepless nights and more worry, and

President Eisenhower, left, and Governor Allan Shivers placed a wreath at the Alamo on Oct. 14, 1952, as the Democratic leader in Texas campaigned for the GOP nominee. Shivers supported Eisenhower again in 1956.

prompted more consultation with friends over the state—and with my family and everyone else concerned—than any other decision I ever had to make," he said.

The dramatic decision was preceded by an earth-rattling conference Shivers had in Springfield, Illinois, with Governor Adlai Stevenson, the Democratic presidential nominee, one August day in 1952.

"I spent a total of six or eight hours there," Shivers recalled, "and had lunch with Stevenson. I had carried a brief on our tidelands situation to him, as he had asked me to do."

Congress twice had passed and President Truman twice had vetoed legislation returning the oil-rich, submerged lands just off the Texas coast to the State of Texas. The state based its case on the Annexation Agreement, which said specifically that Texas would retain its public lands in return for retaining its public debts. Congress, in 1845, thought it would be a poor bargain to take over Texas's public debts, even if it received in return the state's public lands—including those stretching 10.35 miles into the Gulf of Mexico. By 1952, of course, oil—and methods of recovering it—had been discovered beneath the ocean waters just off the Texas coast.

"After lunch," Shivers recalled, "Stevenson asked me to give him some time to really think about the matter and study it. I did. I went back late that afternoon and he told me that he would do the same thing Truman had done—veto the bill—if Congress passed legislation clarifying our title to the tidelands. I asked him to put that in writing and he did, in a handwritten note.

"The press was waiting for me outside when I left his office about dark that evening," said Shivers. "I had told him—and therefore I told the press—that in view of his decision, I couldn't support him. When the press up there asked him for comment, he said, 'Well, I imagine if I were in Governor Shivers's shoes I'd probably feel the same way and make the same statement.'

"Later, when he came to Texas, Stevenson softened his views somewhat—I'm sure at the suggestion of Rayburn and others down here," said Shivers. "He said he was willing to consider some alternatives but never did say he was in favor of the states having the tidelands. What he wanted to do was to give the states some money 'in lieu of' the tidelands.

"I debated the whole thing with myself, and counseled with a lot of friends," he continued. "At the state convention in Amarillo that September, a great many people wanted to keep Stevenson's name off the ballot in Texas. I was not in favor of that. I had told the Democratic Convention in Chicago in July that I would use my best efforts to see that the nominees of the convention were on the ballot in the proper place in Texas. I felt obligated to do that, not only because of the promise—I thought it was just morally right. If anyone wanted to vote for Stevenson, that voter ought to have the right to find the nominee's name in the place he expected to find it.

"I felt we shouldn't use any chicanery or brute strength or anything else to prevent that voter from having the opportunity to vote for his choice," Shivers declared. "But a group of people, most of whom were close friends of mine, came to see me about keeping Stevenson's name off the ballot. That movement was led by Price Daniel, who was then our attorney general and the nominee for the U. S. Senate, and Hines Baker and Arch Rowan. Daniel had given a verbal opinion the night before that the convention could do this.

"I think possibly the convention could have done it—by brute strength, because the convention controls the organization of the ballots. But I tried to talk them out of it. I told them that not only was it morally wrong but, as far as I personally was concerned, I had given my word that I was going to defend the historic position on the ballot.

"They were hell-bent on testing their theory and they thought that with Price's help they could put it over," said Shivers. "They finally made the motion. I spoke against it and it was defeated. Stevenson's name went on the ballot in the proper place.

"I was still in the position where I didn't really know what I was going to do—whether I was going to stay quiet and do nothing, or support Eisenhower, or, as the old term puts it, 'go fishing.' The Amarillo convention did adopt a resolution calling upon all Democratic office holders, party officials and everyone else to support Eisenhower. While I wouldn't say that didn't influence me at all, in my opinion I still had to make up my own mind."

The decision evolved over a period of time, said Shivers.

"I made some statewide speeches, asking people for their opinions. That's always a good thing to do but you still have to make up your own mind, regardless," he said. "When I finally decided I was going to support Eisenhower I felt that, as active as I had been, I couldn't just sit on the sidelines. I had already said that I wouldn't support Stevenson so that left me with just one choice—to support Eisenhower. But that came pretty late in the season."

Once he made the decision, Shivers went all out for Eisenhower and made speeches for him throughout the South as well as in Texas.

Earlier that year, he had rejected requests—including one from Daniel—that he run against U. S. Senator Tom Connally.

"You can beat him and I can't," Daniel told Shivers late one afternoon, on the front steps of the Capitol.

It did not take Shivers long to make his decision on that. After Shivers refused to run, Daniel announced his candidacy and Senator

Connally mailed a campaign advisory to his long list of supporters. The returns convinced Connally he should retire, especially since a large percentage of his letters came back marked either "addressee deceased" or "addressee moved—no forwarding address." During his 24 largely-uncontested years in the Senate, Connally obviously had lost contact with the voters; his withdrawal permitted Daniel to ride the tidelands issue easily into the Senate. Shivers, of course, emphasized it in his own reelection campaign and in the Eisenhower effort.

Shivers led Texas into the Republican column in 1952 for the first time since 1928, planting the seeds for a new political era in the state. Rayburn and Yarborough found this unforgivable as well as unbelievable. Their relentless criticism and needling of Shivers may well have cost Yarborough the governor's chair in 1954, since Shivers really did not want to run for reelection that year.

Rayburn repeatedly insisted that no public official who had supported Eisenhower would ever win public office in Texas again.

"He and Yarborough kept on with that," recalled Shivers, "until they got me in the position—and, of course, Lyndon sided with Rayburn—where I had to either run and risk getting beat or else drop out and let them say they had run me off. I decided I'd rather get beat than have them say they'd frightened me off.

"A lot of my friends, in 1954, wanted me to soft-pedal my support of Eisenhower in 1952 like Price did later, when he ran in 1956—he practically apologized for it and said he just did it to save the tidelands for the school children," said Shivers. "I told them I couldn't do that, that I wasn't built that way and I had to tell 'em the truth about it—that if I had it to do over again, I'd do the same thing."

Shivers's independence was born in the Piney Woods section of East Texas, where life was so demanding that he did not even see a football game until after his family moved to Port Arthur in 1923, while he was a senior in high school. Born in Lufkin on Oct. 5, 1907, he was reared in the little East Texas town of Woodville and, as a boy, sold newspapers and magazines there to earn spending money. He had a typical East Texan's love for spareribs, turnip greens and blackeyed peas—but even some of his East Texas friends couldn't help raising their eyebrows when he ordered watermelon for breakfast.

After graduating from Port Arthur High School, he entered The University of Texas at Austin but lack of money forced him to drop out at the end of the first year. By working two and a half years for an oil company, he managed to save enough to return. But in order to make the grade financially, he still had to clerk in a shoe store and also work as a night watchman in the State Treasury.

He found time, in spite of his jobs and his studies, to make an auspicious debut in politics. His college political life was as stormy as the distinguished career which followed. At The University of Texas, they still talk about the campus campaign which resulted in his election as president of the student body.

One of his detractors in that race wrote some very unkind things about the young man from Port Arthur and printed them in a sort of outlaw scandal sheet. Shivers paid a fine for assault a few days after he encountered the poison pen expert one night and administered what he considered appropriate punishment.

Shivers earned his bachelor's degree in 1931 and his law degree in 1933. He quickly learned to weather turbulent political seas calmly— at least on the surface, although he might be seething inwardly with rage. Sometimes, the inner turmoil seemed greatest when he was upset over trifles because he was astute enough to realize that the most trivial insults and insinuations could be the most dangerous at the polls.

In one campaign for governor, the opposition began spreading the rumor that the handsome, boyish-looking Shivers, who always received a high percentage of the women's vote, wore a toupee. His charming, attractive wife, Marialice, who did not care a whit for politics, spiked that rumor quickly and effectively.

"If he wears one, I wish he'd get a new one," she quipped, "because the one he has looks a little moth-eaten."

Mrs. Shivers was the only child of the late John H. Shary, pioneer developer of the fabulous Rio Grande Valley. Shivers already had engineered a stunning political upset when he met her on a yachting party at Port Arthur in 1935. He had defeated the "unbeatable" Senator W. R. Cousins, Sr., of Beaumont and, at 26, became the youngest state senator in Texas history.

He and Marialice were married in 1937 and, when Shary died in 1945, Shivers became general manager of the mammoth John H. Shary Enterprises. The interests included 15,000 acres of fertile Rio Grande Valley land, nurseries, canneries, oil and gas property, banking interests and a weekly newspaper.

After leaving the governor's office, Shivers devoted his energies largely to expanding his own business empire but took time out for such civic endeavors as serving as president of the U. S. Chamber of Commerce.

He turned down cabinet posts offered him by both Eisenhower and Nixon. Johnson strongly considered him for Secretary of Commerce but apparently abandoned the idea when his scouting reports made it clear Shivers would turn it down—and partly, perhaps, because Johnson did not want to exert the force that would have been necessary to get such an appointment confirmed over Yarborough's objections.

Shivers had not really wanted even the governor's office when he was first thrust into it.

When he returned in 1945 from two years of overseas service as a major in the army, he just wanted to stay in the State Senate and practice law. His Senate colleagues talked him into running for lieutenant governor in 1946—and he gave his campaign staff a bad case of jitters during that first statewide campaign by calmly taking a two-week vacation right in the middle of it. But he won, was reelected in 1948 and served as lieutenant governor until July 11, 1949, when Governor Beauford Jester died in a Pullman berth en route to Houston.

Shivers was in Woodville when he got word of Jester's death—from a Houston newspaper reporter who telephoned him.

"I cried," Shivers said, when asked his first reaction. "Beauford had been a very close friend of mine."

Shivers took the oath of office at the old, 605-acre Shivers farm near Woodville and became Texas's thirty-sixth governor. He quickly organized his staff along the lines of a business firm. His executive assistants were specialists in the legal, public relations, legislative, personnel and budgetary fields but all of them were convinced that Shivers knew more about their individual jobs than they did—and probably could have performed their duties better than they did if he merely had enough time.

He was elected governor in 1950, 1952 and 1954. It was in the 1954 campaign that Yarborough tried to capitalize on scandals involving the collapse of insurance companies regulated by the State Insurance Commission, whose three members were appointed by the Governor.

Part of that problem had been caused by the long illnesses of two Insurance Commission members, both of whom had died before the campaign began. Shivers earned the undying respect of several campaign aides when, in a strategy meeting one night, an adviser suggested that he could dispose of the insurance scandal issue quickly and effectively merely by explaining the facts about those two men.

"No!" Shivers replied quickly and emphatically. "The widows of those two men are still living and I'm not going to have them dragged into a political campaign and embarrassed just to get votes. If we can't win without doing that, we'll just have to lose."

Later, Shivers suffered the greatest disappointment of his political career when two of his own appointees to the Insurance Commission failed to live up to the trust he placed in them.

Shivers stumped the state during the 1954 campaign in shirt sleeves, battling the fierce summer heat. It was the twilight era of outdoor political rallies and stump speaking on the courthouse square; he made the first statewide political telecast in Texas history. He described himself as a Wilsonian liberal who wanted to get the Democratic Party back on the track of Jefferson, Wilson and the "early Franklin D. Roosevelt" principles. He felt that Roosevelt had been "a sick man during the latter years of his administration" and actually had started the trend away from the principles which made the Democratic Party great.

In almost every speech, he described an incident which occurred on the Sunday before the 1952 Democratic National Convention.

"Walter Reuther and Jack Kroll of the CIO Political Action Committee, Walter White of the National Association for the Advancement of Colored People, and others issued a statement that there was no room for me in THEIR Democratic Party," he said.

"When in the name of God did it get to be THEIR Democratic Party?" he roared. "It is not a party that belongs to a handful of cheap political bosses—it belongs to the people! When that little group of political bosses said the Texas delegation could not be seated at the convention, we started fighting them—and we whipped them!"

He went on to tell how the same group, that same day, went to the hotel room of former Vice President Alben Barkley, "the grand old warhorse of the Democratic Party."

"They told him flatly that he could not run for the Democratic nomination for President of the United States," said Shivers.

Few dry eyes could be found in his rally audiences when he bore down on that, recalling that Barkley later admitted "he closed the door and cried after that group left his hotel room."

Yarborough and his supporters staunchly denied that they were receiving money from Reuther and other "out-of-state labor bosses," as Shivers charged.

But late one night, after a staff meeting in Shivers's campaign headquarters to plan his itinerary for the last two weeks of the campaign, Jack Dillard and James H. Blundell, two of his assistants, began chatting about that matter. Dillard finally decided he would call Fagan Dickson, then one of Yarborough's top-ranking campaign workers, and impersonate Reuther. He had a secretary place the call and pretend to be a long distance telephone operator, informing Dickson's wife that "Mr. Walter Reuther is calling Mr. Fagan Dickson."

"I guess I woke him up or I probably wouldn't have gotten by with it," Dillard later admitted. "But I asked him how the campaign was going and if certain CIO employees, whom I called by name, were doing a good job for them. He said they were.

"I asked if they had gotten the last money we sent and he said they had but still needed more. By that time, I was getting kind of carried away because the hoax was working so well and I finally just said, 'Well, we've got to beat this S.O.B. Shivers!' Fagan said, 'Bless your fightin' heart, Walter!' I said I had to go, then.

"It scared me to think how much I'd fooled him," said Dillard. "But it also scared them. They found out about it and I guess they figured we'd probably recorded it because they called all the radio stations and told them the Shivers people had a tape of a telephone conversation that was libelous and they'd better not use it."

Shivers, of course, was much more straightforward than that in dealing with his opponents—just as he had been on the University of Texas campus. In 1955, he went to Washington for both a White House Governors' Conference and a meeting of Democratic governors. After the White House meeting, the young maverick who was counted among Eisenhower's close friends was asked if he intended to stick around for the meeting of his Democratic colleagues.

"Yes," he replied, with a grin. "I suppose I just want to see who will be the most embarrassed—me or them."

He sat through that meeting for hours, listening to his colleagues assure each other that President Eisenhower was losing his popularity and the Democratic Party would win the 1956 presidential election by a landslide. After listening to all of that he could stand, he got up and told the other Democratic governors that they were whistling in the dark.

Shivers declared that some Democrats had "tried unsuccessfully to talk us into a depression" and that such tactics could not be expected to win the confidence of the people. He pointed out that neither party had been able to come up with anything resembling a solution to the farm problem. And he said the Democrats could not expect to win the presidency unless they came up with some positive program for the benefit of the nation.

He made it clear that he felt the fundamental, traditional differences between the Democratic and Republican parties had shrunk rapidly, to such a point that it was difficult to tell one from the other without relying on labels. As a result, he said, voters were no longer blinded by a party label that was "good enough for Grandpa."

Shivers left no doubt that he did not intend to vote for Stevenson if he should win the 1956 nomination. One reporter asked him what Stevenson would have to change in order to get his support.

"A lot of things," said the outspoken Shivers, "including his name."

Candor remains a Shivers trademark.

During the fall of 1967, Shivers and his wife were attending a party at the Sheraton Hotel in Dallas when Eugene Locke, then Deputy Ambassador to South Vietnam, suggested that they leave a little early so they could have a private conversation.

"He and his wife went up to our room with us," Shivers recalled, "and had a couple of drinks. It became obvious pretty quickly that he wanted to talk about the possibility of his running for governor.

"Finally, I said, 'Gene, I guess you're asking me for advice. I've always followed a policy of not giving this kind of advice but let me tell you, I think you've got a long row to hoe. It would cost you an enormous amount of money. I know you've got a lot of money, and you may be willing to spend it on this. You'll raise some money— Connally can raise you some. But in my opinion, your case is almost hopeless.'

"But he had it all figured out," Shivers continued. "He felt he was in exactly the same position Connally had been in when he ran for governor the first time, in 1962—that he was giving up a federal post, just as Connally had, that he was going to build himself up the same way Connally had built himself up and that, with Connally's help, he could win the race.

"I said, 'Oh, hell, Gene, you really don't believe that, do you?' But he did," said Shivers. "He got mad, and I guess he should have. You still can't tell a fellow not to marry some girl he wants to marry, or not to join a church he wants to join, or not to run for a political office when he thinks he can win."

Locke's anger did not last long. It melted away rather rapidly, as has most of that exhibited by Shivers's political foes—with the exception of Yarborough. Hating Shivers is almost an obsession with Yarborough, observed one of their mutual friends, and Johnson's friendship with Shivers is something Yarborough can never understand. Yarborough holds that against both of them.

In 1956, Shivers and Johnson staged one of the roughest precinct convention fights ever seen in Texas. They fought tooth and nail over control of the state delegation to the Democratic National Convention.

Johnson won—and, a short time later, Shivers visited Washington with an old friend, W. E. (Eddie) Dyche, Jr., a Houston lawyer. Shivers phoned Johnson and invited him to come by his hotel suite for a drink. They had a brief argument—over whether Johnson should drop by the hotel or Shivers should go to the Majority Leader's office. They finally agreed on the hotel—and then spent several hours there rehashing the campaign, eating dinner and joking about some of the brickbats they had just spent months hurling at each other.

The night after Johnson accepted the vice presidential nomination in 1960, he phoned Shivers at his home in Woodville and asked for his support, recalling another Washington meeting.

"I haven't decided what I'm going to do," Shivers responded.

"Don't you remember the party in Washington last spring where you told me you'd support me?" asked Johnson.

"I surely do," said Shivers, "but I told you I'd support you if you were nominated for *President.*"

"Well, I *sure* want your support now," Johnson said.

"Lyndon, you and I are friends and we're not going to fall out about this—I hope," Shivers replied. "But I don't know—I just don't think I can support Kennedy."

"Well, now, if that's your final decision, when you reach it, just don't help that other fellow," said Johnson.

A few days later, Johnson had Senator Earl Clements of Kentucky, his predecessor as majority leader and then secretary of the Democratic Policy Committee, call Shivers.

"I told him I would like to help Lyndon but I couldn't support Kennedy," Shivers recalled. "He wanted me to promise I would call him before I made any decision but I wouldn't let him put me in that position—I told him he or Lyndon could call me any time but I was not going to promise to call them. I said, 'I've told Lyndon and I'll tell you: I don't see any way in the world I can support Kennedy.'

"I supported Nixon that year," said Shivers. "Then I supported Johnson in '64 and got cussed more, by more people, for doing that—. A lot of old-time friends would call me up and say, 'tell me it isn't true.' "

But it was true, and Shivers never regretted his support of Johnson's campaign for the presidency.

"I think he will go down in history as a good President," he declared, a few months after Johnson left the White House. "And his critics might even make a martyr of him.

"Lyndon's smart—he knows the game. You can go back to Franklin Roosevelt, who proposed all those things and didn't want to pass them; he just proposed them for campaign purposes. Kennedy was just the opposite. I guess he really believed in them but he just proposed them, then thought of something else to propose.

"But, hell, Lyndon passed all of 'em!" said Shivers. "He could shoulder Congress out of more money for more projects than any of our last ten or fifteen presidents—probably more than all of them combined. Except for the Vietnam War, I think he probably would go down as a *great* President."

Shivers also thought highly of Eisenhower and had no regrets for supporting him in 1952 or 1956. But he disagreed with those who felt Texas Republicans failed to capitalize on the two Eisenhower victories in trying to establish the two-party system in Texas.

"They didn't have anything to capitalize on," Shivers declared. "This was due to a shortage of Republicans, a shortage of candidates, a shortage of organization. The 'Democrats for Eisenhower' won those elections. The Republicans didn't have any organization.

"And you have to remember," he added, "that Eisenhower was not political himself. He thought the presidency was above politics. Certainly Johnson, as majority leader, was one of Eisenhower's strongest

Allan Shivers, left, and the late Governor Beauford H. Jester, who were close friends, enjoyed this personal, informal chat shortly before Jester died on July 11, 1949, of a heart attack, making Shivers Governor of Texas.

supporters in the Senate—and Rayburn, I would say, didn't do anything to hurt him.

"But Eisenhower didn't really begin to believe in politics until after he was out of office. I told him several times, playing golf and on other occasions—and we'd laugh about it a lot—that if he had gotten the political bug, including patronage and organization and everything, during the first couple of years he was *in office* as much as he got it after he got *out of office,* he might have been able to build a strong Republican Party in Texas. But there weren't any Republicans in Texas in 1952—just a handful, and they were fighting among themselves, over Senator Robert A. Taft and Eisenhower.

"The 'Democrats for Eisenhower' was the only organization during the campaign—and after the campaign, for that matter," said Shivers. "And we weren't really interested in Republican patronage, as such."

Shivers was interested, instead, in trying to reshape the Democratic Party. In 1955, he went so far as to boot his erstwhile good friend, Wright Morrow of Houston, out of the Democratic national committeeman's job in an effort to placate the national committee, which had refused to seat him because he had supported Eisenhower. Morrow had offered the state committee his resignation in September, 1952, when he decided to support Ike, but Shivers's hand-picked state committee then refused to accept it.

In an Austin meeting of the state committee on July 25, 1955, Shivers demanded Morrow's resignation, Dawson Duncan noted in the *Dallas Morning News.*

"He said in a talk to the committee that it was necessary in his effort to strengthen the Democratic Party in Texas and in the nation," wrote Duncan. "In effect, he reiterated what he has been saying for some time. That was, to be able to fight within the Democratic Party to bring it back to the conservative theories of Jefferson, Jackson and Wilson that Texas needed a national committeeman with a voice in the national committee. . . .

"There was old-time political oratory as the white-maned Morrow for 40 minutes pleaded his cause, averring that he had done only what Texas Democratic conventions had voted for him to do. He said he was sure he was not qualified to be national committeeman under the rules laid down by National Chairman Paul Butler in his recent speaking tour in Texas 'because I am sure I am not satisfactory to Speaker Sam Rayburn and Senator Lyndon B. Johnson.' "

Duncan noted that Shivers listened intently to Morrow's defense of his political honesty.

"Then, in a 15-minute rebuttal, he expressed regret a controversy had arisen," Duncan reported. "It grew out, he said, of a 'bedroom conference' in Dallas with Morrow, when he asked Morrow to resign, and a 'kitchen conference' in Washington with Butler, in which he sought to make peace with the national party boss.

"Then he gave what he termed his true version of what had transpired. It added up to his summary that 'my chief aim is to try to strengthen the Democratic Party, to work from within, for I consider myself a Democrat."

Shivers never has given up completely on the Democratic Party but he concedes that the Republicans in Texas have made a lot of progress during recent years and may eventually establish a two-party system in the state.

"There are a good many Republicans across the state who are active now and they can do well if they get any help out of the Nixon administration on campaigns and patronage," he said. "They'll also have to do a better job of recruiting candidates. I've always said that you can't take just any kind of candidate, regardless of how sorry he is, and defeat him.

"There's a lot of timing in it, there's a lot of organization in it, and there's the colorfulness of the candidate himself," said Shivers. "Paul Eggers made a strong showing in the 1968 governor's race. He was a hard campaigner and made a nice appearance. But one thing he didn't have was the support of the entire Republican organization. They wanted to carry Texas for Nixon more than they wanted to elect Eggers.

"There's no question that the Republicans in Texas have been preoccupied with the national scene. And sometimes they get into power plays of their own and lose their organization."

Oddly enough, Eggers ran what appeared to be a less effective campaign in 1970 than he had in 1968—but garnered almost 47 per cent of the vote in 1970, compared with 43 per cent in 1968.

It may be significant, however, that all during 1969, people were talking primarily about Bush and Barnes—not about Eggers or any other Republican hopeful. And Shivers was one of many who hoped Bush and Barnes would not wind up running against each other.

"I think both of them, if they keep their noses clean, have very bright futures," he declared.

"I think Barnes's field actually is more legislative than administrative, that he makes a better legislator than he would an executive— although I don't really know, since I've never seen him operate as an executive. But I do know he has a knack for legislative activity. And he's young—if he went to the Senate, he would be there a long time. I do think it's obvious that he's modeling his whole career after LBJ.

"Johnson was lucky in that he never had to face a crisis at the same time he faced an election," said Shivers. "Barnes is going to need the same kind of luck. Thus far, Barnes hasn't had a crisis—he's been riding waves. But this gets back to timing. If a man gets caught at

the low stage of his popularity during an election year, he's likely
to get beat. But if that low stage comes between elections, he might
be high enough the next time to win reelection or he might luck out
and not have a strong opponent.

"Waggoner Carr is a good example," he declared. "He made the
wrong judgment at times. He could have been elected governor, if
he had run for reelection as attorney general in 1966 instead of running
for the Senate against Tower. He would have come up for governor
then in 1968, probably riding at his highest. But he picked the wrong
race. The Tower organization was riding as smooth as it could be and
it ran the smartest campaign I had ever seen in Texas. They just
played it low and cool, where Carr didn't have any issue he could
raise with them at all.

"Will Wilson's another example," said Shivers. "He's not the strongest campaigner in the world—but then neither is Preston Smith. But
they're both tireless workers. Will resigned from the Supreme Court
to run for a lot of offices he couldn't win."

Wilson served as attorney general of Texas from 1957 until 1963,
after winning distinction as district attorney in Dallas and then as a
member of the Texas Supreme Court. After his unsuccessful race for
governor in 1962, he switched to the Republican Party. Early in 1969,
he was appointed Assistant U. S. Attorney General in charge of the
Justice Department's Criminal Division.

Shivers always believed that in politics, as in Southwest Conference
football, it takes a lot of luck as well as skill and other factors to win.

"Johnson wound up having both sides mad at him at all times,"
said Shivers, "but he was able to put together in every election year
a combination that was a winning one. He's supposed to be a great
liberal but the liberals cuss him more than the conservatives do—if
that's possible.

"Barnes is good at contacting people. And, like LBJ, he can make
trades with various segments, then convince one segment that he *had*
to do something for the other group. Barnes is doing that just like
LBJ always did."

Another thing Barnes and Johnson had in common was an intense
dislike for Senator Yarborough. Once, while he was President, Johnson
was visiting with Shivers and, in one of his more jovial moods, quipped,
"I think I'll appoint you to something—just so Yarborough can bust
you."

Shivers enjoyed the joke—even though there still was no appointive
job even within the power of the President of the United States which
he was willing to take. He was as mystified as some of Johnson's
other friends, however, by the President's kindness toward Yarborough—particularly in 1964.

"He told me," Shivers said of Johnson, "that he had promised George Meany he would help protect Yarborough and he was going to do it. I said, 'You don't need George Meany—he needs you.' Lyndon was in office without any obligation and he knew he couldn't trust Yarborough. He knew he could trust Joe Kilgore. He did say that Meany had promised him Yarborough would vote for everything Lyndon wanted him to vote for and that Joe wouldn't do that. My answer was that 'you can depend on Joe more than you can depend on Yarborough.' Basically, Kilgore would have been of much more help to Johnson than Yarborough was."

But that, of course, was just another case of political "might have been." Hindsight is just as good in politics as it is in any other field, or perhaps even better.

Once, during the long, grueling 1954 campaign, Shivers and one of his aides, Wick Fowler, the noted war correspondent, chili mix manufacturer, wit and newspaper columnist, were driving by a Port Arthur oil refinery when Shivers announced proudly: "That's where I used to be assistant timekeeper."

"Too bad you left," sighed Fowler, wearily. "If you'd stayed there, you'd probably be *head* timekeeper by now and you wouldn't have to put up with all this."

Chapter 10

OIL, INK AND TEARS

A s a front-line war correspondent in both Europe and the Pacific during World War II, then twice in South Vietnam, Wick Fowler won high praise for courage. In his own mind, however, he reached his personal pinnacle of bravery in a suite at the Adolphus Hotel in Dallas while watching the start of the 1954 Rose Bowl football game.

Fowler was there with Shivers, his boss at the moment, and Kilgore, then a state legislator. H. L. Hunt, often described as the world's richest man, dropped by for a visit. When Shivers made the introductions without explaining that Fowler was a member of his staff, Hunt apparently thought the jolly, rotund humorist was an oil man. Just as the Rose Bowl game began, Shivers took a telephone call in an adjoining bedroom.

Fowler, more to make conversation than anything else, asked, "Well, Mr. Hunt, who do you like in this game?"

Hunt thought that over for a minute or two, studying the television screen intently. Finally, he replied, "Michigan State."

"Fine," said Fowler. "Just to make it interesting, I'll take UCLA and bet you a quarter."

Fowler delights in telling how Hunt pondered that proposition for several moments and then said: "I don't think I want to bet on this game—I'll just give them my moral support."

"After he left the suite," Fowler recalled, "I told Kilgore to be sure and spread the word around that I had made the world's richest man back down on a bet."

"You idiot!" Kilgore replied. "Mr. Hunt thought you meant a *quarter of a million!*"

Michigan State won, 28-20—a fact which may support the widely-held theory that Hunt generally is too conservative for his own good. Years later, Fowler continued to flinch when he thought of how many wars he would have had to cover, or how many packages of his chili mix he would have had to sell, in order to pay off a $250,000 bet on a football game. That probably would have been one of the few situations which Fowler could not joke his way out of, despite his casual attitude toward money.

After returning from overseas duty for the *Dallas News* during World War II, Fowler neglected to file an expense account for months, creating great consternation in the newspaper's accounting department. Finally, in response to repeated requests, he did turn in his expense account—on the back of an envelope. It said simply, "covering war: $2,000."

Hunt's feelings about money always ran to the opposite extreme. He took his lunch to his office in a paper sack even while his fortune was being estimated at well over two billion dollars. But he poured tons of money into "Facts Forum" and "Life Line," a pair of public information projects he originated to sell his right-wing views to the public through radio, television, newsletters and newspapers.

Hunt's direct contributions to political campaigns generally have been overrated and overestimated, according to most Texas politicians. So have those of other Texas oil millionaires. Although many of them are counted among the "fat cats" in campaigns, the select circle of financiers covers so many diversified interests—such as insurance, banking, contracting and ranching—that oil money controls Texas politics only in the minds of the "instant experts." These usually are pundits from other states who visit Texas for a few days and then write lengthy, detailed explanations of its complicated, ever-shifting political crosscurrents.

Naturally, because of Texas's reputation as the land of the big rich, these "foreigners" are inclined to paint the picture in terms of well-publicized millionaires. Hunt, undoubtedly the world's foremost example and exponent of the Horatio Alger theory, is a favorite subject, particularly because of his right-wing views; but his actual political influence seems almost negligible, since he generally is regarded as an extremist. His open support of the Kennedy-Johnson ticket in 1960, strangely enough, did little to alter this image.

Multimillionaires Sid W. Richardson and Clint Murchison, both from the little East Texas town of Athens, and Hugh Roy Cullen, Jesse H. Jones and James M. West, all of Houston, were cited for many years before their deaths as key political kingpins in Texas. But while they were being publicized, usually against their wishes, the greatest array of political power was concentrated in the "8-F Crowd" and went almost unnoticed. During the 1940's and '50s, this handful of millionaires compiled an enviable—perhaps even undefeated—record in statewide races without being detected by many people other than the candidates themselves.

The group drew its name from the fact that it met regularly to play cards and discuss politics in Herman Brown's suite, 8-F, at the Lamar Hotel in Houston. The members included Jesse Jones, publisher of the *Houston Chronicle;* Gus Wortham, an insurance magnate; William A. Smith, who made a fortune out of railroads; Judge J. A. Elkins, a lawyer with far-flung banking interests; Leopold Meyer, a merchandising king; James Abercrombie, a famous lawyer and oilman, and George Brown, Herman's brother and his partner in the well-known contracting firm.

While the financing this combo could pump into a campaign was important, most candidates ·considered its influence even more so. When the "8-F Crowd" took to the telephones and began contacting associates in other parts of the state on behalf of a candidate, that candidate suddenly became the toast of the Texas business community. The seven men, among them, had enough employees of their own to form a fairly substantial bloc of voters—but, despite this and their vast financial resources, they did not have a monopoly on political power. They did, however, take a great deal more interest in partisan politics than did many of the other money men in Texas.

Among the more influential millionaires have been H. H. (Pete) Coffield of Rockdale, the world's greatest host and a man who always took more pride in serving as chairman of the Texas Board of Corrections than he did in having pulled himself up by his own bootstraps; French Robertson of Abilene, who also served on the state prisons' governing board; John Mecom, a Houston oil man and sometime friend of LBJ; H. B. (Pat) Zachry, a San Antonio contractor famed for never finding anything that couldn't be done; Morris Jaffe, another San Antonio contractor, who built his fortune on uranium and wound up with Billie Sol Estes's assets; Walter Hall, a banker in the little town of Dickinson and one of Senator Yarborough's staunchest supporters; Corbin J. Robertson of Houston, Cullen's son-in-law; Pat R. Rutherford, another Houston oil man; Walter Mischer, a Houston banker; Arch Rowan, a Fort Worth oil man long active in Texas politics, and Dallasites E. O. Cartwright, investment broker; Benjamin H. Carpenter, whose wealth was based primarily on ranching and insurance; Jim Aston, a banker; Sam E. Wyly, a computer king, and Earl Hayes, one of the state's best-known automobile dealers.

Most of these names long have been synonymous with money, even in such faraway places as Washington, D. C. But most successful politicians in Texas would trade three millionaires for one substantial publisher almost any day of the week, figuring that newspaper editorial support—especially in the major cities—is an essential campaign ingredient which money cannot buy.

Thus, the candidates covet the friendship of such newspaper publishers and executives as Joseph M. Dealey and Ted Dealey, of the *Dallas Morning News;* James F. Chambers, Jr., and Felix R. McKnight, *Dallas Times Herald;* Oveta Culp Hobby and William P. Hobby, Jr., the *Houston Post;* Everett D. Collier, the *Houston Chronicle;* Amon G. Carter, Jr., *Fort Worth Star-Telegram;* Houston Harte of San Angelo, who owns a chain of newspapers that includes the *San Antonio Express-News,* the *Corpus Christi Caller-Times,* the *Abilene Reporter-*

News and the *San Angelo Standard-Times;* Harlon Fentress of Waco, owner of the *Waco News-Tribune,* the *Austin American-Statesman,* the *Port Arthur News* and the *Lufkin News;* Sam Wood, editor of the *Austin American-Statesman;* Harry Provence, editor of the *Waco News-Tribune;* S. B. Whittenburg, publisher of the *Amarillo News-Globe;* Charles Guy, *Lubbock Avalanche-Journal;* James N. Allison, Sr., *Midland Reporter-Telegram;* Mrs. Carl Estes, *Longview Journal;* Charles K. Devall, *Kilgore News-Herald,* and Rhea Howard, *Wichita Falls Times-Record-News.*

One reason the publishers rate such a high priority when candidates solicit support is simply that most of them operate in a monopoly situation. They may have the only newspaper in town—and quite a few of them don't mind acting like it. Oil millionaires, on the other hand, are not exactly considered expendable but they can be replaced if necessary.

Senator Tower is one of the successful politicians who believe that oil men play "a tremendously important role—but not always a decisive role—in Texas politics."

"For instance," said Tower, "most of the oil men backed Coke Stevenson against Lyndon Johnson in 1948. Jester, of course, was aligned with the oil men, and Shivers was.

"I didn't have their support—but, well, the oil fraternity is *not* a monolith," he declared. "I had the support of some oil men in my original campaign but by no means a majority of them. In my second campaign, I didn't have the active opposition of the oil fraternity because I had gone to bat for the independent oil men on a number of occasions. As a matter of fact, I would say the majority of them supported me against Carr—because I was a known quantity.

"But the oil men certainly made their peace with Lyndon, in due course, and I think they have to be considered a *part* of the establishment," Tower added. "Their influence is waning, just as the oil industry is on the wane as an element in our economy. It's still a *major* element but, proportionately speaking, it's not as great as it was. I think that's due to the industrialization of the state as well as to the decline in oil exploration. We're so industrially oriented now—we're the home of some of the great conglomerates. Texas capital, a lot of which came out of oil, has been channeled into other areas."

Despite this, the public's fancy always will be captured by such a man as Cullen, who founded the University of Houston. He once became so ecstatic over a football game the school won from Baylor that he gave it another $2,250,000. Making a football victory that profitable provoked so much criticism that Cullen subsequently donated $1,000,000 to Baylor. Cullen, who died in 1957 at the age of 76, built a personal fortune of more than $200,000,000 but gave away $180,000,000 before his death—explaining that he was "selfish" because he wanted to give away his money while he was alive so he could see people enjoying it.

Richardson was much more inclined to invest his money in politics. He reportedly made the largest single political contribution in American history—and it may have resulted largely from rain that fell in Fort Worth one late summer day in 1941, producing pennies from Heaven for Dwight D. Eisenhower.

Richardson had planned to fly to Washington that day with Elliott Roosevelt, then a captain in the Army Air Corps and formerly his partner in four Texas radio stations, and with Bill Kittrell. Richardson refused to fly in inclement weather, however, and when it began raining in Fort Worth he insisted that they take the train.

Shortly after the train passed through Louisiana, the three men decided they would like to play bridge and Kittrell went back to the lounge car seeking a fourth. When he asked for a volunteer, his invitation quickly was accepted by a young colonel who introduced himself as Dwight D. Eisenhower.

The four played bridge during much of the remainder of the trip and arrived in Washington early one morning. Roosevelt, like Richardson, had quickly developed a great respect for Eisenhower—and the President's son took his three companions to the White House for breakfast.

"I remember that my father was quite impressed with Eisenhower," Roosevelt recalled 28 years later. "I'm a little vague on the details but, of course, Father's chief of staff was General George C. Marshall and he was a good friend of Eisenhower's, so they had good rapport.

"Just after that, my father chose Eisenhower to be a brigadier general and sent him to England to check on such things as transporting supplies over there," he added.

A short while later, President Roosevelt picked Eisenhower to serve as Allied Commander in Europe. This prompted Stuart Long to write later that "if it hadn't rained in Fort Worth one day in 1941, Eisenhower might never have become President of the United States."

Richardson tried to get Eisenhower to run for President in 1948, then made a trip to Paris early in 1952 to talk him into running. He reportedly backed up his friendly persuasion with a pledge that he would donate $3,000,000 to his campaign. There are conflicting opinions on whether or not Richardson actually contributed that much but there is little reason to doubt that he did.

The late Jesse Jones was one of the truly big spenders so far as the Democratic Party was concerned and reportedly contributed $50,000 to help cover its 1924 presidential campaign deficit. He served as Board Chairman of President Roosevelt's Reconstruction Finance

Corporation from 1933 until 1939 and as Secretary of Commerce from 1940 until 1945.

Jones wanted the vice presidential nomination in 1944. So did Sam Rayburn, who was being prominently mentioned for the post until Texas Democrats spoiled his chances with one of their typical donnybrooks. This one occurred at their state convention in Austin on May 23, 1944, at the capitol, with oil purportedly at the root of the controversy. The resultant rhubarb created cleavages which still exist within the party.

Anti-Roosevelt forces won control of the convention and refused to instruct their national convention delegates to support FDR's fourth-term bid. Former Governor Moody was named to head the delegation to Chicago after his anti–New Deal contingent won the key vote, 940 to 774. That came on a motion by Wirtz to elect former Governor James V. Allred, instead of Moody, as temporary chairman and to recognize in the convention only delegates who would take a loyalty pledge to support the party's nominees.

Mass confusion surrounded the rostrum when the vote was announced. The late William M. Thornton, for many years chief of the *Dallas News* Austin Bureau, wrote:

"Youthful Congressman Lyndon Johnson of the Austin district was also a platform visitor and sought to whisper or prompt the chair. The crowd noticed his presence and shouts went up, 'Get that yes-man off the platform,' 'Get Lyndon Johnson out of there,' and 'Throw Roosevelt's pin-up boy out of there.'

"Only last week, at Dallas, Johnson said he never attended state conventions and did not expect to attend this one," Thornton commented. "He has been a loyalist to the Roosevelt administration."

Johnson told the crowd he would not walk out, declaring: "When I bolt a convention, it's going to be a Hoovercrat Republican convention."

But his old friend, Wirtz, joined about 250 others, led by Mrs. Alfred Taylor of Austin and Joe T. Steadham of Fort Worth, in marching out of the Senate Chamber to hold a rump convention at the other end of the capitol, in the House of Representatives. Mayor Tom Miller of Austin was elected temporary chairman of that group, which regained control of the party machinery at the September convention in Dallas and helped Roosevelt win another landslide victory in Texas.

"I didn't bolt a Democratic convention," said Mayor Miller, at the rump meeting. "I left a Republican convention."

According to Richard M. Morehead, in the *Dallas News*:

"C. F. Richards, an oil man and former state senator, complained in a speech that much of the dissatisfaction against Roosevelt in Texas came from oilmen wanting the price of crude raised 35 cents a barrel. He called them men whose patriotism is gauged in barrels."

Some of the anti-Roosevelt Democrats formed a new party, the Texas Regulars, which offered no candidate for president but presented a slate of electors pledged only *not* to vote for Roosevelt under any circumstances. The Texas Regulars did not have to worry about making any decision, since they received only 135,439 votes to Roosevelt's 821,605 and Thomas E. Dewey's 191,425.

The Texas Regulars quickly assumed their place in oblivion but the oil issue continues to haunt Texas politicians, despite the fact that they are for oil just as strongly as they are for flag, motherhood and country—if not more so. Even Senator Yarborough proudly proclaimed his support for the depletion allowance on domestic oil, although he contended U. S. producers do not need it on oil produced abroad.

The summer of 1969 kept Congressmen Bush and Burleson, Texas's two members of the important House Ways and Means Committee, busy defending the depletion allowance during the "tax reform" movement. They were hampered to some extent by the average Texan's failure to realize the importance of the indirect benefits he derives from this long-heralded, little-understood tax advantage which provides an incentive for exploratory drilling. Only a few Texans own any direct interest in oil wells. Perhaps because the image of the wealthy, flamboyant, free-spending oil man—who actually represents a small minority of those engaged in the business—is as prevalent in Texas as elsewhere, most Texans actually feel little sympathy for the industry which claims it pays 41 per cent of every tax dollar collected in their state and provides more than 200,000 jobs in Texas.

Bush termed some of the attempts to cut the depletion allowance "hysterical."

"We recognize that depletion on oil has become a symbol—an idol that some feel must be toppled—but in the light of the unrefuted testimony on the serious resources shortages, we simply suggest that taking about $600 million out of an industry at this time is not in the public interest," he said in a statement issued jointly with Congressman Rogers C. B. Morton of Maryland, the Republican National Chairman. "The loser here will be the consumer—gasoline prices must rise sooner or later. This industry, not now disproportionately profitable, cannot be expected to absorb these additional costs."

Bush, who achieved great success in the oil business before going to Congress, said oil industry testimony before congressional committees was "never challenged and never questioned, but fell on deaf ears."

Bush had divested himself of his personal interests in the oil business when he was elected to Congress but said he resented strongly the efforts to make a whipping boy of an industry so important to the economy of Texas. He admitted that few Texas voters realized the importance of such technical taxation tactics but, even while representing officially only one portion of Harris County, he felt compelled to protect as best he could the interests of "non-oil" Texans, who outnumber so greatly the relatively small handful of "oil-rich" Texans.

He was one of 30 congressmen who voted against the so-called "tax reform" bill, admitting at the time that, "Politically, quite clearly, you should vote for it."

Margaret Mayer, Washington correspondent for the *Dallas Times Herald*, said Bush was not too surprised after the vote when a colleague passed him on the floor of the House and remarked, "Well, I see you've quit running for the Senate."

"Maybe I have," Bush mused, according to Miss Mayer. "People will say, 'Rich Republican, voting for special interests and against the people.' I lose politically—but I feel pretty good inside."

Miss Mayer added: "A week later, the Houston congressman and others who try to puzzle out how the voting public's mind ticks had to acknowledge they did not know. The congressman's vote against tax reforms and against tax relief, both supposedly popular with the public, had aroused only one constituent to comment and he sent a telegram of congratulations."

Bush had received an advance briefing on President Nixon's welfare revision message and knew it would cost $4 billion—and that it could not be financed with a tax bill which created a $2.4 billion deficit. But he realized that his vote against the bill would be interpreted as a regional desire to protect the oil industry, said Miss Mayer.

Few people outside the oil business—and politics—realize it but just as there is a broken heart for every light on Broadway, there probably are at least a dozen broken hearts for every producing oil well in Texas. Many of them belong to investors and wildcatters who have lost $40,000 or $50,000 drilling a single dry hole, and some to financiers who have hit dry holes in politics. Some belong to erstwhile politicians whose careers have been abbreviated by failure to combine successfully such essential ingredients as financing, organization, newspaper support, timing and the same type of luck it takes to strike it rich in oil.

Former State Senator Jimmy Phillips of Angleton is one of those who scored an apparent near miss in the governor's race, without ever getting on the ballot, when he made an abortive bid for the office in 1956 while riding a wave of favorable publicity.

Phillips enlisted the aid of an oil man who was a close friend, Floyd

Karsten of Houston, who never had taken an active interest in politics before. Karsten believed in Phillips, however, and was willing to back him to the hilt. So were many others until Senator Daniel decided to return from Washington and run for governor.

The flamboyant Phillips, considered by many a diamond in the rough, began his ill-fated bid for governor early in 1955 while leading the Senate General Investigating Committee in a probe of the veterans land scandals. State Land Commissioner Bascom Giles had originated the Veterans Land Program shortly after World War II ended. It enabled veterans to buy farmland on long-term, low-interest loans with small down payments; the State actually bought the land, with funds raised through special bond issues, and resold it to the veterans.

The program proved so successful that Giles, elected to nine consecutive terms as land commissioner, was being considered a strong contender for governor until it blew up in his face and he resigned. Although the State never lost any money on the program, the disclosures of large "bloc deals" involving Giles—and through which land promoters took advantage of both the program and individual veterans—led to his conviction on theft charges. Giles, who had made a fortune earlier in Austin real estate, served a six-year sentence in the Texas penitentiary.

Phillips's relentless pursuit of the facts in the veterans land scandals, along with the attention he had attracted through several long Senate filibusters, convinced him—and, initially, at least, a good many political kingpins—that he could win the governor's race.

The people of Galveston, the largest city in his district, gave Senator Phillips a huge appreciation party on Sept. 1, 1955. It featured a parade and a barbecue, complete with tons of adulation for the one-time shoeshine boy who had made good.

William H. Gardner, in the Sept. 18, 1955, *Houston Post*, declared:

"Old Horatio Alger, who used to write books by the dozen about street urchins who ended up as governors, senators and corporation presidents, would have doted on the story of Jimmy Phillips.

"In fact, Alger could have written the Phillips story without changing a single fact and it would run true to form. And if Jimmy's political hopes are realized next year it will have the Horatio Alger climax—shoeshine boy to governor. . . .

"Sen. Phillips has a flair for attracting attention. He lets his hair grow longer than most men, dangles a big handkerchief from his breast pocket, smokes a long cigar, talks in a loud voice and laughs boisterously. He doesn't mind when people jokingly refer to him as Sen. Klaghorn, and he revels in his title of the talkin'est man in Texas.

"Behind the blustery front, however, he is a warm-hearted, even sentimental, individual who has a sincere sympathy for the poor and

State Senator Jimmy Phillips watched his gubernatorial ambitions go down the drain and decided he had been a victim of "technology and timing—and luck."

unfortunate. His eyes sometimes fill with tears when he talks about the need for more charity beds to treat children with cleft palates and twisted legs, and for years he has resisted fiercely any effort by the Legislature to raise college tuition.

" 'I remember only too well when I had to quit college in midterm because I couldn't raise $25,' he says. 'Times are better now, but there are still some boys and girls in the same spot.'

"He is irascible and antagonizes many of his Senate colleagues with his bull-like roars of indignation or his needling remarks, but he has many devoted friends, among them Houston's Sen. Searcy Bracewell. Newspapermen generally like Jimmy Phillips—for one thing, he never yells that he's been misquoted, even when he has been. The friendship of working newsmen is a valuable thing for any candidate to have," Gardner declared.

Ironically, it was the loss of the *Houston Post's* editorial support which finally prompted Phillips to withdraw from the 1956 race. Former Governor William P. Hobby (who died in 1964) had told Phillips he would support him long before there was any indication that Daniel would run. After Daniel made his decision, Hobby informed Phillips that he felt compelled to switch his support.

While Daniel also siphoned off much of Phillips's financial backing, it was the loss of the *Post's* endorsement that broke the back of his campaign. With the *Post* and the *Houston Chronicle* each reaching a large percentage of the voters in Texas, he felt he needed at least one of them on his side to win.

"Newspapers are a key factor in any race," Phillips noted many years later. "I'd always had a good image in the press. The Capitol Press had been friendly to me and that was my big asset.

"But I never will forget that one columnist, Charlie Guy, the editor of the *Lubbock Avalanche-Journal,* wrote a glowing column about me and what a great man I was. Then, after Price got in the race, he wrote another one saying that if I stayed in the race I could be nothing but a hatchet man who would split the vote and enable Ralph Yarborough to get elected."

That view was shared, apparently, by Rayburn. He sent word to Phillips that he did not want to see the party divided and would pledge him the same support, if he would switch to the attorney general's race, that Daniel would have for governor.

"I felt if I could win the attorney general's race, I could win the governor's race," said Phillips, in explaining his rejection of that offer.

He had told Daniel himself essentially the same thing several months earlier during an unpublicized rendezvous in a small, private dining room at the Houston Club. Daniel said he was considering the race and asked how, if he decided to run, Phillips thought he could win.

Phillips responded by asking Daniel how he thought *he* could win.

"As far as I'm concerned," Phillips snorted, "you're looking at the next governor of Texas."

In retrospect, Phillips decided that perhaps he always was a little too independent for his own good—and that he was a "victim of technology and timing—and luck."

"I made the mistake the whole time I was in the Senate," he said, "of acting on my own and not relying on, or even getting acquainted with, the lobbyists. I guess I didn't know as many as five of them personally, on a first-name basis, when I tried to run for governor. I was generally considered a conservative but I never asked for their advice.

"Of course, I didn't have any organization at all when I tried to run and that really hurt," said Phillips. "Now, a group picks an individual to run and he has a ready-made organization backing him. I came along during the transition period—at a time when they were switching from such individuals as Allred and O'Daniel getting out and getting votes on their own to the present, when groups pick a candidate and back him. I had a lot of people who knew me, through the newspapers and so forth—but I didn't know who those people were.

"My timing probably was off," he added, "but if I'd had good relations with the 'Third House' and had had their support, I probably could have stayed in the race."

When he decided to withdraw, Phillips mailed back approximately $2,000 in contributions—mostly in $1 and $2 donations sent to him in response to a tabloid newspaper he had published and sent to rural box holders. He also refused to collect sizable campaign contributions which had been promised him and, as a result, spent the next 12 years draining his successful law practice for enough to pay off his campaign debts.

"My campaign cost me about $40,000 of my own money," said Phillips. "It wouldn't have cost me anything if I'd collected from all the people who had promised money to me, and who had it to give, but I wouldn't take it after I decided not to run."

Phillips noted that the "money in Texas politics still comes from Houston" but there have been some changes made.

"You've got new blood and new titans of industry calling the signals now," he declared. "You have people 30 or 35 years old who are the real leaders—many of them people you never hear about."

In 1956, however, it was easier to pinpoint the real powers behind the scenes in Texas politics. When they, including an oil industry that was grateful for his successful efforts to regain the oil-rich Texas tidelands, decided to throw their weight behind Daniel, discretion obviously was the better part of valor for anyone as realistic as Phillips.

The realists, in this case, included Phillips's pretty wife, Esther, who had never wanted him to run in the first place.

Shortly after Phillips entered the race, he asked his public relations director to draw up a candid list of "do's and don'ts" for his guidance during the campaign. It included a number of general philosophy and campaign mechanics suggestions, such as emphasizing his "middle-of-the-road" views and trying to contact personally someone in every county to serve as a campaign manager. It recommended personal visits with as many newspaper editors as possible, keeping the door open for possibilities other than the governor's race and, in connection with finances: "Anytime anyone offers you some campaign money, try to collect it on the spot. A buck in the hand, in this game, is worth five or six in somebody else's bank account."

The "personal" suggestions included going to church regularly, listening more and talking less, being more charitable to his political enemies, dressing neatly, keeping his hair trimmed and being careful to display good table manners. ("You'll feel like you are going to starve at some of the luncheons you will have to attend. Just keep quiet about it and figure on getting a hamburger later.")

Mrs. Phillips read the entire list with a great deal of interest.

"All I want to know," she then told her husband, politely, "is why you have to hire a public relations man and pay him a lot of money to tell you the same things I've been trying to tell you for 18 years!"

Chapter 11

TIME AND TIDES

One day early in 1953, Senator Price Daniel of Texas made his maiden speech in the U. S. Senate. It concerned state ownership of the tidelands, the issue which had prompted him to run for the Senate in the first place, and the response was almost as gratifying as having the boss double your salary after your first day on a new job.

Daniel still likes to recall some of the glowing tributes paid him that day by such Senate stalwarts as Harry F. Byrd of Virginia and Walter F. George of Georgia. They were in the forefront of those who congratulated him upon a great speech, contending that he had put the tidelands controversy in the proper perspective for the first time.

Daniel's wife, his favorite barometer of public opinion and political reaction, was thrilled to hear of the compliments.

"But just wait," she told him that night, "until they find out that's all you know anything about."

Sixteen years later, Daniel chuckled as he related that story and admitted, "She was pretty near right."

"If it hadn't been for the tidelands," he said, "I probably never would have gone to Washington at all. I had never had any desire to go to Washington and it was only because of the tidelands that I did go up there."

Ironically, Daniel felt that his victory in the 1952 race for the U. S. Senate signaled the end of his political career because he had supported Eisenhower's successful bid for the presidency.

The short, cigar-chewing lawyer from Liberty had served three terms in the Texas House of Representatives, including one term as Speaker, and then entered the army for World War II service during which he rose from private to captain. After leaving the army in May of 1946, he won a whirlwind campaign for attorney general while Jester was winning the governor's chair and Shivers was moving into the lieutenant governor's office. All three of those top-ranking state officials were reelected in 1948 and Daniel felt confident that he would be able to win the governorship in 1950; he thought Shivers probably would either retire from politics or seek reelection and that, in the event he did run for governor, he, Daniel, could beat him.

But Jester died on July 11, 1949, and Shivers became governor automatically.

"When Jester died," said Daniel, "I figured I hadn't been living right."

143

Marion Price Daniel had announced openly his eventual candidacy for the governorship in September, 1927, when he entered Baylor University and modestly admitted that he first hoped to become president of the freshman class. He did—and, in addition to becoming one of the few Texas governors ever elected for three consecutive terms, he established a record as the only one in history who ever had to go through Washington to reach the executive mansion.

"His greatest triumph," wrote Allen Duckworth in the *Dallas Morning News* on Dec. 9, 1962, as Daniel prepared to surrender the governor's office to John Connally, "came after a long fight through the courts and through Congress: a quitclaim by the federal government to Texas's ownership of its tidelands and the potential riches for the permanent state school fund. . . .

"While Daniel won himself international note as a lawyer during the tidelands suits, his early background was in journalism. He was a newspaper carrier in Liberty for the *Houston Post* and the *Beaumont Enterprise* while in grade school, and during a few years' residence in Fort Worth he edited a high school newspaper, then became county debating champion and was a cub reporter on the *Star-Telegram*.

"In Baylor, he was a bundle of campus energy. They called him 'Bigger and Better Daniel.' He was editor of the Baylor newspaper, the *Daily Lariat,* and the yearbook, the *Round-up.* He was awarded a journalism degree in 1931 and a law degree in 1932.

"Although he couldn't read a note of music," Duckworth added, "Daniel organized and led a dance band, to finance his college education."

Even that did not require as much nerve, in Daniel's opinion, as did his active support of Eisenhower in 1952.

"Deciding to go for Eisenhower was the toughest political decision I ever had to make," said Daniel. "But the night I learned that Adlai Sevenson had told Governor Shivers he would follow the same course Truman had and veto quitclaim legislation, I told reporters who called me at my house in Austin that I would not support Stevenson."

Daniel was then attorney general and a candidate for the U. S. Senate on the Democratic ticket.

"Sid Richardson called me one day while I was in Fort Worth, at the Texas Hotel," said Daniel. "I already had decided I would *vote* for Eisenhower but I hadn't decided to get out and campaign for him.

"Sid said Governor Hobby had called him and wanted him to deliver a message to me—and that he joined in Governor Hobby's hope that I would introduce Ike when he came to Texas for his birthday celebration, because they thought it would be worth thousands of votes.

"I told him I wanted to think about it a little bit more," Daniel recalled, "but I decided that if I was really interested in getting the tidelands bill signed I'd better help get that man elected. And I'd already pretty well burned the bridges, anyway. It's one thing just not to support the Democratic nominee and another to actively support the Republican nominee, but I figured I might just as well go all the way.

"I also felt that by getting into the thing, I could have some influence on what Eisenhower said about the tidelands. And I did wind up helping to write that part of his Houston speech.

"I called Governor Hobby the next day and told him I'd do it—but, under the circumstances that existed at that time, I really figured it would be the end of my political career," said Daniel. "I didn't think I would ever be elected again to any office. This was all before the big push. You know, the Democratic state convention later went on record for Eisenhower but this was some time before that.

"When I introduced Eisenhower on his birthday, in Houston, it seemed certain that would be the end of politics for me. But I thought it was more important to have a president who would let Congress restore to us this 3,000,000 acres of land for our Public School Fund and win that battle than for me to stay in politics and get re-elected.

"I didn't realize then," Daniel declared, "that supporting Eisenhower would turn out to be the popular thing in Texas.

"I really felt this would be the last election I ever won," he said. "I wasn't worried about this one, of course, because I had both the Democratic and Republican nominations. The Republicans had nominated all the Democratic nominees, without even checking with us, so this was just free gratis. John White, the State Agriculture Commissioner, was the only one who took any affirmative action to get off the Republican ticket.

"I was all wrapped up in the tidelands, even though at first my best friends didn't think the battle could be won," said Daniel. "My own wife, who has a pretty good 'John Q. Public' sense, didn't think we'd ever be successful. She just didn't know that an Eisenhower would come along."

During the early stages of the fight, no one else did—and the cause seemed so hopeless that a wedge of proposed compromise was driven between Texas's top-ranking state officials. It caused what Daniel considers "the biggest strain" in his frequently stormy relations with Shivers.

"That happened while he was lieutenant governor and I was attorney general," Daniel recalled, "when he came out for the compromise. The oil companies that had been through it for so long—they were the whipping boys—finally decided they wanted to get a compromise worked out through Tom Clark, who was then U. S. Attorney General, and Sam Rayburn. They got Philip B. Perlman of the Solicitor General's office in on it.

"They thought they could get a compromise worked out whereby we'd get a share of the revenues on the outer continental shelf in exchange for giving up some of our inner boundaries, and get it over with," he said. "After they worked it out with Mr. Rayburn, they came down and tried to get Jester to go for it but he wouldn't. Then they tried to get Bascom Giles, the Land Commissioner, to go for it and he wouldn't.

"We met over at the Governor's Mansion with some representatives of the industry and both of us, Jester and I, told them together we wouldn't go for it. So then they ended up going to Shivers, and explaining it to him. Without checking with us and finding out about the trap this could get us into, he came out for it.

"That threw us into the terrible position of fighting each other," Daniel declared. "Until Jester died, we had pretty open warfare on that issue—for about a year.

"I took the position that it would be all right if they vested title in whatever we were given. I think the federal government was to get 27½ per cent of the revenue from within our boundaries and we'd get 27½ per cent from the outer continental shelf. I said this would be fine if they would recognize our boundaries for other purposes, and recognize the principles involved—making it an exchange of property that would be good forever.

"But just an Act of Congress, giving us a percentage of the revenue out there, would be good only for as long as Congress wanted us to have it—the next Congress could come along and take it away. It would have been foolish to go for that.

"After Jester died and Shivers became governor," said Daniel, "I figured the best thing to do was to put all my eggs in the basket of trying to get Shivers to change his position on compromising the tidelands and work together, and forget my idea of running for governor."

Weldon Hart, who had been the top-ranking member of the governor's staff under Jester and continued in that capacity under Shivers, had long been a friend of Daniel's—even though he had managed the unsuccessful campaign of Pat Neff, Jr., for attorney general in 1946.

"I called Weldon in," said Daniel, "and told him there was only one thing that could make me run for governor in 1950 and that was for Shivers to continue his position on the tidelands.

"I told him that if we gave Shivers the facts he would change his position and I wished he would work on this. Weldon arranged for a meeting and Shivers came to my office. By that time, Giles had changed and favored the compromise. That's when my wife said it was hopeless—there were three of us on the Texas School Land Board and two of them were against me.

"But when Shivers saw how flimsy the compromise was, and that it would ignore all the principles involved, he became as strong an advocate as I was of fighting it all the way through," said Daniel.

They fought it to the U. S. Supreme Court and lost. Then, with Shivers high in popularity and seeking reelection in 1952, Daniel decided to take the fight—and his political career—to the U. S. Senate. His easy victory, after Senator Connally declined to seek reelection, prompted him to do a bit of muscle-flexing as he entered the Senate.

Stephen A. Mitchell, chairman of the Democratic National Committee, provoked that by threatening reprisals against Daniel because he had campaigned actively for Eisenhower. It was, at best, an ill-timed threat since Daniel's vote would have been enough to throw control of the Senate to the Republicans. It seemed typical of the costly accusation frequently made by Texas Democrats when someone disagrees with them on some issue: "You're a Republican!" Although many Democrats still do not seem to realize it, this is an extremely poor way to win converts to their party.

Daniel delayed his decision almost until the last minute, explaining that he did not want to "join up with any group which intends to visit reprisals that would hurt Texas."

Duckworth later noted in the *Dallas News*: "Senate Majority Leader Lyndon B. Johnson told Daniel that the National Committee didn't run the Senate. Daniel took his seat on the Democratic side of the aisle, thus winning a place on the Senate Interior and Insular Affairs Committee—which handled tidelands matters. Under Daniel's prodding, the tidelands bill passed House and Senate and was signed by President Eisenhower."

That was one of the first bills approved in 1953. For a while after that, the junior U. S. Senator from Texas found little to interest him. There must have been times when he felt that the most important thing he was doing in Washington was substituting occasionally for his son, 12-year-old Price Daniel, Jr., in throwing a morning newspaper route. A lot of U. S. Senators have delivered newspapers—but few of them *after* being elected. (Fifteen years later, in 1968, Price, Jr., was elected to the Texas House of Representatives from Liberty, Texas.)

"But then I found something else to work on hard, and that was the narcotics problem," said Daniel. "A fellow needs a challenge to really sink himself into."

Shortly after Daniel was named to the Judiciary Committee, State Senator Charles F. Herring of Austin wrote him a letter about the increasing narcotics traffic in his district and said he thought something should be done about it. About the same time, Daniel received a similar letter from a Houston grand jury. As a result, Daniel launched a nationwide committee investigation of the problem and noted later that "it occupied me quite well the rest of my time in the Senate."

"I still had in my mind that I wanted to be governor of Texas," he said, "and I didn't want to serve in the Senate more than six years. After I'd been there four years, it looked like the time was ripe—because a new governor was going to be elected in 1956, since Shivers wasn't running, and whoever won probably would get a second term in 1958. So I decided I was going to run, provided I could get a 'feel' from the people who had sent me up there for six years that it was all right to come back after four years. Also, I had made up my mind I couldn't resign before the election. So I went on statewide television and asked the people what they thought."

On March 12, 1956, Daniel told a statewide television audience that he would rather serve as governor of Texas than hold any other office in the country. Two weeks later, in another statewide telecast, Daniel said he had left the final decision up to the voters.

"You employed me to serve in the Senate, and I did not feel free to seek a change while serving in this employment without your whole-hearted approval," he declared. "In a tremendous out-pouring of letters, postcards and telegrams, you have given your approval in no uncertain terms. Accordingly, I hereby announce my candidacy for the Democratic nomination for governor of Texas."

Daniel won the Democratic nomination, in a runoff with Ralph Yarborough, by only 3,171 votes. He refused to support Eisenhower's reelection bid that year but did not take an active part in Adlai Stevenson's campaign.

"I could just barely vote for him," he explained later. "The big issue on which the scales were tilted against Stevenson in 1952 had been settled. I told Rayburn and Johnson that if Stevenson would call me up and assure me that he would not try to revive the tidelands issue, that he would consider it settled, that I would support him. He called me one afternoon down at my ranch in Liberty, and I remember taking the call on a phone in the kitchen and hearing him say he would make that assurance to me. He said he disagreed with the way we had settled the tidelands issue but he had no idea of reviving it.

"That brought me back into the Democratic fold but I was not active in the campaign because I still appreciated what President Eisenhower had done in signing that bill," said Daniel.

Stevenson's telephone call came shortly after the September Democratic State Convention in Fort Worth.

"Some of the so-called loyalist Democrats, who have since gone against some of the Democratic candidates, nearly tore up that convention," said Daniel. "Only by Rayburn and Johnson and me joining

President Dwight D. Eisenhower, at a White House ceremony, presents to U. S. Senator Price Daniel the pen with which he had just signed the controversial bill restoring to Texas ownership of the state's oil-rich tidelands.

forces were we able to keep control of the convention for the new governor. Had it not been for them joining with me, I would have lost that convention without any doubt."

Yarborough liberals had tried to take over the May convention that year in Austin. Rayburn and Johnson feared that if they did, they would prevent Johnson from getting his own state's support in his bid for the presidential nomination.

"Labor was trying to take over the party," Daniel recalled, "and this was at the time of Johnson's big fight with Shivers for control of the party machinery. Johnson won it with labor's help but when it came down to picking the Democratic National Committee members, they wouldn't listen to Rayburn and Johnson much. They insisted on Mrs. Frankie Randolph of Houston against Johnson's choice of Mrs. Lloyd Bentsen, Jr., of Houston. When Johnson and Rayburn came back to Washington, they had had enough and were ready to help me gain control over the Democratic Party in Texas.

"So we joined forces and John Connally became the main 'go-between' between Rayburn and Johnson and me," said Daniel. "He spoke for Rayburn and Johnson at every convention from that time on. He was their representative on the working angle with me."

Meanwhile, however, the September convention marked only the start of Daniel's pre-inaugural problems. He and Shivers, who was preparing to leave office, conducted a running feud that fall which centered around the timing of Daniel's resignation.

On Sept. 26, 1956, Daniel submitted a conditional resignation from the Senate to Shivers, effective Jan. 15, 1957, the date of his inauguration, "or such earlier date as my successor has been elected and qualified." Daniel contended that this would permit Shivers to go ahead and call a special election before the first of the year, enabling him to carry out his campaign promise to time his resignation so that even his temporary successor would be chosen by the people instead of being appointed.

Shivers, however, insisted that the conditional resignation did not create a vacancy until Jan. 15 and refused to call an election before that date. He accused Daniel of trying to control the offices of both senator and governor.

In a letter to Daniel on Nov. 12, 1956, Shivers said: "I must and do accept your resignation as of Jan. 15, 1957, but respectfully suggest that in fairness to the people of Texas and to yourself, you should submit a resignation effective immediately and without conditions."

Shivers said he would call the special election at the earliest date permitted by law if Daniel would submit an "unconditional resignation, effective immediately."

"If you do not resign effective immediately, with no strings attached,

I must agree with many of your friends that, in spite of your promises to the contrary, you now seek to control both offices—Governor of Texas and the United States Senate—and plan to appoint your own successor," said the letter.

It also noted: "Incidentally, you promised the people of Texas that you would not appoint your successor in the United States Senate nor allow me to do so. The date of Jan. 15, 1957, selected by you, is the only date on which each of us would have the opportunity to do what you promised would not be done."

Daniel immediately accused Shivers of deliberately delaying the special election so that he might name a pro-Eisenhower appointee to the Senate, in which the Democrats then held a precarious 49-47 majority.

"The unfriendly tone of Governor Shivers's letter, his long delay in announcing his decision, and his present proposal leave me no alternative than to conclude that he has deliberately delayed action so as to try to appoint a senator on Jan. 3 rather than to have him elected by the people," said Daniel.

"I do not know Governor Shivers's motive," he added, "unless it is to help the Republicans organize the Senate. He may want to defeat Senator Johnson for majority leader, but if successful in that he would also be denying the South control of the Senate's most important committees."

The sniping continued until the inauguration—and intensified a few days before it took place, when Shivers filled vacancies on the University of Texas Board of Regents and the Texas A&M Board of Directors. Daniel contended that those appointments should have been left for the incoming governor. He tried to withdraw them after he took office but the Senate permitted him to do so only on the condition that he reappoint the *same* individuals—which he did.

Shivers, meanwhile, appointed William A. Blakley of Dallas to the U. S. Senate on the morning of Jan. 15, shortly before the noontime inaugural ceremony. He also called the special election for April 2. Blakley, a self-made millionaire who never had sought or held political office before, was a close friend of Daniel as well as of Shivers. He did not run in the special election, which Yarborough won, but sought the office unsuccessfully in the 1958 Democratic Primary.

Daniel later praised Blakley's service and commented that if he ever had the opportunity, he would send him back to the Senate. While that "promise" was made in good faith, there was no reason at that time for Daniel to suspect he would ever have such an opportunity. He was surprised when it came—by virtue of Senator Johnson's being elected vice president—and even more surprised when Blakley accepted the appointment.

Daniel thought about the appointive possibilities quite a bit during the 1960 campaign. He discussed the matter with Attorney General Wilson, with whom he later was to have a bitter rift, and with John Connally, whose liaison work on behalf of Johnson had strengthened his friendship with the Governor.

"What I was doing," Daniel recalled, "was trying to talk it over with those that might have a good chance of getting elected. Wilson told me one night, when we were coming back from a rally in Longview where Senator Kerr spoke, that he didn't want to be considered because he had just gone through a reelection campaign. It was then down to Blakley and Connally.

"At that point, we didn't really think it was in the cards for Kennedy and Johnson to win," Daniel admitted.

When the Kennedy-Johnson ticket did win, Daniel told Connally he would name him to the Senate if Blakley turned down the appointment. He felt he owed Blakley the courtesy of offering it to him but did not think Blakley would be willing to run in the subsequent special election.

"There were no strings attached to the offer," said Daniel, "but I think it was pretty well understood that I thought whoever accepted it should make the race and that it ought to be considered with that in mind. I was surprised when Blakley accepted it, only because I considered his acceptance an indication he would run."

Connally, however, said he was not particularly surprised—nor too disappointed—when Blakley accepted, adding that "going to the U. S. Senate was not something I was just dying to do."

But by late 1961, becoming governor of Texas was in that category for Connally—and he told Daniel so. Daniel, nearing the end of his third term, was not at all averse to the idea of having Connally succeed him. A public opinion poll by Joe Belden Associates, Inc., early in 1962 helped convince Daniel that Connally could not win but that *he* could win a fourth term, despite the fact that he had been whipsawed by the first retail sales tax in Texas history.

Daniel had fought the sales tax relentlessly, incurring the wrath of business interests which insisted upon it. When the Legislature finally passed it over Daniel's protests to solve the state's fiscal problems, the public blamed him for it. Cashiers in restaurants, for instance, almost inevitably seemed to say, upon being confronted with a check for, say, $4, "and eight pennies more for Price."

Daniel finally decided that Connally could not win and that if he did not run for a fourth term, Attorney General Wilson probably would succeed him. By that time, he and Wilson were at dagger points.

"He had come out for the sales tax when I was trying to beat it, early in the 1961 legislative session, for one thing," Daniel explained. "He was attorney general and had no business getting mixed up in legislation but he came out criticizing me. He just asked for that fight. He made life miserable for me, and for nothing but political reasons.

"He got me on the defensive," said Daniel. "He got me to feeling that I didn't want *him* to be governor because he was opposing so many things I favored."

He chuckled as he recalled the tense feeling that resulted.

"At the time, I felt those things were awfully important," he said. "Now I can't even remember what they were."

Daniel, with his keen sense of history, undoubtedly was aware, too, that Shivers—who probably had done more to make his life miserable than had Wilson—then had served as governor of Texas longer than anyone else. A full fourth term would have given that honor to Daniel. But Daniel still insists that he would not have run in 1962 had he thought Connally could win.

"I talked to Connally about it frequently and we went over everything," said Daniel. "We went over various issues and found we were in agreement on them. I always kept the door open but I encouraged him to talk to newspaper editors and publishers and to 'feel out' the situation. I told him that if I thought he could win I wouldn't run—but that if I didn't, I would run.

"That Belden Poll showed me with nearly 50 per cent of the vote against the field," Daniel recalled. "With that, with my mail and all, I thought I had the pulse of the people.

"I was," he admitted ruefully, "mistaken."

Chapter 12

LONG SHOT

John Connally survived an assassin's bullets on Nov. 22, 1963, without any serious scars, mental or physical, although Lee Harvey Oswald's shots came within a few inches of killing him. That is roughly the same distance by which Connally's friendship with Lyndon B. Johnson missed slaying him politically in 1962.

Connally's opponents still believe Johnson "put him in" the 1962 governor's race. Connally always insisted that just the opposite was true—that Johnson had done his best to talk him out of running. Nevertheless, the accusation that Johnson was trying to install a personal puppet in the governor's office—that Connally was "Lyndon's Boy John"— proved the biggest handicap Connally had to overcome. But it was only one of many he anticipated when he resigned as President Kennedy's first Secretary of the Navy in December, 1961, to run.

"That was one of the toughest political decisions I ever had to make," Connally recalled, "because, by any reasonable standards, I had no chance to win."

The former governor settled back in an easy chair in the library of his palatial Houston home as he recalled the details of that fateful decision—one which almost cost him his life. The plush River Oaks house exemplified his love for the outdoors, since every room on the first floor opened onto a garden. Even the bathroom adjoining the library and his bedroom featured a sliding glass door leading onto a small patio lined with tropical plants and surrounded by high, brick walls.

It was mid-afternoon on Saturday, July 26, 1969, and from the vantage point of six months out, Connally felt he could view objectively his three terms in the governor's office—as well as the political struggle which put him there. And he made it clear he had no regrets about surrendering voluntarily the chief executive's chair he had sought so eagerly just seven years earlier.

"In spite of the odds against success," he declared, "I felt that running for governor in 1962 was something I really should do. Looking back on it now, I guess it's fairly difficult to explain. It *was* an awfully tough decision—but another tough one was whether or not to run for a third term, and another was whether or not to run for a fourth. . . .

"I don't know that there was any one compelling reason why I decided to run for a third and not for a fourth—but I never wanted, and certainly do not want now, a long political career," said Connally.

154

"I've always viewed participation in politics as more of a duty and obligation than as the fulfillment of any personal ambition."

He admitted that his long, close friendship with President Johnson turned out to be a millstone around his neck during the 1962 campaign.

"Johnson did not want me to run," he declared flatly. "He discouraged me every way he could, advised me against it in every way he could and said he thought I was foolish to do it. He thought if I wanted to stay in politics, I had every opportunity to do so at the Washington level instead of coming back to take on an incumbent governor and an incumbent attorney general—who, on the face of it, had every advantage over me.

"I suppose his judgment, like everybody else's at the time, was probably right—that I did have a very poor chance to win," Connally admitted. "In one way, I thought I had only one chance out of 10 or maybe 20. But in my own mind, I really thought I could win; if I hadn't, I wouldn't have run.

"We had an unusual situation, you'll recall. I thought the people were disturbed and frustrated. You have to remember the atmosphere of the 1960 presidential campaign, which was a bitter one in Texas. You go back to the spring of 1960 and the state was overwhelmingly behind Johnson to contest Jack Kennedy for the nomination. Then, when Johnson went on the ticket in Los Angeles, the reaction was immediate and bitter and vocal. This left a very, very strong resentment in the minds of a lot of people and the presidential election was close.

"It just wasn't a real popular thing to admit you were a Democrat," said Connally. "In fact, if you lived in certain areas of town, your kids got picked on. People kind of looked down their noses at you. Feelings were running very high.

"Well, Kennedy and Johnson won the election nationally by one of the smallest margins in history. They carried Texas by only about 46,-000 votes. Then we came along to fill Johnson's seat in '61 and had the topsy-turvy election which Tower won.

"I didn't have any great desire to run against Price Daniel," said Connally. "As a matter of fact, I had been very friendly with him. But I never thought he'd run. He kept saying he would decide by October—but October came and he didn't decide. Then he said he'd decide by November, and he didn't, and then by December, and December came and he still hadn't decided.

"I finally told him that he could wait until the last minute but I couldn't. I said, 'You're the governor, your name is well-known and you have the contacts; but I know I have a long row to hoe.'

"I don't think it was just the Belden Poll that kept him from thinking I could win. A number of people kept telling him I couldn't win and that he was the only one who could—and, of course, this is understandable.

"And I suspect," Connally added, "that he had a lingering ambition to run again, anyway. He and Governor Shivers had locked horns and fallen out. They were certainly not on the best of terms. Shivers had served longer than any governor in the history of the state and if Daniel served four full terms, he would have served longer than Shivers.

"This probably was just a part of his thinking. Then, too, people kept telling him, *as they tell every governor,* 'You're just as strong as horse radish! You can sure do this and you can sure do that and, yes, sir, *you're* right!'

"I think Price believed it—and he had good reason to believe it," said Connally. "I think the Belden Poll accurately reflected what the situation was at the time it was taken. But most people read polls the way they want to read 'em. Instead of analyzing a poll in terms of the time in which it was taken and the questions that were asked, they want to project it six months forward and read the results of an election into it. And this is the great mistake they make in poll-watching.

"I knew what the poll showed but I actually felt pretty confident. I knew the odds were against me," he declared. "But in any political situation, you cannot look just at the situation which exists at any particular moment. You have to analyze the individuals involved— their basic strengths and weaknesses.

"And by that," he added, "I mean not just their visible political positions. I'm talking about their personal strengths and weaknesses. This includes everything—their appearance, their size, their age, their looks, their voice, mannerisms, dress, political positions, background, acquaintanceships, and the intangible things, such as whether or not they come across as forceful, as personable, as sincere, or whether they have a false smile or instinctive characteristics that are displeasing to people.

"These are the things that ultimately determine whether, in the final analysis, you have a candidate that will run well or one that won't run well. A part of this, too, is his ability to lead and inspire people because, in the showdown, during the last two or three weeks of a campaign, this is what makes the difference—the enthusiasm of the people in your organization."

Organization? Connally apparently had none when he first entered the governor's race but this, he contended, was somewhat deceiving.

"Basically, the old Johnson organization was built in 1941 and 1948, largely out of people whom I had known. It basically was a *Johnson-Connally* organization, because I organized the young fellows who were my contemporaries, starting in 1941. Joe Kilgore, for instance, ran a sound truck all over West Texas during the 1941 campaign for Johnson—and Johnson had never heard of him at that time. This was just prior to the war and you had Mac DeGeurin, you had John Single-ton, you had Jake Pickle, all of whom went up there in the Johnson or-ganization and all were fellows whom I had known."

The fact that Connally had been president of the student body at The University of Texas and his wife, Nellie, the former Idanell Brill, had been the "University of Texas Sweetheart" in 1938 also helped tremen-dously.

"The basic organization arose out of friends whom I had made at the University and, of course, Nellie had a tremendous acquaintanceship," said Connally. "My last year in school there were about 10,000 students in the University and I dare say that I could call over half of them on that campus by their first names. Then, during the War, I saw a lot of them, and I renewed acquaintances and solidified a lot of them."

Connally, born Feb. 27, 1917, at Floresville, was one of seven chil-dren. His father, J. B. Connally, was a tenant farmer and cattle-raiser who knew Johnson quite well by the time John entered The Univer-sity of Texas.

"I first met Johnson in about 1936, I guess," Connally recalled. "He was National Youth Administration director in Texas and I was in school. With the help of Mr. Sam Fore, Jr., who was publisher of the Floresville newspaper, I went down to see him about getting a job with the NYA while I was in school. I subsequently got on—working at the Supreme Court Library in the capitol, at 17 cents an hour.

"Many of those who were in the NYA I came to regard as close friends—people like Jesse Kellam, Sherman Birdwell, Bill Deason, Fen-ner Roth, Victor Yeagli. . . .

"Then, in the spring of 1939, Eddie Joseph and one or two others who had stores on 'The Drag' [Guadalupe Street, adjoining the UT cam-pus] started asking me if I had my job yet," said Connally. "They knew this was my last year in law school so I didn't think much about it at first. But I finally asked Joseph what he was talking about and he said he thought I'd applied for a federal job because they had been checking on me. It turned out that Johnson, who was then in Congress, was re-sponsible for that. He hadn't even talked to me then but he came home a short while later and offered me a job on his staff, because Birdwell was leaving.

"I took it and stayed in Washington until February of 1941, when I came home to open a law office," said Connally. "I opened one but I hadn't been home six weeks until Senator Sheppard died and Johnson decided to get in that 1941 race. And, of course, I got right in the mid-dle of it and basically organized the campaign."

Connally had no idea at that time that he actually was taking his first step toward the Governor's Mansion. And, that fall, when he began a four-year tour of active duty with the U. S. Navy, he never dreamed that this World War II duty, including combat aboard aircraft carriers, would be a factor 20 years later in his selection as Secretary of the Navy.

Back home in 1946, Connally and a group of other close Johnson friends established an Austin radio station, KVET. The founders included Kellam, who was to become general manager of the Johnson family's Austin radio and television stations, KTBC; Robert L. Phinney, who later became Austin's postmaster and, after that, district director of the Internal Revenue Service; Pickle, who succeeded Judge Thornberry in Johnson's 10th District congressional seat after serving on the Texas Employment Commission; Willard (Bill) Deason, whom President Johnson appointed to the Interstate Commerce Commission; Birdwell, whom Connally named to the Texas Employment Commission; W. E. (Ed) Syers, who became a public relations consultant and then a newspaper columnist; Merrill Connally, Floresville rancher and one of the Governor's brothers, and Ed Clark, already a prominent Austin attorney.

All of them, along with Austin Mayor Tom Miller and a handful of friends, showed up early for the 6 a.m. dedication of the 1,000-watt station the day it went on the air—but not the future governor, who was to double as a disc jockey while serving as manager of the station.

Connally raced up to the scene, panting, just at air time—and wearing house slippers instead of shoes.

"My alarm didn't go off," he explained.

Connally took time out later that year to manage Congressman Johnson's reelection campaign, and then to quarterback his dramatic 1948 Senate race. And it was then that Connally had to make his first major decision about seeking public office himself.

"When Johnson came home early in 1948," said Connally, "there was no question but what he had made up his mind *not* to run for the Senate. Several of us talked him into it. We met in the Driskill Hotel. As I recall, Jake Pickle, Ed Syers, Senator Wirtz and, I think Ed Clark and Bob Phinney, and two or three others were in on this particular meeting where he changed his mind and decided to run.

"After he made the decision to run, there obviously was going to be a vacancy because he couldn't run for both offices in 1948. There was a lot of discussion about who was going to run for his congressional seat. Kelly McClain from Georgetown had been mentioned and Creekmore Fath of Austin was talking about it, and a great many people were talking to me about it.

"Homer Thornberry's name came up and he discussed it with me," said Connally. "He said if I wanted to run, he wouldn't. I told him no, that I didn't want to run. But if I had wanted to go into national politics, that would have been the best opportunity that I could have had because I knew that 10th District. The odds were as strongly in my favor to win that congressional seat, if I ran, as they were *against* me to win the gubernatorial race in 1962.

"But I had worked in Washington and a great deal of the glamor, the excitement, had worn off it," he declared. "I knew the job from the inside. I knew how much hard work it was and how little glamor and excitement. And I felt that any man who went up there should do it with the idea of spending the rest of his life, or at least a substantial part of it, in the federal picture.

"Now, there was one other factor that weighed heavily on my mind," Connally said. "This was just two years after I had come home from the navy. I had gotten out Jan. 3, 1946, and hadn't had time to make any money or do anything else. Fortunately, during the years between '46 and '61, when I became Secretary of the Navy, I had been able to make a little money so I had some feeling of independence.

"One of the overriding considerations I had in mind in 1948 was that I was never going to become an active political office holder or seeker of public offices unless and until I had accumulated a little money. I gave no thought to being rich or anything of that kind but simply to having some kind of security, some kind of independence. Actually, it wasn't a question of security; independence was the key to it, where you didn't have to have the job to live and to pay your bills, and you didn't have to have it to feel that you were not destitute.

"I just always had the feeling that until I could feel I was financially independent, I would never seek public office. And that was one of the main reasons I didn't run for Congress in 1948."

Money again was a key factor in 1962 but, by then, the question was one of campaign finances rather than personal finances.

"I tried to analyze carefully everything involved in making that race," said Connally. "I decided that, given help, if I could get enough people in an organization working fast enough and if we could raise enough money to make the impact that obviously I had to make to get my name known, then I would have a good chance to win.

"My work in the Johnson campaigns of 1941 and '48 gave me a familiarity and acquaintanceship statewide that not many people knew I had," he said, "and so not much weight was given to it. But there wasn't a publisher in the State of Texas that I hadn't known, and known pretty well. There wasn't a one that I couldn't call on or go see. This doesn't mean they were committed to me but at least I had an entree. I'd had some working relationship with nearly all of the top editors and publishers in the state during those two statewide campaigns for Johnson."

This was one of the major differences, Connally noted, between his situation in 1962 and Locke's in 1968.

"I tried to tell *him* that," said Connally.

Still, he added, he thought Locke had a chance to win, depending entirely on "how he performed as a candidate."

"You can't tell that about anyone until you actually get him in a race," said Connally. "I didn't encourage Gene to run; I discouraged him. I told him the odds were he couldn't win—for all the reasons that people gave me in '62, and they were all sound reasons. Now, it so happened that circumstances broke to where I overcame the odds but Locke couldn't and none of these other fellows could."

Connally led the ticket in the first Democratic primary of 1962 and was forced into a runoff by Don Yarborough, the Houston lawyer who Connally later declared "was in his prime as a candidate" that year. Getting into the runoff was a remarkable feat for Connally since the vote was split between him, Yarborough, Governor Daniel, Attorney General Wilson, former Highway Commissioner Marshall Formby of Plainview and Major General Edwin A. Walker, a noted right-winger, in that order.

Connally borrowed a page from the past to help dramatize, very successfully, his runoff campaign against Yarborough. He made a three-day, 800-mile whistle-stop campaign tour by special train across the state, from Texarkana to El Paso, reaping surprisingly good crowds and tons of publicity.

He won the runoff from Yarborough, 565,174 to 538,924.

Yarborough, who had run unsuccessfully for lieutenant governor in 1960, ran against Connally again in 1964. Then, in 1968, he led Smith in the first primary, 422,823 to 382,488, but lost in the runoff, 771,648 to 617,063.

Connally, despite his early and unsuccessful efforts to recruit a candidate of his own political philosophy who could win, wound up with so many personal friends in the 1968 race that he refused to take sides openly. He admitted later, however, that he thought "most people knew that, out of a sense of loyalty and obligation, I probably preferred Gene Locke."

"But to say that I went all out to help Locke—I didn't, and I couldn't," said Connally. "I explained my position to all of them: to Gene, to Dolph Briscoe, to John Hill, to Waggoner Carr. I told them that I was just going to work on the conventions and not take any active role in the primary.

"Actually, I tried to discourage them all. I told them all the same thing: that if you go into this, you have to do it with the assumption that you can't win and that it's going to cost you some of your own money. You're going to have to go into it with your mind made up that if you lose, you can lose gracefully, and it's not going to hurt you—it's not going to hurt your personality, it's not going to hurt your family, and it's not going to make you bitter or sour. You'll have to be man enough to take defeat.

"Then," said Connally, "I tried to analyze the political situation for each of these individuals and I told most of them they could stand to lose because they'd never made a statewide race. So many people have lost and later come back to win. But at no point did I encourage any of them to run."

Locke's campaign started in house-afire fashion, Connally noted, with catchy radio jingles, countless television spots and colorful billboards.

"Financing has to be a major problem in any campaign but it takes more than financing," said Connally, "and Gene didn't husband his resources. The first six weeks of his campaign, he made great headway, then he faltered. He faltered, I think, because of financial circumstances. He didn't time his campaign properly. I think he felt he could raise more money to keep up the pace he'd set—but he couldn't, and he didn't. Then Briscoe started making a run.

"I don't know why it works that way, but it does—just like a horse race. You can watch the Kentucky Derby, the Preakness or any of 'em and you rarely see a horse that starts in the lead finish in the lead. This is true in politics. The guy who is out in front early rarely wins.

"While Gene was faltering, while he was trying to raise money to finish the campaign, Briscoe started coming on," said Connally. "There was about a three-week lag in the Locke campaign—three weeks to a month that was just lost. During that time, Briscoe came on strong and Gene never could regain the momentum. I think he actually lost votes. Gene was stronger six weeks before the election than he was on election day.

"You take a field where you have a Carr, a Locke, a Briscoe, a Smith, a Hill and a Don Yarborough and the voters will shift. They will shift off one candidate onto another to a remarkable degree, in a week or 10 days. It depends a lot on who they think is going to be in that runoff and who's moving and how things look. And if you ever lose that timing—

"Just like in a national campaign," said Connally. "Nixon had the thing won right after the Democratic Convention and Humphrey didn't have a prayer. But Nixon almost played it coy too long. He just almost lost the election because Humphrey started gaining ground. He started building momentum and Nixon began to slow. In a national campaign, or in a state campaign, it takes a month to turn something around—if you *can* turn it around. If you ever lose that momentum, it's nearly always deadly.

"To win, you not only have to have a candidate, you have to have excellent political advice," Connally declared. "You have to have someone around you, both in terms of organization and press, and otherwise, who is able to sense the timing of the campaign. Because it doesn't matter how you run in March or April—you've got to run on election day. Very few campaigns ever peak on election day—but you try to come as close to it as you can."

Partly because of his experience as a campaign manager, Connally feels he probably spent more of his own time during the 1962 campaign on organization, fund-raising, speech-writing, public relations and various mechanical details than anyone else who has been elected governor in modern times.

"I had to," he said. "Gene Locke is awfully smart, has tremendous capacity and unbelievable powers of concentration, almost more than anybody I know of, but he had never had any seasoning in a campaign.

"But this fit the image of the type of campaign I was going to run— the presentation of a bunch of new faces in Texas political life," Connally declared. "I tried to disassociate myself from the old established lines. Then, too, there were no experienced individuals with the necessary qualifications to run a campaign.

"Back in the 1930s, you had some people available who were pretty well regarded as the 'pros' but in the 1960s there weren't any," he explained. "Times had changed. You could attract the younger people to politics in the '30s and '40s because everybody was looking for a job; everybody was available. You could get a guy to take off and work in a campaign because he figured if he did, it might mean a good job for him. In the 1960s, you were in a different world economically and people weren't available.

"Plus, I felt our strongest position was in coming not only with fresh faces but with a little different approach—a little different look at the state's problems. I hoped to talk during the campaign about the opportunities the state had. I didn't think it was necessary to identify myself with the pros. And, furthermore, I didn't know where you could find one."

Connally did, indeed, use a different approach, not only during the campaign but after he took office. As is generally the case when Texas changes governors, almost the entire executive department staff was replaced. It took many months to achieve a semblance of organization, especially since Connally's staff faced a backlog of several weeks' mail when it moved into the Capitol, only to be greeted by a deluge of congratulatory correspondence and recommendations for appointive positions.

Connally also displayed a rather casual approach toward members of the Legislature. Many of the lawmakers became irked when they were unable to see him on a moment's notice, as they traditionally had been able to do with other governors. He aroused the ire of the Senate

John B. Connally and his wife, Nellie, sewed up his 1962 Democratic nomination for governor with a three-day, 800-mile whistle stop campaign by special train.

Wives Club (its name indicates its tremendous influence) even before taking office, when he scheduled a Democratic Party "Victory Dinner" for the evening before the inauguration. The Wives Club traditionally held a party of its own on inauguration eve.

Despite such handicaps, Connally compiled an enviable record. He went to bat for higher education more, and more enthusiastically, than had any of his predecessors.

"I think, and I hope, we initiated movements in many different fields," said Connally, reviewing his administration, "such as education, water planning, industrial growth, tourist development, a consciousness of the arts through creation of the Fine Arts Commission, and an awareness of the need to improve libraries in both large cities and small. And, more than anything else, we tried to awaken the minds of the people, including legislators, to the fact that our potential is basically untapped. We have to dream bigger dreams and we must have the courage to make the changes that will enrich the lives of the people who live here.

"Many of these things are intangible but they reflect the fierce pride we have in this state," he declared. "We've tried to promote dignity, pride and respect. We've tried to instill in the minds of State employees the fact that their work is vital and critical. Their decisions and their actions are vital to the existence of a democracy, and fairness must be part of every decision they make. They must be aware that you can't please everyone; you have to be willing to suffer disapproval in the minds of men because human nature resists change, even though it might be for the better."

Connally declared emphatically that he never entertained any doubt that he could win a fourth term if he sought it.

"I didn't know anybody that would run against me except possibly Preston," he said. "I had to assume, in light of what he had said, that he would run regardless of what I did. But that had no bearing at all on my decision because it never entered my mind that I couldn't win a fourth term.

"Nearly everybody seemed to agree with this—but that was not the problem," said Connally. "The problem, the question, was did I owe that much more? Now, you start on the basic assumption with certain things: that my own time as an active office holder should have a limit on it, because I had other things I wanted to do. Holding public office was too consuming. It consumed my physical and mental energies almost to the exclusion of everything else.

"Secondly, realistically, you had to come off any idea that you were an indispensable person. I never had that idea. I always approached it with the idea that no matter what problems I might solve, there would be new ones arise the next day and that no one was going to stay there long enough to 'carry out his program.' If he did, he would have

A jubilant John Connally, who had resigned six months earlier as Secretary of the Navy, received the 1962 Democratic Primary returns at his campaign head-quarters. He still insists that LBJ did not want him to run.

stayed there too long because that would mean he didn't have a program the last two years. You'd have to be a dictator and stay there the rest of your life to carry out your program because you ought to always be looking two, four or even ten years ahead. If you stayed long enough to solve all the problems you started out to solve, you had the wrong attitude to begin with.

"So the question in my mind was simply whether I was leaving the state, or leaving the party, in a lurch—was I leaving either in a situation that was unfair? I didn't think I was. But to answer that question, you had to look at the prospects, and you had to realize that you can never dictate your successor. All you can do is try to create an environment where you've attracted at least a few good people into the political arena.

"So, at least there was a choice available and you had stability within the party. By '68, we didn't have people quitting the Democratic Party and going Republican the way they were in 1960 and '61. The Democratic Party was basically strong, at least within our state. It was a strong, coherent, unified body. Oh, we still had frictions and factions within the Party but the Party wasn't in disarray.

"I felt that no matter who won the governor's race," said Connally, "he could control the state convention, he could basically carry out his policies and he could have a Democratic Executive Committee with whom he could work. So I felt there wasn't a better time for me to leave the political arena."

It is an arena that will forever bear his mark—and one which he really could not escape. Close friends of Connally say that Humphrey approached him early in 1968 on the possibility of being his running mate. Connally turned him down—and there are those who believe that, had he accepted, the Democratic ticket might have won.

Despite Connally's support of the Humphrey-Muskie ticket, he was approached by an intermediary for Nixon on the possibility of becoming Secretary of Defense. Connally refuses to discuss that unpublicized incident but well-informed sources say flatly the appointment definitely would have been offered to him had he not made it clear that he would not accept it. He was simply tired of holding public office, however, and wanted to quit the political scene. But after another taste of private life, he accepted enthusiastically the post of Secretary of the Treasury.

Perhaps his biggest regret, upon leaving the governor's office, was that he had never been able to throw Senator Yarborough to the lions. He undoubtedly enjoyed tremendously the role he played in Bentsen's 1970 upset of the liberal leader.

Connally disliked Yarborough intensely and the feeling was mutual. Yarborough contended that Connally never would have won even a second term had he not been shot while riding with President Kennedy. And Connally was convinced that his own good friend, President Johnson, had saved Yarborough's political hide in 1964.

"I'm one of the few men," said Connally, "who ever served three terms as Governor of Texas without having a U. S. Senator he could really talk to. That made it very difficult.

"Oh, I don't mean we didn't have telephone conversations, of course. I mean we didn't have the rapport that's helpful to a governor, and to a senator, in doing a job for this state. Unfortunately, that was the situation the entire time I was governor, through no fault of mine. I'm not going to take the responsibility for it.

"Tower was elected in 1961, before I was elected governor; actually, we got along fine together, even though we were in different parties. As for Yarborough, the Yarborough-Connally feeling was really nothing but a Yarborough-Johnson feeling.

"And Yarborough," said Connally, "carried on this feud with Johnson right up to the time of the assassination."

Chapter 13

THE LITTLE THINGS

"I heard the shots," said Nellie Connally. "I had an awful feeling but I couldn't truthfully say I knew they were gun shots—until I looked at the President. Then I knew he had been shot. I heard all three shots. John just heard two. He didn't hear the one that hit him.

"I pulled him over into my arms and put my head down on his. I thought he was dead. But then he moved his hand—it was almost an imperceptible movement—and I knew he was alive.

"I whispered to him over and over, all the way to the hospital, 'Be still, it's going to be all right.' I must have sounded like a broken record. He would come to for a few seconds but I think he was mostly unconscious on the drive to the hospital. . . ."

That is the way Mrs. Connally described the ordeal of Nov. 22, 1963. Later, Connally explained that the assassin's bullet entered his back, just to the left of his right shoulder blade, and came out on the right side of his chest, tearing a gaping hole there after destroying a rib. When he slumped over, he said, his right arm happened to fall over the hole in his chest.

"That probably saved my life," he declared. "The hole in my chest was larger than the nose and throat opening. With a hole that big, when you try to breathe, you suck air through the hole and it tends to collapse the lung. You can suffocate—strangle yourself—pretty quickly. My arm happened to cover up the hole."

Still, Connally almost bled to death before he reached Parkland Hospital in Dallas.

"I don't know how much blood I lost," he said, "but they gave me two and one-half quarts. That's about one-third of the body's supply.

"I am," he added, "a very lucky man."

That thought apparently came close to dominating the remainder of Connally's tenure as governor. No man could endure the traumatic experience of being wounded, almost fatally, in a presidential motorcade without having it affect his philosophy and, to some extent, his personality. In Connally's case, it seemed to make him believe more strongly than ever in the adage that it's the little things that count—such little things as being able to tie your own shoes, for instance.

"I'm just so glad that we have ol' John Connally here," his wife said one day in January of 1964, "that I'm as happy as I can be to tie his shoelaces—even when I don't tie them exactly to suit him and he fusses about it!"

She was even glad to hear him fuss, she added, because that was a sure sign his condition was improving. That sentiment was not necessarily shared by Connally's staff members, some of whom had to help dress him when she made a brief shopping trip to Houston.

"It was quite a project," one of them recalled, shaking his head. "Finally, when we got through, he grumbled, 'I'll sure be glad when Nellie gets back.'"

"It's nice to know I was missed," said Mrs. Connally, when she returned. "He reminds me of that television commercial where they say, 'Mother, I'd rather do it myself!' That's just the way he is. He'd rather do everything himself, cast or no cast. And he's gotten now to where he can do everything for himself except tie a bow knot.

"He can even tie a four-in-hand tie with his left hand," she said, with obvious pride. "He doesn't like for us to do things like cut up the meat on his plate before we bring it to him but we do—because it's awfully hard on him to do it."

Meanwhile, the governor was perfecting a left-handed offense for defensive purposes during the 1964 hand-shaking season. His defense was bolstered by his doctors' insistence that he keep the cast on his right hand and wrist longer than he normally would have, strictly as a precaution against over-zealous handshakers, and use his left hand for handshaking.

Actually, said Connally, he had learned early in his political career that the best defense in the handshaking league is a good offense. He estimated that he shook hands with between 140,000 and 180,000 people during his 1962 campaign. He developed heavy calluses on his right hand—one in a half-moon shape between his index finger and thumb, another of similar shape on the side of his hand, just behind the little finger.

"Both calluses stuck up about an eighth of an inch and were just as tough as boot leather," he declared. "You know how tough your feet got when you were a kid going barefooted? Well, that's about the way these were.

"You have to learn to protect yourself shaking hands—it's really an art, a science, for a politician," said Connally. "You have to react very quickly. It's something nobody ever thinks about but it's awfully important when you do a lot of handshaking. For instance, some people make a quick grab and squeeze your fingers before you can grip their hands. That can really hurt. You have to be just a little quicker than they are and grab their hands first.

"Some people, of course, try to overpower you; they really almost crush your hand," he added. "With a person like that, you have to grab his hand quickly and apply counterpressure, primarily with your thumb, and little finger. I try to respond in kind and always have a fairly strong, firm handshake."

Connally had the opportunity to do quite a bit of firsthand research on this while serving as Secretary of the Navy.

"I found then that we could shake hands with about 1,000 people an hour in a fast-moving line, such as one at a formal reception," he said. "But you can't shake hands that fast in politics. For one thing, you usually don't have the precision of a formal receiving line; and, generally, you do a little more visiting with each person."

Connally also learned, after being shot, to sign his name with his left hand.

"It quickly got to the point where I could sign my name with my left hand almost automatically," he said, "but when I'd try to write anything besides my signature, I almost had to stop and think about how to form each letter."

A few weeks after the assassination, Connally seemed almost as proud of his lefthanded achievements—signing his name, brushing his teeth, dressing himself and tying his ties—as he did of his political accomplishments.

"Just try putting on your socks with only your left hand when you're used to using both hands," he challenged. "Try it and you'll see that even little things like that can be quite a problem."

Connally was still trying to cope with such problems when Johnson went to the aid of Yarborough—and when the President first began trying to bury poverty, ignorance, racial discrimination and Republicans all under tons of federal money.

Connally denied it but some of his closest friends insist that he became so angry with President Johnson early in 1964 that he gave serious thought then to running for the U. S. Senate or quitting politics. Time has tempered his feelings but there is no doubt that he was infuriated when one of his best friends, even if he did happen to be President of the United States, declared that another of his closest friends could not run for the U. S. Senate.

President Johnson told Congressman Kilgore that if he ran against Senator Yarborough he would fight him and could "assure" his defeat. One of Johnson's close associates spelled it out, telling Kilgore that the President could "cut off" his campaign financing and could "handle" the Texas newspapers, persuading them to oppose him editorially. Kilgore, a conservative, also was told that the national welfare might hinge on his decision and that Johnson could do more for Texas as President than Kilgore could do as a senator.

Johnson also talked Bentsen out of running in 1964.

The President had assured labor leaders that he could promise Yarborough's reelection. Failure to deliver on that promise, he felt, might lead to his being defeated for the 1964 presidential nomination.

Five years later, Connally tried to minimize the incident—although it obviously had been one of the major squalls in his frequently stormy relationship with Johnson.

"I think he did his best to talk Kilgore out of running," admitted Connally, in one of the most glaring understatements of the decade. "That irritated me, because I thought he owed Joe more than that. I thought that was where his basic loyalty was; it damned sure wasn't to Yarborough. And it irritated me because by keeping Kilgore out, Johnson was helping Yarborough and he was doing it deliberately.

"It wasn't a matter of bitterness between us," Connally added, "although I don't think there was any question that we disagreed on it, that he was irritated with me and I was irritated with him."

Connally said he always had felt that George Meany was responsible for Johnson's going to bat for Yarborough in the 1964 Senate race but said he had never questioned LBJ about it because "it would serve no useful purpose."

"I've always assumed that, in 1964, the President felt that he was on trial, so to speak, as a candidate himself," said Connally. "No one knew what the feeling of the country would be and these decisions had to be made less than three months after the assassination, because the deadline for filing to get on the primary ballot in Texas was Feb. 1. Johnson was nervous and jittery and the country was in a state of chaos and uncertainty. He was trying to pass the Kennedy program through Congress, he was trying to solidify his own situation and he was looking toward a convention and a campaign.

"Obviously important to him was the labor crowd—and, at least as far as Texas was concerned, Yarborough was their darling, a guy they could depend on under any circumstances. So I'm sure they moved in with everything they had on the national level to try to make Johnson stay off Yarborough and try to keep Yarborough from having any substantial opposition.

"That was the only time Johnson had any choice about Yarborough. He felt he couldn't unseat him then and, after that, the guy had a seat until 1970. At that point, Yarborough was a senator and sometimes his vote made a lot of difference on some of the programs. Whether it made a difference or not, he was the senator who had a say on the patronage in Texas and he did have a seat in the Senate. This was the tragedy of it and this is what I tried to say in 1964.

"Johnson didn't say it to me but he told some of those around him up there that I wouldn't even talk to him, that I wouldn't even discuss it with him and I wouldn't consider his problems," said Connally. "He said I was trying to crowd Joe off into a race he couldn't win.

"I wasn't trying to crowd Joe at all," he declared. "He had indicated he was tired of Congress and was either going to run for the Senate or get out. I never try to make another man's decision for him. But Joe talked with me about it. He told me about the discouragements he had had, directly and indirectly, from the President, and he was disappointed about it. But I told him I still thought he could win the race.

"I said, 'Maybe the President *will* be against you. But I don't think he can be. He can be against you now, and he can discourage you now, but publicly he can't be against you. There's no way he can because you were for him in 1941 and you were for him in 1948 and you've always been his friend. You've always supported him and you've always helped him; you did that in 1956 against your neighbor, Shivers, in the precinct fight. He can't, regardless of what he wants to do or regardless of why he's trying to help Yarborough, he can't publicly be against you. He can't even privately be against you if you get in this race.

" 'Now until you make a decision,' I told Joe, 'he can discourage you. But you just have to forget that. You have to analyze the position he will be in if you actually announce—and he would be confronted then with a completely different situation. All I can tell you is, I can't believe he'd oppose you. I can't believe he'd even hurt you or try to hurt you and I don't believe he could. Because the only people he could hurt you with are the people who are close enough to both of you to understand what you've always meant to him and how loyal you've been to him. Since they have that knowledge, he can't hurt you with those people. All he can do is hurt himself if he even tries to hurt you with them.

" 'But if you do run, you can't win it the easy way,' " Connally said he told Kilgore. " 'You're going to have to make up your mind that it's going to be the fight of your life and that you're going to have to put everything you've got into it—money, marbles and chalk.' "

Connally said he also warned of the sacrifices which Kilgore's wife, Jane, and their children would have to make.

"I said, 'Janie's got to like it and she's got to make up her mind that she's got to move your family home next week—that you're going to sell your Washingon house, that you're going to take a house down here, that she's going to have to campaign, every day and every night; that all your kids are going to have to campaign—Mark and Dean and Bill and Shannon—and it's going to be a dog's life for you. Unless you are willing to make that kind of commitment, you have no right to expect other people to support you—and you can't win.'

"I said, 'Now, if you're willing to do that, I think you *can* win. And if you make that decision, I'll support you. I'll do everything I can to help you, including publicly endorsing you if that will help. But unless you're willing to do that, you shouldn't run.'

"In fairness, I must say that if Joe had had the all-out support of the President, he might have run but I'm still not sure he would have," said Connally. "He was never as enthusiastic about it as he needed to be to win."

Kilgore, even at that, displayed more enthusiasm about running for the Senate in 1964 than Connally did for many of Johnson's legislative proposals during the next few years.

"I had a very deep concern that Johnson was going too far too fast," said Connally, "not in terms of what was wrong or in terms of whether a program was good or evil. But I felt he was generating too many programs that were easily conceived, fairly readily passed and very, very difficult to administer. As a matter of fact, this remained a problem after he left office.

"During the past eight years, we'd had over 400 new programs and no one understood them," he said. "People were frustrated because money was being wasted and there was overlapping—no question about it.

"Everybody who knows anything about it knows that in the aftermath of the assassination, Johnson went too far in terms of what was wise—not too far, perhaps, in terms of what was right or what was needed. But he created expectations where there obviously could be no fulfillment, resulting in frustration, criticism, disagreement, disappointment. And I knew this was coming. It had to come, the way he was going. But it was neither necessary nor wise that he do it.

"He was listening to a great many of these fellows who were dreaming up all these new programs and he was trying, as he frequently did, to capture his enemies," said Connally. "And you just don't do that. You never leave an old friend to make a new one—and get by with it. You obviously want to have as few enemies as you can but you don't want to forsake your past, forsake your friends, forsake your own record, in order to create new friends."

But disagreements with Johnson on such philosophical matters, and even on the Kilgore case, paled into insignificance, Connally said, when compared with those which disrupted their friendship during the 1941 and 1948 campaigns. In both cases, the credibility gap type of unnecessary secrecy—which appears to have been one of Johnson's most glaring liabilities, throughout his career—was responsible.

"During the 1941 campaign," Connally recalled, "he got laryngitis and went to Scott and White Hospital in Temple, because he could just barely talk. Gordon Fulcher [former editor of the *Austin American-Statesman*] and I went out to his house in Austin, just before the election, and asked him what we should say about it. He told us just to get other people to take over his speaking engagements and say nothing.

"We told him we couldn't do that, that we had to tell them he was sick, and this provoked an argument. Of course, at that point, he could barely talk, he was running a fever and he was not as rational as he might have been. We told him we were going ahead and tell 'em he was sick—that he was a candidate for the U. S. Senate and we couldn't keep it a secret that he was sick. I told him that we didn't have any choice, that you couldn't cancel a bunch of speaking engagements without giving an explanation.

"He ordered us out of the house, and said he didn't ever want to see either one of us again. Lady Bird was standing there crying when we left.

"It may sound juvenile and childish now," said Connally, "but it was pretty serious then. We went ahead and put out a press release about his sickness. I didn't talk to him for about 10 days, and this was right during the campaign. He would phone in and talk to someone else and they would relay the messages to me.

"In 1948, he had kidney stones—and apparently he had a phobia about not announcing that he was sick. Warren Woodward [a Johnson aide who later became an American Airlines executive] was with him and they were getting ready to fly from Dallas to the Mayo Clinic. Johnson didn't want anything said about it.

"We put out a statement against his instructions that he was sick and was going to Mayo's and he got mad as hell. He said he was going to resign. He told Woody to call in the press, that he was going to withdraw from the race—but Woody wouldn't do it. Woody called me and I told him not to do it. I said to just keep him in the hotel and not let anybody see him.

"He went on to Mayo's and for two weeks we didn't talk to each other. He'd call back and talk to everybody in the office except me but we wouldn't talk to each other," said Connally. "Again, we'd relay messages back and forth."

During the summer of 1967, Connally went to Africa on a six-week safari, sponsored by the American Broadcasting Company, which seemed to convince him that a great many messages are unnecessary, anyway. He was out of contact with the governor's office most of the time.

"When you get out there," he said later, "and have that much time to sit and think, when you're not under pressure and not in a hurry; when you sit there and watch the sun come up in the morning, then sit around a campfire at night, and you can look up and see the beauty of the moon and the stars; when you really take time to see the wonders of nature and to hear its sounds, it gives you a perspective you're inclined to push aside in normal, everyday life.

"It tends to bring into focus the fact that, whether you live the biblical three score and ten or not, your time is limited.

"Nothing can be more dramatic than the evidence you see all around you," said Connally. "Life is fleeting, at best, and you regain a sense of values. You tend to acquire an almost abstract objectivity in relation to problems and you realize just how minute, how inconsequential, you are in the overall scheme of things.

"You are profoundly impressed, no matter how great your effort or how consuming your desire, with the fact that you can't solve all the world's problems. All you can ever hope to do is to leave some measurable contribution, no matter how minute it might be.

"I wouldn't say that this experience is why I decided not to run for a fourth term," said Connally, "or even that it was while I was over there that I decided not to run. I cannot pinpoint exactly when the decision was made. But, beyond question, this provided the longest period that I'd had during my adult life to pause and reflect.

"And those circumstances," he added emphatically, "did not argue very eloquently for me to continue in public life."

Chapter 14

DOUBLE PLAY

Nine o'clock in the morning came to Miami Beach awfully early on Thursday, August 8, 1968, according to most of the Richard M. Nixon supporters who were awake to witness it. His first-ballot victory seven hours earlier at the Republican National Convention naturally had provoked extended celebrations. For Nixon, it also touched off a marathon round of strategy conferences on selection of his running mate and he managed to get only two hours' sleep before the meetings resumed at 9 a.m.

They took place at the Hilton-Plaza Hotel. A dozen of Nixon's close friends, advisers and key campaign workers gathered in the Jackie-of-Hearts Room (named in honor of Jackie Gleason) for the 9 a.m. conference. They included the two leaders of the Texas delegation, Senator Tower and State Chairman Peter O'Donnell.

At that point, both Tower and Congressman Bush still were in the running for the vice presidential nomination, but ironically, and perhaps fatally for their chances, both still were being "endorsed" by O'Donnell. Solid backing from the Texas delegation certainly would have enhanced the chances for either one. As it was, Bush reportedly was among the last four survivors in the elimination process, along with Gov. John A. Volpe of Massachusetts, U. S. Senator Howard H. Baker, Jr., of Tennessee and Gov. Spiro T. Agnew of Maryland.

It also seemed ironic that Texas Republicans had two strong prospects for the vice presidential nomination when they did not have a single candidate considered likely to win a statewide race in 1968. But preoccupation with national politics long had been considered both a trademark and a major fault of the Texas GOP, which had earned a reputation for fumbling on the goal line.

The ridiculous idea of trying to support two Texans for one vice presidential nomination in Miami Beach reinforced that reputation. It also caused a bitter rift, which both men later tried to minimize, between Tower and Bush.

As the only Texas Republican to win a statewide race in several thousand years, Tower obviously was an exception to the party line. He even describes himself as a "victim of circumstance" when he won his Senate seat in a 1961 special election to choose Vice President Johnson's successor. Although he was opposed in 1968 by the Northern liberals, that hurdle could have been overcome had Nixon decided that he needed Tower's eloquence and Southern identification on the ticket. But Tower still discounts—publicly, at least—the theory that he might have been Nixon's running mate had it not been for the "help" he received from the Texas delegation.

Bush still had Eastern identification despite more than 20 years of business experience in Texas. He also possessed the youthful image and eloquence which many Nixon advisers felt was needed to thwart the George Wallace threat. And, probably most important of all, his selection would have triggered a flood of large campaign contributions from former Senator Prescott Bush's wealthy friends in New York financial circles.

Tower, of course, could not come close to matching that last qualification. He is a former professor of government at Midwestern University in Wichita Falls and the son of a Methodist minister. Although he is only 5 feet 6 inches tall, it did not take him long after reaching Washington to achieve national stature as an eloquent, outspoken and entertaining champion of the conservative cause.

As the youngest member of the Senate when he took office, the 36-year-old Tower patiently let Washington and the Republican Party nationally discover his speaking ability for themselves—and that did not take long. During his first 10 months in office, he made more than 130 public speeches and appeared on nine network television shows.

Felton West, then chief of the *Houston Post* Washington Bureau, noted at that time: "A Tower speech is usually right out of his head. He rarely ever writes one, which is hard on his public relations assistant because a speech has a better chance of getting in newspapers if texts are available. Tower does not even outline his speeches on cards to be held in hand.

"The 5-foot-6-inch former Midwestern University political science professor quickly warms up a banquet-circuit audience with quips about his height.

" 'My name is Tower, but I do not,' he often begins. Or he starts by saying he can represent Texas because he has a Texas Chamber of Commerce permit allowing him to be 'one foot less than the legal minimum height for Texans.'

"But he usually gets down quickly to the business of preaching his brand of conservatism and saying what conservatives must do to win.

"The boyish-looking Senator, exuding self-confidence, speaks with well-developed vocal chords."

West noted that Tower took pride in his "100 per cent Americans for Constitutional Action voting record rating and his zero rating from the liberal Americans for Democratic Action."

Tower's popularity as a speaker, along with his reasonable approach to national problems, his conservatism and his Texanic appeal to both the South and the West, his work on the Senate Armed Services Committee (including several trips to Vietnam), and his early campaigning for Nixon propelled him into the vice presidential picture. He took himself out of it at that 9 a.m. meeting in the Hilton-Plaza on August 8, 1968.

"I was certain I could not get the nomination," Tower explained later, "so I took my own name out of contention in order to throw more weight behind the ideas I had on other people."

He did that at the meeting in the Jackie-of-Hearts Room.

"After that," said Tower, "several of us adjourned upstairs, to Nixon's penthouse suite, to meet with Nixon. The final decision was made there, about noon."

The participants in that final meeting included Congressman Morton of Maryland, who would nominate Governor Agnew that night; Robert Finch, one of Nixon's closest friends, who later was appointed Secretary of Health, Education, and Welfare; John Mitchell, the New York lawyer and Nixon campaign director who became U. S. Attorney General; Peter Flanigan of New York, deputy campaign director; Robert Ellsworth of Kansas, a key political strategist and organizer; H. R. (Bob) Haldeman of California, who headed Nixon's personal staff, and Tower.

Tower's name came up again as a vice presidential prospect during that meeting but when it did, he quickly squelched the idea. He did, however, bring up Bush's name once more.

"I think that what eliminated George," said Tower, "was this: They figured if they were going after a Southerner to counter Wallace, they'd need a more bonafide Southerner than he was. If they were going after the more liberal element that wanted the appearance of youth and that sort of thing, they'd want a Northeasterner. So George just didn't quite fit either pattern."

He did have such obvious assets, Tower added, as a youthful, handsome appearance, excellent speaking ability and a reputation for energetic campaigning.

"He was not abrasive as far as the more liberal element of the party was concerned but he still couldn't have been regarded as a sop to the liberals in the party," said Tower.

He scoffed at the idea—widely held by Texas delegates when they left Miami Beach—that Bush's failure to remove himself from the vice presidential picture and O'Donnell's endorsement of both men strained his own relationship with Bush.

"I think there's no question but what the potential of both of us was diluted by the state's failure to associate with either one or the other," said Tower. "But, in retrospect, I don't think either one of us would have gotten the nomination, anyway. So in the final analysis, it didn't make any difference.

"Unfortunately, some people conveyed to George the idea that I had scotched his chances of getting the Number 2 spot—which I did not do. As a matter of fact, I re-introduced his name myself in the last inner circle meeting.

"George and I talked it out later, on a plane trip, and some of those who had been present in that last meeting told him the facts. There was no strain as far as I was concerned and if there was any on his part, it was due to misunderstanding. Actually, George and I have always been associated politically and we're good personal friends. I backed him for the Senate in '64. I have always regarded him as a political ally and still do. We counsel with each other regularly and we've never had any major disagreement on anything."

For two such prominent leaders of the Texas GOP, that fact in itself seems a rarity. While harmony and serenity usually prevail on the surface, undercurrents of division and dissension have boiled inwardly among the party faithful for years—mainly over strategy and philosophy, particularly in choosing candidates. Party leaders have been accused of precluding victory several times by picking "a new face," an unknown without political experience, to run against some prominent, well-known Democrat.

As one member of the Republican State Executive Committee put it in January, 1968, during the search for a gubernatorial candidate: "Some of the party leaders had rather lose with an old-guard, lifelong Republican than to win with a well-known 'convert' from the Democratic Party."

At that time, Party leaders had just received rather coolly a suggestion that they try to persuade former Congressman Kilgore to run for governor on the Republican ticket. When Ken Towery approached him on the idea, Kilgore indicated he was at least willing to consider it. O'Donnell was not at all enthusiastic about the possibility but he did invite Kilgore to meet him at the Austin Club one day to discuss it.

Kilgore told O'Donnell immediately that he could not consider the proposal seriously unless all the Republican Party leaders approved of it. When O'Donnell indicated that this might be arranged, Kilgore noted another obstacle. The Governor of Texas should be his party's leader, he said, and he could never support a GOP candidate against one of his old congressional friends, such as Mahon, Teague or Roberts.

"Under those circumstances," said Kilgore, "I don't see any way this could work."

O'Donnell, probably anxious for it *not* to work, quickly agreed.

That brought to an abrupt end a rather brilliant idea for the Repub-

licans to "draft" for governor a man whose philosophy was closely akin
to their own and who offered their best chance for success. The GOP
leaders could easily have granted "amnesty" to Kilgore when it came
to endorsing *all* Republicans and could have assured him that all they
really wanted was good government which represented their philosophy—at least until they really became entrenched in state government.

But many of them had never quite forgiven Jack Cox and Will Wilson for having once been Democrats. That was one factor which prevented either Cox or Wilson from being anointed as the GOP nominee for governor in 1968, although Cox had made three statewide races
and Wilson had served as Dallas district attorney, as a member of the
Texas Supreme Court, and as attorney general before switching his allegiance to the Republican Party.

Either Cox or Wilson would have had a headstart over Paul Eggers,
the eventual choice, in both name identification and knowledge of campaigning.

Many Republicans apparently had forgotten that Tower, their most
successful candidate, also had been a Democrat—and that he lost a
U. S. Senate race in 1960, when he was a "fresh new face." It was the
exposure he gained then that enabled him to win the special election
in 1961.

Tower had switched to the Republican Party 10 years before that.

"I decided in 1951 that being a Democrat because Granddaddy was
a Democrat was foolish," he recalled, "and that tradition had nothing
to do with the current postures of the two parties. Being basically conservative, I felt I should associate myself with the party that most nearly represented my views. And that was the Republican Party, nationally. Then, too, I think I had matured in my thinking to the extent that
I felt we should have a two-party system in our state instead of an out-
worn one-party system. My being an academic political scientist had
something to do with that."

Tower, a native of Houston, had graduated from Beaumont High
School in 1942 and then enlisted in the navy, serving aboard a gunboat.
After World War II, he earned a bachelor's degree from Southwestern
University in 1948 and a master's from SMU in 1953. He also did post-
graduate work at the University of London.

As a recent Republican convert, he ran for the State Legislature in
1954 against Representative Vernon Stewart of Wichita Falls.

"I ran against him at the end of his first term and I got clobbered,"
said Tower. "He slaughtered me—about an 8 to 3 ratio. We're still not
very strong up there but I carried Wichita County in 1966."

Tower taught at Midwestern University for nine years before his
work within the GOP led to his 1960 candidacy. Neither Bruce Alger,

then a Republican congressman from Dallas, nor Thad Hutcheson, a Houston lawyer and GOP state chairman, wanted to run against Senator Johnson, Tower recalled.

"The only reason I became a candidate was because of the paucity of candidates," he said. "I had said that I would be available if one of the better-known figures in the party didn't choose to make the race. And that I'd be glad to do it, even knowing there wasn't much chance of winning.

"We sort of felt we had a moral obligation at that time to take on Lyndon Johnson, who was then the Senate majority leader and running for reelection. He was a potential national candidate but had not been named one at that time. We felt we had to mount responsible Republican opposition. I could articulate the party line pretty well—I had been a figure in the party leadership, was chairman of the committee on education and research for the party and editor of our little monthly poop sheet, so we were all pretty well in tune philosophically. That's how I became a candidate.

"It was pretty well settled by the party leadership in advance but the actual decision was made by the state convention in McAllen on May 30, 1960," said Tower.

He had made up his mind in advance to accept the nomination.

"I've always loved politics," he said, "and I had known, since I became a Republican, that I would be fighting an uphill battle all the time so that didn't bother me. I really didn't have anything to lose. I was a $5,000-a-year school teacher. I didn't have a business or a law practice to worry about and I thought if I lost I could always get another job teaching.

"Of course, the race took on added significance after Lyndon was nominated for the vice presidency," he said. "It probably would not have been nearly so significant a race had it not been for that, because then he became a national candidate. I was campaigning not only against a U. S. Senator from Texas but the Democratic nominee for vice president and my campaign attracted more interest then," he said.

"As I got around the state and got a little more exposure, I began to attract a little more money," said Tower. "We never really had enough money to run that thing on. Toward the end of it, quite a few people decided to throw a little more money into it. We bought a lot of TV time late in the ball game. I got about 42 per cent of the vote—and got the exposure that carried me through the special election."

Johnson polled 1,306,625 votes in that senatorial race to Tower's 926,-653. Tower led a huge field in the subsequent special election, after Johnson resigned to become vice president, and defeated Blakley in the runoff, 448,217 to 437,874, despite financial problems.

"I think we raised and spent somewhere in the neighborhood of

$250,000 in that first successful race—and that was pretty much a shoestring operation," said Tower.

In 1966, Tower admitted, it was a different story. While he declined to name an overall figure, there were estimates from informed sources that his campaign involved expenditures of about $1,500,000 on the state level—and that Waggoner Carr probably also spent about that much.

"We didn't have very great difficulty raising money," Tower admitted. "I was an incumbent and a known quantity and we had what might be called 'built-in' resources. We raised a lot of money and we spent a lot of money. I'm sure my opponent spent as much as I did. As a matter of fact, he might have had even more television than I did.

"But one thing I think a politically-savvy Republican has over a Democrat in Texas, in a hotly-contested election," he said, "is that Democrats are so accustomed to running in Democratic primaries that they're not oriented to running in general elections—while we're totally oriented to general elections. Waggoner Carr ran his campaign against me like a Democratic primary campaign.

"The emphasis he put on being a Democrat, and the fact that this didn't help him any, I think is adequate evidence of the fact that people aren't any longer hidebound by the brass-collar tradition in this state," said Tower. "The Democrats are used to getting a few of the old party bosses who run various areas, lining them up and saying that's an organization. They haven't developed the technique of working precincts the way we Republicans do.

"Of course, ordinarily it is easier for them to get financing—simply because there are more of them and the 'establishment' in this state is principally conservative Democrat-oriented."

Despite this, Tower believes it "almost inevitable" that Texas will become a two-party state.

"I think that if it had not been for powerful figures like Johnson and Rayburn and their predecessors, we probably would have moved further in that direction than we have," he said.

"When they had the speakership of the House and the majority leadership of the Senate, nothing could emanate from Washington to Texas without the approval or forbearance of Johnson and Rayburn," said Tower. "I think this was one of the factors in keeping Texas a one-party state. Another is the establishment—the big businessmen, the publishers, the prominent lawyers and political leaders who have found it comfortable to have the one-party situation in which they were the dominant influence."

Johnson and Rayburn were quite effective at cutting off financing for prospective Republican opponents, he noted.

"After all, with the power they had, they didn't have to make a positive effort to discourage contributions. People just normally are not going to contribute to someone who is going up against the apex of the power triangle."

By the same token, Tower admitted, his relations with the Democratic power structure improved considerably after Nixon's election in 1968, "but it was just a continuation of the changing attitude that has existed ever since I won reelection in 1966."

"I think everybody decided then I was there to stay," said Tower. "And even though we had a Democratic President during the two years after that election, I think they came around to the idea that it was good to have some influence in both parties.

"As a matter of fact, I was able to do things for the state from time to time that a Democrat couldn't have done," he declared. "There were marginal issues on which I could influence some Republicans to vote with us—for example, on something such as the oil depletion allowance—so it was helpful for the state to have somebody in the opposition camp, even though we were the minority party in the Congress and didn't have the White House. It had some value. . . ."

Robert Baskin, in the June 15, 1969, issue of the *Dallas Morning News*, noted that Tower's workload had "just about doubled" since Nixon took office.

"Tower's stature has risen considerably as a result of the election of a Republican President," said Baskin. "And the fact that Tower was strong for Richard M. Nixon in the pre-convention period and ensuing months of last year gives him some authority when he has dealings with the White House.

"Some Texas Republicans are concerned over the fact that there have not been more Texans appointed to high positions in the Nixon administration.

"But as Lt. Gov. Ben Barnes remarked here this week the state has been 'politically spoiled' by having had a heyday of Washington power for a good many years, thanks to the prestigious positions occupied by such giants as John Nance Garner, Sam Rayburn and Lyndon B. Johnson. It's a little hard to get used to being just another state in the Union," said Baskin.

Tower discounted the theory that Texas Republicans had "muffed" opportunities during the Eisenhower years to promote the two-party system in Texas.

"It's not so much that we muffed it," he said. "It's just that Eisenhower felt more beholden to the conservative Democrats who supported him than he did to the Republicans. And Eisenhower was not politically-oriented—he was not a party-builder, because he didn't understand the party leadership responsibility the President has. He was non-political and only late in his second term did he realize that he had a party leadership responsibility.

"Our party declined in strength during the Eisenhower years nationally; we gained in Texas, but not to the extent we should have. That was a transitional period for us—going from the old, small patronage clique to the modern, rival party organization."

Tower felt that the election of Nixon would help attract more people into the Republican Party.

"As a matter of fact," he said, "a number of Lyndon's friends have told me that they feel they can now identify with us. I think the centralization of leadership power in the hands of the very liberal element nationally, in the Democratic Party, is going to drive 'em into our party, without our doing anything in a positive way to attract them."

The Texas GOP still faced the chicken-or-egg dilemma, trying to decide if you get a lot of members first and then candidates or if you recruit top-notch candidates in an effort to attract members.

"Our strategy has been," said Tower, "and I think must continue to be until we grow more, to use a 'rifle' on the opposition and pick 'em off one at a time, rather than a 'shotgun' and try to get a bunch. We've run full slates before and you just dissipate your resources without getting anywhere when you do that. For example, our running candidates for state offices below that of governor has proved to be pretty fruitless. Until we can elect a governor, I think it's going to be very difficult for us to pick off one of those subordinate offices. But we've always run slates. . . ."

Tower said he doubted that anyone else would have fared better on the Republican ticket in 1968 than Eggers did.

"He turned out to be a good personal campaigner," said Tower. "I never saw anybody who has been around Paul who disliked him. His mass media style leaves something to be desired but he's a helluva lot better personal campaigner than I am. As a matter of fact, by ordinary, objective political standards I'm not a very good one. I'm just not particularly good at the back-slapping and hand-shaking type of thing."

Jim Lehrer of the *Dallas Times Herald* noted this on Nov. 9, 1967, in discussing Tower's vice presidential possibilities and declaring that he probably was hurting himself in promoting a conservative for the presidential nomination, since an all-conservative ticket seemed unlikely.

"There are some friendly critics who say it might be just as well if Tower put his national ticket aspirations aside anyhow," said Lehrer.

"While a tireless man, they note of Tower, he is not the natural campaigner type. He doesn't enjoy 'feeling the flesh,' mixing with crowds of people and doing those many other things that a candidate on the

U. S. Senator John G. Tower receives a certificate of his initiation as an honorary member of the Montagnards, South Vietnam tribesmen famed for helping U. S. troops. The Senator has made frequent trips to Vietnam.

stump must do. He would much rather discuss things with intellectual equals in small groups.

"As a national candidate, this abhorrence for the glad-hand, the small talk and the big smile might hurt him when put under the glare of a rigorous coast-to-coast campaign," said Lehrer.

Tower admitted that "personal campaigning" seemed to come much easier to both Eggers and Bush than it did to him. He felt Bush's knack for it would be a big asset in a 1970 Senate race but, like nearly everyone else, he assumed that the Democratic nominee would be either Yarborough or Barnes.

"I must admit that I'm not entirely objective about it because I would like for George to run," said Tower. "I want us to mount a good, strong campaign. As chairman of the Republican Senatorial Campaign Committee, it's my job to recruit the best possible candidates.

"But I realize that George has a lot of things to consider," he added. "He has a spot on the Ways and Means Committee and he's the first freshman congressman to get on it in 50 years. And that's an important spot so far as Texas is concerned—especially as far as the oil industry's concerned—so it's a tough decision for him to make.

"You have to consider everything and usually you don't peg your decision on any one factor, but on a combination of factors," said Tower. "Now, if Barnes got in a bruising primary with Yarborough, and managed to beat him, he would completely alienate all the liberal element in the party without consolidating all the conservative support—because George certainly has great acceptability to that faction. He would eliminate the 'lib-labs' and probably by no means consolidate conservative support. In effect, he would be in the same position my last two opponents were in.

"On the other hand, of course, if there were a bruising primary between Yarborough and Barnes and Yarborough beat Barnes, the establishment—the conservative element in the state—would immediately consolidate behind Bush. There would be no question about it. He would have the endorsement of virtually every newspaper in the state. He would have the backing of the business and professional community.

"I think George is, by far, the strongest candidate we could offer," said Tower. "He has run one statewide race, he's a popular congressman and there was speculation about him as a vice presidential candidate in 1968. He's got a lot of moxie. He's conservative enough to be sound, so far as the average conservative is concerned, but not dogmatically conservative enough to become offensive to the more moderate or liberal element.

"The liberals," he declared, "would *not* be inclined to mount any crusades against him."

Chapter 15

BIG LEAGUE

George Bush probably weighed his decision to enter the U. S. Senate race in 1970 as carefully as any politician ever did any decision. But, despite his high intelligence, expert judgment and excellent advice, he guessed wrong—in a classic demonstration of the fact that Texas voters remain unpredictable.

Bush, of course, came out much better than do most politicians who make a wrong move. After his defeat by Lloyd M. Bentsen, Jr., Bush was appointed Ambassador to the United Nations. But even if he had known that a defeat would produce such a tremendous consolation prize, he might still have preferred to stay in the House of Representatives.

Like nearly everyone else, Bush made the mistake of assuming that Senator Yarborough would again be the Democratic nominee in 1970.

Robert Baskin, chief of the *Dallas Morning News* Washington Bureau, noted in his May 16, 1969, column that Congressman Bush seemed to be "quietly but persistently laying the groundwork for a campaign for the Senate in 1970."

"He is alert to every political situation that arises and is prepared to comment gracefully and forthrightly," said Baskin. "The 45-year-old Republican naturally would like to follow in the footsteps of his father, Prescott Bush, who served with distinction as a senator from Connecticut within the last decade. . . .

"If Bush is going to take on Sen. Ralph Yarborough in the 1970 general election, he will have to have the full support of the Texas GOP, which has a tendency to split at crucial times. And beyond that he will need a great outpouring of conservative Democratic votes to win.

"It is a matter of alarm to some Republicans that conservative Democrats have shown a tendency in the last year or two to amalgamate with the liberal wing of the party when the chips are down.

"This occurred in the 1968 presidential election when then Gov. John B. Connally, a longtime foe of Yarborough, embraced him as a friend in the last days of the campaign and swung a large body of conservative Democrats, who were inclined toward Richard Nixon, into supporting Hubert H. Humphrey.

"The developing political power of Lt. Gov. Ben Barnes is viewed as a coalescent factor for the Democrats in the general election contests. Barnes appeals to both conservatives and liberals," Baskin wrote.

"Yarborough has been in the Senate since 1957. That is enough time for a senator to acquire important seniority. The senior Texas Senator is now chairman of the Labor and Public Welfare Committee and is a member of the prestigious Appropriations Committee.

"Texas Democrats, attuned as they are to the signs of political power and traditionally appreciative of the seniority system in Congress, are going to be attentive to Yarborough's position and less disposed to go tearing off down the road with the Republicans.

"There is also apparent an instinct against having two Republican senators from Texas on the part of many conservatives. It is better, they feel, to have access to both parties, for this is built-in protection when national administrations change. It may be well and good to have John G. Tower in the Senate, they reason, but it is likewise beneficial to have even a liberal Democrat with some seniority also serving in that body.

"Thus there are complex factors to be faced by Bush when he contemplates running for the Senate next year. There are large question marks before him. At the same time, he realizes that he probably can be reelected indefinitely to the House from his Houston district. Eventually, that will bring him political power that could gain him national recognition. And who knows what that would lead to?" Baskin concluded.

It seems doubtful that it would have led to the UN, where Bush quickly made a highly favorable impression.

Bush, the All-America boy type, a handsome, dynamic young millionaire with a Phi Beta Kappa key, a fine family and a genuine love for his congressional seat, appreciated fully the complexities involved in his "now or never" decision to run for the Senate in 1970.

For many, many months Bush weighed all the factors involved in his giving up almost certain advancement in the House of Representatives to run for the Senate. He had to work, of course, on the assumption that his opponent in a Senate race would be either Barnes or Yarborough. When Bentsen came out of nowhere to upset Yarborough in the Democratic Primary, it became a whole new ball game; but, by that time, Bush already was in it.

The many similarities between Bush and Bentsen molded their race more along party lines than the Republican nominee wanted it to be. From the moment he first began considering the race, Bush tried to shape it to the idea that Texas would vote "for the man—not the party." Long before he made his fateful decision, he bemoaned the fact that many of his prospective backers could not boil the question down in their own minds simply to this: "Who would be the best senator?"

"I sometimes get frustrated," he told me one Sunday morning in mid-August of 1969, at his Houston home, "by this feeling many people have that they have 'too much at stake' in Austin to antagonize somebody by supporting me, even though they say I'd make a much better senator than Yarborough or Barnes.

"We're still in a Democratic state, of course. And we still have big-shot names who could be most helpful if they would say publicly what they tell me privately. They'll say, for instance, 'You'd be the best of anyone being mentioned, in terms of experience or ability or background—the best guy we could have in the Senate—but be careful, because you recognize that I won't be able to help you publicly. I will do what I can privately.'

"You get this kind of feeling: it's one thing to make the commitment yourself but it's another thing to get some other people to make commitments," said Bush. "This is what troubles me. And yet I understand it in a way. I mean, their lives are being regulated and controlled in Austin to a degree, and they're Democrats—although their party nationally has moved off from them. They're going through a big transition.

"The thing that fascinated me about this poll we made recently is that it showed there is considerable change taking place in Texas. There is a change away from party labels and towards voting for the man. To the degree that Nixon is popular, I think this change will be hastened in 1970.

"We polled specifically, too, on the two-Republican senator argument," said Bush. "Now, when you sit down with a group of politicians at the Forty Acres Club or the Headliners Club, they'll tell you this is a big factor. But we polled the people, not the politicians, and the poll showed emphatically this was not an issue.

"Barnes could probably make a better issue out of that than Yarborough could—but the people who made the poll say it definitely is not an issue. I hope to heck they're right. If they're wrong, and if it is an issue, then you're starting with a handicap you don't need. Of course, in a campaign, I wouldn't say we need another Republican senator—I'd say that I'd be the best man in the Senate."

That is exactly what Bush did say during the campaign—but the voters obviously reacted strongly to Bentsen's contention that Texas needed a "voice in both parties." Bentsen's conservative supporters knew this theory would rise up to haunt them in 1972 but it probably was the deciding factor in the 1970 race. And they knew they needed to exploit it in order to win.

But most of them, like Bush, did not suspect a year earlier just how potent that issue would be.

"It's flattering," Bush said during that August, 1969, interview, "for a lot of people to tell me to be careful, that they don't want to lose me from public service. Some of this comes from very close friends who think I have a good future—and it's not a case of their thinking I've gone as far as I can go and just wanting me to look after their Houston interests. It's more flattering than that. They're just saying, 'Be damned sure you can win before you get in the race.'

"I think Yarborough is tough," Bush declared. "I think he's less controversial today than he was. On the other hand, he's older. You get a postal reform bill up and, immediately, he's against it. I think my campaign would be more for change—such as implementing President Nixon's welfare program. I think I would campaign on who could bring the right kind of progress to Texas. Is it the guy who's 68 years old and kind of wed to the past and resisting change or is it the guy that Nixon would be down here to put his arm around, no matter who the opponent might be—Barnes, Yarborough, Kilgore, Locke, anybody?

"Nixon would be here and he would say, 'This is the guy I want—and we've got to have control of the Senate.' To the degree he's popular, this could be rather compelling. It might *not*, of course, because you can't assign popularity. But we underestimated the value of Johnson's putting his arm around Yarborough in 1964. And I do know that Nixon would go all-out for my candidacy."

Nixon did go all-out for Bush and may have killed him with kindness. But such a backlash did not seem even remotely possible as Bush pondered another Senate race, analyzing his earlier campaigns and noting that his entering politics now seemed as though it had been inevitable.

Born June 12, 1924, in Milton, Massachusetts, Bush was graduated in 1941 from Phillips Academy and in 1948 from Yale, where he captained a baseball team that won the National Collegiate Athletic Association's Eastern Championship twice.

He was only 18 when he won his Navy pilot's wings and a commission as an ensign at the Corpus Christi Naval Air Station. He earned the Distinguished Flying Cross and three Air Medals while serving as a World War II carrier pilot in the Pacific, before being shot down in 1944 near the Bonin Islands.

After graduating from Yale, he moved to Midland and became an oil field supply salesman, then helped form an oil development firm in 1951. Two years later, he helped found the highly successful Zapata Petroleum Corporation—but he divested himself of all his oil holdings when he was elected to Congress in 1966.

He was reelected in 1968 without opposition—a remarkable feat for a Republican in Texas.

"I always wanted to get into politics," said Bush. "In 1964, an unusual opportunity came along. It was a long shot and the odds-makers were correct. But, on the other hand, I think if I hadn't made that race for the Senate, I would never have gone to Congress. I got the feel of it and got interested in it. But I've never shared the view that

I wouldn't want to get into politics, that all politicians are corrupt. I have a much more idealistic view than that. I just think it's so important that it wasn't very traumatic for me to decide to get into it.

"I would like very much to be in the Senate," he declared. "I am ambitious and I don't mind admitting it. I don't think there is anything wrong with a politician being ambitious so long as it doesn't lead to selfishness or ruthlessness.

"I think 1970 would be the best year possible for me to run," said Bush. "If I could survive three more elections in the House, that would be 1976—the only other logical time for me to run for the Senate—and that would be 10 years on the Ways and Means Committee. I wouldn't want to give that up. I could be fourth or fifth from the top of the Committee by then—and that means a lot. I like the work on it and this really is the biggest inhibiting factor in my decision.

"But Yarborough is older, if he's the opponent; if Barnes is the opponent, you'd have a bruising primary there. Neither one of them would look as good after that. You've got an off-year, which is the best time for a Republican to get elected in Texas, and you've got a Republican President who could be awfully popular then.

"Certainly," said Bush, "that would be more of an asset than having a popular Democratic President, who won by 63 per cent, put his arm around a guy he didn't like to help perpetuate him in office.

"Nixon is awfully interested in what happens in Texas," he added. "He needs seven seats to control the Senate. I don't think anyone ought to underestimate this. He's not going to say, 'Well, Ben Barnes is a conservative and therefore I'm not going to be unhappy if he wins.' To hell with that—this is national politics, this is the big league."

Bush expressed confidence he could raise the money necessary to finance an all-out campaign against either Yarborough or Barnes. He estimated the amount at a minimum of $1,500,000 and said as much as $2,000,000 might be required. And, this time, he said, he would expect the Republican Party to furnish part of the funds although it "didn't give me a nickel" in either the 1964 or the 1966 campaign.

"But we waged a reasonably well-financed campaign in 1964," he said. "Now, part of that was pure anti-Yarborough money, since I was totally unknown. But the whole Party effort in '64—and I'm not saying it shouldn't have been—was directed toward Goldwater.

"The money *we* raised, we raised ourselves—guys who were amateurs, such as Fred Chambers of Houston, Bill Clements and Ralph Rogers of Dallas, Ike and Flo Kampmann of San Antonio. I had never been promised anything but I'm not so sure this isn't the way it ought to be. The candidate ought to be able to raise the money to finance his campaign. I think part of being the kind of guy who is going to exert leadership is the ability to raise money.

"Now, in Yarborough's case, he can get the financing because the unions come through big," said Bush. "No one should sneer at that. I think that's a credit to him—it shows he has stature. He may be in a different philosophical bed from mine but this is a 'plus' factor. By golly, when Yarborough's in there, he cries poor mouth but his campaigns are pretty well-financed. The Democratic Party of Texas is not doing that for him but he can attract the dough.

"Too often, we're naive," he declared. "A candidate for the Legislature or some other office gets beat and then wants to know where the money was. They figure all you do is throw your hat in the ring and someone comes charging in with a bunch of checks. Well, it just doesn't work that way. But I've made enough general contacts to know I could raise the money for a U. S. Senate campaign."

Bush said he had received "pretty good support" in the past from contributors in the $100 to $250 range.

"I still think of $1,000 as a pretty darned big contribution in politics," he said. "I've never seen the corporate gift and I don't really know how that works—maybe I'm *still* a little naive. Maybe they just don't like me but, from what I've seen, the corporations are a lot more scrupulous than they are given credit for being."

With complete candor, Bush admitted that the early polls showed he would lose to either Yarborough or Barnes in a 1970 race. But, he added, the early poll on his first congressional race also indicated that he would lose and yet he defeated Frank Briscoe, a popular Houston district attorney, by more than 15,000 votes.

His comments on the polls were among the things which prompted Leslie Carpenter, the Washington columnist, to describe Bush in early June of 1969 as a "unique politician."

"He is totally honest—even to the extent of volunteering information which might be politically harmful or, at least would be better left unsaid for political reasons," said Carpenter. "When Bush meets the press, he doesn't dodge questions, resort to double-talk or use that tiresome phrase, 'no comment.'

"This is not intended to suggest that other politicians lie, but most of them do duck embarrassing questions at times. The time would be rare—if it ever occurred—when Bush did."

Carpenter also noted that Bush was convinced that Johnson was responsible for his defeat in the 1964 Senate race.

"When President Johnson came to Texas and put his arm around Ralph Yarborough, that was the end of me," said Bush. "The President was and is enormously popular in Texas."

Despite that, Bush and his wife, Barbara, both admire and respect the former President and Mrs. Johnson very much.

"They were wonderful to us when I first went to Congress," Bush recalled, "and they had no reason to be. One thing that troubles me about the Johnson presidency is the personal abuse he took on the war. I can differ with him on policy—anyone can—but this left-wing stuff about 'how many kids did you kill today?' really offended me.

"The day he left Washington, I went out to the airport. I just felt that here was a guy who had served his country for 35 years, who had served with my father and was from my state. I just thought it would be courteous for me to go out there. His cabinet was there but there were only four or five members of Congress there. I later received a note thanking me and saying he would like for me to come by the ranch sometime when I was in Texas."

A lot of eyebrows were raised when Bush accepted that informal invitation several months later. Bush described the visit as "strictly social" but some political observers wondered how much significance to attach to his statement later that he did not think the former President would "get involved" in the 1970 race.

In view of 1964, this prospect—along with Nixon's assurance that he definitely *would* get involved—had to be considered encouraging to Bush.

"Our biggest mistake in '64," said Bush, "was in running without a track record—without any experience in lower office. Inexperience was important and this wouldn't be a problem in 1970.

"Our other big mistake, in retrospect, probably was in being a little too negative—talking more about what I was against than what I was for," he declared. "And I think this, to a degree, has been the disease of Republicans in Texas. We've been opposed to this or opposed to that and, as a result, we haven't identified with the people.

"I feel I would wage a different kind of campaign in 1970 against whoever the opponent happened to be and I'd feel more comfortable doing it. I feel more comfortable as an advocate than as a critic. I think people want to know what you believe in, what you're for. So I think we ran too much *against* Yarborough rather than *for me.*

"Now, maybe that was necessary then because I didn't have a track record. I had been in business. But in 1966, when I ran against Frank Briscoe, a very able fellow and very popular, we never ran against him at all. And I felt so much better about it. I didn't assail Lyndon, either, although I had very broad differences with him and still do on certain points.

"One of the secretaries who works in my office told me a while back that before she met me she didn't like me—that she had the impression I was a kind of special interest, rich, no-sensitivity, no-humor, no-concern-for-people type of person. Now, this was back in 1964 and she knew me only from my campaigning. If that was the impression I left with people, we made a major mistake because I don't consider myself that kind of person. And I think that where I did meet people—whether they were Democrats or Republicans or even Yarborough supporters—I don't think I left that impression with them personally.

"But I think the big mistake was in being too negative and I don't think it has to be that way," said Bush. "For example, Yarborough is making outrageous statements about postal reform legislation which I've supported. To me, here's a great example of where we would have a major difference.

"I think the guy who is for postal reform is for change—he's for improvement, he's for the people; and the other guy, who is flailing away at it, is for the special interests. He's for the negative—he's for not doing a thing to drag this Post Office Department into the '70s, you see. I use this as an example of how we approach things differently—not to assail Yarborough.

"To a degree, I respect him," said Bush. "I've gotten to know him and I respect certain things about him. But I think he's wrong for Texas. I think he's old and out of it. His liberalism is not tied to anything exciting but it's almost a special interest liberalism. He's not free to opt in favor of change—and I am. I am free to do that. I don't want to be classified as liberal or conservative. But I think if Nixon follows up on some of these ideas—new federalism, block grants, revenue sharing, tax credits, the kind of moderate but progressive approach to moving the country ahead—it will be a much more comfortable kind of position to be in.

"I think Nixon's going to give us something to be *for*," he added, "but I don't mean that I would be running just on being a Nixon Republican.

"I view Yarborough differently than I did before—perhaps because I've gotten to know him better. I don't view him as a wicked, mean guy or as a corrupt fellow. I don't think he's dishonest.

"In '64, I viewed him pretty much as a real left-wing guy," said Bush. "I had no understanding—and still don't—of such traits as storming out of a press conference or of getting into a wrestling match in the Senate with Senator Strom Thurmond, as Yarborough once did. I thought anyone who would let himself get so worked up might be a push-over.

"I still feel we're under-represented in this seat in the Senate. I still feel I could do a better job for Texas and for the country—but there's nothing personal in it. When Yarborough gets up and calls me names, I'm a little surprised because I haven't made up my mind to run. You know, in athletics, when a guy knocks you down a couple of times you generally say, 'Well, let's go at it.' If a guy wants a fight, he usually can get it.

"But I do think Yarborough's less controversial now than he was, partly because time has helped on some of the positions he took," said Bush.

He noted, too, that Yarborough had been "campaigning like mad" for many months.

"I want to do my job in the Congress even if I'm running," said Bush, "and that's going to be hard. I have a good attendance record, a good voting record and I've had an excellent record attending the committee meetings. I think the people in my district are entitled to this and yet if I get in the Senate race, it will really be tough to do both."

After Yarborough's defeat in the primary, Bush declared that he did not intend to make the same mistake the Senator had "of spending too much time in Washington during the campaign." As a result, he missed several important votes in the House during the summer and fall but this never became a campaign issue.

In the aftermath of the general election, some observers felt strongly that Bush had picked the wrong race and that he could have defeated Smith. Although he did not consider seriously that possibility in 1970, the thought of running for governor had crossed his mind—and it may do so again. He believes Texas cannot achieve true two-party status, which he thinks is badly needed, until the Republicans elect a governor.

"After Claude Kirk was elected Governor of Florida," Bush noted during a 1969 interview, "there were an awful lot of 'instant Republicans' down there."

He also recalled that the possibility of his running for Governor of Texas once had been suggested to him by one of the state's most influential insurance executives and financiers.

"Gus Wortham told me one night at a dinner that if I were a Democrat I'd be Governor of Texas and that he would like to see that," Bush recalled. "I told him I didn't want to make a civics speech but that I'm in politics for matters of conviction and I'm interested in national government. 'I just feel so much more at home in my party than I do in your party on the national level,' I said.

"He really paid me a high compliment and I hardly knew him at the time. Subsequently, I got to know him quite well and I have great respect for him. He's never asked me for a thing. He has a great sense of history about Texas and I've often thought about his comment—and wished we could look ahead to see if this is what would be best for Texas. But I feel strongly that I'm on the right track.

"Some people say we have two-party government, liberals and conservatives. But that's not good enough. In terms of responsive government, you need the balance in the Legislature that comes from reasonably close apportionment between parties. The people are better served with a balance there.

"Sometimes, I think if I'm going around and preaching the new federalism, and talking about decentralization and stuff, maybe I should apply myself and try to make some contribution on this level—maybe some day run for Governor of Texas. I think there's a lot to be said for trying that some day. I think it would take something like that to see if my theory is correct, that we'd get more responsive government with a true two-party system.

"It's like running for mayor of a city, in one way. You know, it's hard to get mayors like Erik Jonsson of Dallas—but if successful business-men like him are going to preach their philosophy of government around the country clubs, and if they believe in it, by golly they ought to do like he did and get in the ball game."

At that time, however, Bush was thinking only about the 1970 Senate race.

"I don't object to getting beat," he told newsmen during a May 28, 1969, press conference, "but I don't want to make a stupid decision."

When Bush and Tower visited the "Western White House" at San Clemente, California, in late August of 1969, President Nixon joined those who were assuring Bush that a decision to run for the Senate would not be a stupid one.

Bush continued his methodical assessment of the Texas political cli-mate with the help of such trusted advisers as James N. Allison, Jr., deputy chairman of the Republican National Committee and son of the *Midland Reporter-Telegram* publisher; Jack Steel, a Houston in-surance company executive, and Fred Chambers, the Houston oil man who managed his 1966 campaign.

One of Yarborough's aides ridiculed a statement by Allison in early June that the 1970 Senate nominees in Texas probably would spend $2,000,000 each on their campaigns.

"I've never seen that kind of money in a campaign and I don't expect to," said the Yarborough staff member. "The Republicans will have the newspapers' endorsements and all the money—but money is a dim-inishing return unless you've got the power with the people. I think they could pave the west side of San Antonio with all that green lettuce and would lose—but they will try."

Bush ridiculed just as vehemently a claim from the Yarborough forces during the spring of 1969 that the Republicans already had raised a $2,000,000 "war chest" for a Bush campaign. If that were true, he said with a laugh, it probably would not take him so long to make up his mind.

As it turned out, the Bush campaign probably cost between $2,500,-000 and $3,000,000. The lion's share of that went for television, prompt-ing an agonizing reappraisal of that medium's effectiveness after Bush polled only about 1,000 votes more than Eggers—when he had spent probably three times as much on television as Eggers had.

Former Congressman George Bush found his "coat over the shoulder" a trademark—and also that defeat could lead to one of history's greatest consolation prizes since Nixon appointed him Ambassador to the United Nations.

Despite the expert direction and production of Bush's television efforts, at least a few minutes of them wound up at the eleventh hour on cutting room floors—in television stations throughout the state. Bush taped and sent to the stations an impressive, 30-minute program for showing on election eve. It included four and one-half minutes of film on President Nixon's visits to Longview and Dallas the previous Wednesday.

The President, appearing with Bush and Eggers, drew huge crowds and tremendous ovations. But Bentsen had prepared well for this in advance. He said the President was always welcome in Texas but that Bush had to surrender his independence in return for the all-out invasion of the state by the Republican administration. He pictured Bush as a "coattail candidate" who would be a rubber-stamp for the administration, reiterating his oft-expressed theme that he would support the President when he felt he was right but would be free to give him responsible opposition when he felt he was wrong.

By Monday, the day before the election, the reaction to Nixon's visit was such that the Bush forces telephoned television stations which had the election eve film and asked them to delete the four and one-half minute segment depicting that visit.

The second-guessing may go on for years but, so far as Bush is concerned, not publicly. Gracious in defeat, he said on election night that he had no regrets although "I don't like coming out second."

"But the country is in good hands and the Senate is in good hands with Lloyd Bentsen," he declared. "I have a horrible problem in figuring this thing out. I can't think of anyone to blame except myself.

"Like Custer, who said there were just too many Indians, I guess there were just too many Democrats."

Chapter 16

ANATOMY OF A CAMPAIGN

The polls had been closed less than an hour on Nov. 3, 1970, when Walter Cronkite announced that CBS computers had conceded the U. S. Senate race in Texas to Lloyd Bentsen. Cries of shocked delight immediately echoed throughout the Bentsens' palatial Houston home, where scores of friends and staff members had gathered with the family to await the results of his 10-month campaign against Yarborough and then Bush.

B. A. Bentsen, the candidate's lovely wife, had been sitting beside a battery of three television sets, tuning in the appropriate sound upon any visual indication of a report on the Senate race. She jumped up excitedly just as someone declared, "It's too early for them to tell. They don't even have any returns yet."

She spotted George Christian, who was wearing a broad grin.

"George, how often are they right?" she asked.

"About 99 per cent of the time," he replied happily.

During the hubbub that followed, few of the guests were aware that CBS backed down a few moments later, saying it was too early to predict the outcome of the race. But it didn't matter; Bentsen took a lead in the first returns and stayed ahead, winding up with 53.3 per cent of the vote in a race which most observers had been insisting was a tossup.

One of those least surprised by the results was Lloyd Millard Bentsen, Jr. For weeks, he had been telling skeptical staff members that he was confident of victory and that, everywhere he went, he saw more unity and enthusiasm in the Democratic Party than he had ever seen before.

He stressed that theme shortly after 10 p.m. that night, when he appeared at the Sonesta Hotel before newsmen and celebrating supporters. He admitted frankly that he could not have beaten Bush without the help of many Yarborough backers.

"We saw people in campaign headquarters working together in the Democratic Party who hadn't walked the same side of the street in a general election for 15 or 20 years," Bentsen declared.

He added that he felt he had been a unifying force within the party and he hoped to play a similar role in the Senate, helping to bring together a divided and troubled country. After his two giant-killing accomplishments within six months, few doubted his ability to do anything he made up his mind to do.

Most newsmen were not even inclined to take him seriously when he announced on Jan. 6, 1970, that he intended to run against Yarborough in the Democratic Primary. Although he had served three terms in Congress and then retired voluntarily to enter private business, in which he spent 15 years constructing a fortune, he was not widely known when his campaign began.

Born Feb. 11, 1921, near Mission, Bentsen grew up on a farm in Hidalgo County, where his father already had attained considerable wealth. He earned a law degree from The University of Texas at the age of 21, then entered the Army Air Corps to become a bomber pilot. After 50 combat missions over Europe during World War II, he emerged with the Distinguished Flying Cross, the Air Medal with three Oak Leaf Clusters, and the rank of colonel.

At 25, he became the youngest county judge in Hidalgo County history and, at 27, the youngest member of the Eightieth Congress. After three terms without an opponent, he left to enter private business in Houston, where he built Lincoln Consolidated, a prosperous holding company specializing in banking and insurance.

During his primary campaign against Yarborough, Bentsen admitted that he was not exactly "drafted" to run but said a lot of people immediately began asking, "Who is that fellow I'm going to vote for who is running against Yarborough?"

Bentsen, with masterful timing, attacked Yarborough for endorsing the war moratorium demonstrations, for missing an important vote on school busing, for voting against Senator Everett Dirksen's proposed constitutional amendment to authorize voluntary prayer in public schools and for voting against confirmation of U. S. Supreme Court nominees Clement Haynsworth and G. Harrold Carswell.

"Did he represent your views when he voted against voluntary prayer in public schools?" Bentsen asked in devastating television commercials.

"Did he represent your views when he endorsed the war moratorium?" he asked in a TV spot showing films of violence at the 1968 Democratic National Convention in Chicago.

Yarborough cried "Foul!" and complained bitterly that Bentsen was distorting his record.

When Yarborough said his vote on the prayer amendment merely was one to preserve separation of church and state by prohibiting anyone from prescribing the terms of prayer, Bentsen countered with the text of the proposal—putting special emphasis on the last sentence:

"Nothing contained in this Constitution shall prohibit the authority administering any school, school system, educational institution or other public building supported in whole or in part through the expenditure of public funds from providing for or permitting the voluntary participation by students or others in prayer. Nothing contained in this article shall authorize any such authority to prescribe the form or content of any prayer."

Yarborough's opposition to that was difficult to explain in the "Bible Belt," where he always before had been strong. The same area found it difficult to understand his votes against Haynsworth and Carswell.

And, meanwhile, Bentsen was making points by saying the same things, no matter how monotonous they seemed to those traveling with him, everywhere he went.

Jon Ford noted in his *San Antonio Express-News* column on April 26, 1970:

"Bentsen, at 49, still as pencil slim as he was as a 23-year-old World War II pilot, is a striking, articulate, indefatigable and unflappable candidate. He looks the part of the millionaire corporation executive he quit Congress at 33 to become.

"He delivers The Speech almost casually, with infinite variations. He can recite it off the top of his head, forward, backward or from the middle. His frequent injections of humor are often so subtle that they go over the heads of his audiences which seldom burst into spontaneous fits of rapture. Yet, he is deeply impressive.

"Bentsen prides himself on laying down the same set of principles everywhere, even though his consistency sometimes gets him in hot water.

"He is perhaps at his best before an unfriendly crowd. A tiny MAYO (Mexican American Youth Organization) group applauded him in Waco when he defended his positions vigorously amid a volley of antagonistic questions. A black school teacher found he would not budge an inch in his stand for confirmation of Judge Harrold Carswell to the Supreme Court. A mixed black and white gathering in a swinging Dallas bachelor's luxurious pad gave him a generous hand after he stated his case, confessed to being rich and added:

" 'Some people can write great books. Some contribute great art. Public service is my bag. I would like to be remembered more for what I have done for people than for how much money I have in the bank.'

"He is seldom, if ever, visibly ruffled, even at the end of a (standard) 16-hour working day," said Ford.

One of Bentsen's most impressive performances during the primary campaign was his confrontation—in a Negro funeral home chapel, of all places—with the Waco school teacher who insisted that a 1948 campaign speech by Carswell "proved" he believed in white supremacy.

"Justice Hugo Black was once a member of the Ku Klux Klan," Bentsen declared, looking his belligerent questioner in the eye. "But when he got on the Supreme Court he leaned over so far backwards that those white robes turned to black.

"I believe a man can change his mind. I'm tolerant enough to believe that and to think that a man can grow. So I guess I just have more tolerance than you have.

"I have an interest in a $15 million hotel in Houston and, when we opened it, I insisted that it be integrated—just because I thought that was the right thing to do. It was one of the first major hotels in Texas to do this—so I bet a $15 million investment on integration.

"I went through East Texas last week and answered questions for whites and I was just as blunt and honest with them as I am with you," he told the Waco blacks. "My answers didn't satisfy them, either, but I told them what I believe. I am not going to give you any false promises and I am not going to give them any false promises."

Bentsen added that Yarborough had "accused me of having some money and he thinks that is wrong."

"But I left Congress in 1955," he said, "because the salary then was about $12,000 a year and my expenses serving in Congress were about $10,000.

"I have been fortunate and made some money in business and now I can afford to go back into public service. But I will be taking quite a cut in income when I go to the U. S. Senate."

Bentsen defeated Yarborough in the primary on May 2 by 92,000 votes. Among those most shocked by that development was Bush, who contended that he preferred to run against Bentsen, anyway—although his "game plan" obviously had been aimed in the opposite direction.

Bentsen was established early as a slight favorite over Bush but observers immediately began searching for some major "difference" between the two, other than their party affiliations. The similarities were striking. Both were Houston millionaires who had made their own fortunes although neither had to do so, since they came from wealthy families. Both were war heroes—and pilots who had been shot down in combat. Their philosophical views were remarkably similar. Both were handsome. Both had attractive families. Both had served in Congress. Both even loved to play tennis and were members of the River Oaks Country Club in Houston.

Ironically, both candidates were hampered to some extent on fund-raising by a widespread feeling among many well-heeled donors that "they're both good men so it doesn't matter which one wins."

That theory was attacked quite eloquently by former Governor Connally on Aug. 27, 1970, at a meeting of about 60 trade association executives in the Villa Capri Motor Hotel at Austin. He urged them forcefully to buy as many tickets as possible to Bentsen's $100-a-plate fund-raising dinner in Houston on Sept. 10.

"I told some people back in the spring," Connally said in opening his remarks, "that if they would help in the primary, we would not call on them in the fall."

He paused dramatically, looking over the crowd. Then he grinned and quipped: "But none of those people are here. I didn't tell any of *you* that. I only said that to about five people and I know who they are!"

Connally noted that many of those present did not believe him when he told them in the spring that Bentsen could win the primary.

"Some of you are inclined now to say that his opponent is a nice guy and you get along with him and it doesn't matter who wins," he declared. "Some of you are inclined to feel that you could be at home in the Republican family. But the trouble is, they won't give you a key to the house. It's not an easy family to join—and if you doubt that, just ask Jack Cox.

"You know, in the cattle business, I've learned that you generally go back five generations to establish a pedigree," said Connally. "In the Republican Party, you have to go back further than that. This isn't a group that will let in just anybody who wants to join it. If you think you can move in and have any influence with the Republican Party, you are making a bad mistake.

"And don't make a mistake about this: you may think that politics is expensive now, but the Republicans can win the governor's race or the U. S. Senate race or both. And if they win either one, the price of poker will go up. If they do, there will be contested races all up and down the line from now on, for all the legislative and congressional seats as well as for all the state offices.

"Some people talk about the advantages of the two-party system," said Connally. "But no state has had better representation in the Congress than Texas has had with Democrats."

He went on to give a rundown of the committee chairmen who would be replaced if the Democrats lost control of the Senate. With deft thrusts of sarcasm in his voice, he ran down the list again in his speech at the Sept. 10 dinner.

"Aeronautical and Space Sciences, which is slightly important to Houston and to Texas, is headed by Clint Anderson of New Mexico," he noted. "If he were replaced, Margaret Chase Smith of Maine would replace him—and I really believe Clint Anderson knows a little more about Texas and is a little more concerned about the Southwest than Margaret Chase Smith is."

On down the list he went.

"Let's take Foreign Relations. What can I say?"

A round of laughter greeted that question.

"We'd lose Senator William Fulbright of Arkansas and they'd get Senator George Aiken of Vermont—and the only difference I can see is that the President would be even further hamstrung, because then he would have a man of his own party and he couldn't criticize him like he can Fulbright."

Bush drew highly favorable crowd reactions in his campaign speeches when he said that Republican control of the Senate would remove Fulbright from his chairmanship. Bentsen responded that Bush didn't finish the story and did not tell his audiences that Aiken would be the replacement and that "there's not one iota of difference between them on their foreign affairs views."

When Vice President Agnew emphasized the Fulbright matter on his Texas visit, Bentsen suggested that he "ought to go to Arkansas if he wants to run against Fulbright."

Connally was followed on the Sept. 10 dinner program by President Johnson, whose timing in delivering a speech was never better. Johnson paused dramatically after almost every sentence as he said:

"Now, I think I should tell you that I know Lloyd's opponent in this race very well. And I'm not going to say anything ugly about him. I knew his father well. I served with his father in the Senate. His father was a Republican Senator. He sat across the aisle with the minority.

"He was from New England—I believe from the state of Connecticut. And if his son were running for the United States Senate from Connecticut, and I lived in Connecticut, and I wanted a New England Senator to represent New England, and if he would change his party and join the Democratic Party—then I would sure go down the line and support him for the Democratic nomination for Senator from Connecticut!"

Johnson went on to describe Bentsen as competent and fearless, as a man who "does what's right" and as "the Number One man for the job."

"Lloyd Bentsen is steadfast, he is a man of integrity, he says what he means, he always means what he says, and he says the same thing in every part of Texas," Johnson added. "I admire him, I respect him and I salute him."

The appearances by Connally and Johnson led Bush to charge later that he was having to fight the "Connally-Johnson machine" and "the entire Democratic establishment." Much of this came in response to Bentsen's accusation that the Republican establishment in Washington was trying to coerce and bribe Texas voters with a massive power play.

Bentsen's fund-raising dinner, ramrodded by Fred Hofheinz of Houston, who had been a strong supporter of Yarborough, proved a great success. Nearly 3,000 persons attended, providing the bulk of the funds Bentsen used for his radio and television advertising. Many of his spot announcements, however, were taped and sent to his county campaign coordinators for use as often as they could finance them locally. Most of Bentsen's newspaper advertisements were handled in the same manner and local workers also bought the time for the 30-minute question-and-answer television programs, on which viewers phoned in questions and which proved one of his best campaign weapons.

One of the most obvious differences between the two candidates during the campaign showed up in their sharply contrasting approaches to the use of television.

Bo Byers of the *Houston Chronicle* said in his Nov. 8, 1970, column that Bentsen's victory proved that " 'TV image,' no matter how skillfully developed and heavily financed, won't win for Republicans in Texas."

Said Byers:

"Few dispute the opinion that Bush, under the direction of Harry Treleaven of New York, came across in great style on the tube. Much better than Bentsen, so far as appearance was concerned.

"But you can get arguments from a good many people on whether 'image' is enough to satisfy the person trying to make up his mind how to vote.

"The Bush commercials depicted the candidate as an energetic, youthful, concerned man, dedicated to helping solve the problems that beset this nation.

"And as the TV 'spots' faded out, the Bush campaign slogan superimposed on the screen said, 'He can do more.'

"The slogan may have been part of Bush's undoing. It was a claim that you kept seeing over and over but one which the candidate never seemed to support with specific illustrations.

" 'How can he do more? In what areas? On what problems? How has he shown that he can do more than Bentsen?'

"This was the reaction of many who viewed Bush's TV image even though they conceded he 'looks great.'

"Bentsen, shorter on funds than Bush for the fall campaign, feared the Bush TV blitz might do him in. He proposed to Bush that they agree on limiting the amount to be spent for TV, but Bush turned him down.

"Bush took the position that Bentsen's heavy TV campaign in the Democratic Primary last spring was a major factor in the defeat of U. S. Sen. Ralph W. Yarborough.

"He said Bentsen had derived widespread identification with the voters through that earlier TV while Bush, of course, was holding his funds for the general election contest.

"You can't argue with Bush's refusal to hold down his TV spending since he and his strategists obviously thought TV image was their strongest weapon.

"You can argue with the desirability, from the voters' viewpoint, of having to make up your mind on the basis of how a candidate looks and acts on TV, finding little of substance on which to base your opinion.

"Bentsen's TV image was poor compared with Bush's, but he managed to convey the impression that he was talking more about issues than was Bush," said Byers.

Ironically, two of Bentsen's main issues were blown up out of proportion—by Bush. He reacted rather violently when Bentsen said his opponent had voted for the "Gun Control Act of 1968" and for the "guaranteed annual income" which was a part of President Nixon's welfare reform "Family Assistance Plan."

Bush denied that the "Gun Control Act" was a gun registration act and that the "Family Assistance Plan" was a guaranteed annual income. His denials prompted more detailed study of the Gun Control Act by State Senator Jack Strong of Longview, who discovered that it gave the Secretary of the Treasury the authority to ask any question he wanted on a form which anyone who bought a new gun was required to fill out.

The Bentsen forces pointed out, perhaps most forcefully in a press conference by Strong a few days before the election, that new guns had to be registered—and the Secretary of the Treasury could even require the purchaser to list descriptions and serial numbers of any guns he already owned.

Bush, who had antagonized right-wing Republicans with his vote for open housing, got into hot water with a much broader segment of the electorate in trying to deny that Nixon's Family Assistance Plan included a guaranteed annual income. He failed completely in his efforts to convince the voters than Bentsen had invented the "guaranteed annual income" phrase.

But the most important issues appeared to be those of "pocketbook" and independence. Bentsen kept pointing to rising unemployment, a sagging stock market, high interest rates, tight money and inflation.

"Everything that ought to be going up is going down and everything that ought to be going down is going up," he said.

Bentsen said Bush had been forced to embrace Nixon's economic policies and exploited the "independence" theme.

"I intend to support the President when I think he is right but I intend to give him responsible opposition when I think he is wrong," Bentsen repeated over and over. "The Republicans are urging you to vote for the Republican Party but I am urging you to vote for Texas."

Bentsen continually called attention to the statement by Senator Tower in 1966 that Texas "needs a voice in both parties." That battle cry undoubtedly had a tremendous effect on the Bentsen-Bush race—and it may be a haunting refrain in Texas for many years to come.

A good time was had by all when Lloyd M. Bentsen, Jr., Lyndon B. Johnson and John B. Connally got together at Bentsen's "Victory Dinner" during his 1970 campaign. The dinner financed Bentsen's radio-TV schedule.

Bentsen's constant pounding on independence and the poor state of
the economy probably deserves much of the credit for his carrying 227
of the state's 254 counties and winning by 155,334 votes out of 2.3 million.

He complained vigorously of the Republican administration's "power
play," being careful to avoid as much as possible any direct criticism
of President Nixon.

When Vice President Agnew paid visits to Lubbock, Amarillo and
Dallas, Bentsen was quick to note that he "has trouble trying to explain
the Republican idea that a Republican President needs a Republican
Congress but a Republican Governor is needed to work with a Democratic Legislature."

"The Vice President said in Dallas that it is wise to maintain a constructive adversary climate in government so the public will have an
opportunity to know what's going on," said Bentsen. "He was trying
then, of course, to get a Republican Governor elected in an overwhelmingly Democratic state. If you need a constructive adversary climate
in state government, I think you also need one in the federal government."

Bentsen complained strongly that a majority of the Republican Cabinet members were coming to Texas to "twist the arms" of voters. Surprisingly, the administration played into his hands through such incidents as Secretary of the Interior Walter J. Hickel's announcement in
Houston on Friday night, Oct. 16, that a sale of oil and gas leases on
127 tracts of submerged land off the Louisiana coast would be held on
Dec. 15. Hickel made the announcement of that governmental decision at a $50-a-plate fund-raising dinner for Bush.

Bentsen promptly labeled it "a rather crass demonstration of the Republican establishment's power play—its attempt to coerce and bribe
Texas voters into giving the Republicans both of our votes in the Senate."

This came just a few days before Bentsen discovered that White
House staff members had been telephoning Democratic campaign
workers, and probably other Texans, in an effort to switch their support
to the Republicans.

"We have proof," Bentsen declared in a Houston speech, "that at
least two different assistants to Harry Dent, President Nixon's top political aide, are calling Democratic campaign workers in this area in
an obvious effort to intimidate them.

"They say they are 'calling from the White House to let you know
how interested the President and Mr. Dent are in the campaign.' They
urge our workers to vote for George Bush to help the Republicans win
control of the Senate and for Paul Eggers because a congressional redistricting bill will have to be passed next year.

"I think Texans resent this type of pressure from White House aides," Bentsen said. "The President has every right to campaign for his party, and they expect this, but they don't appreciate sledgehammer politics of this nature. It is beneath the dignity of the Presidency for the White House to be used in such tactics."

On Nov. 1, Margaret Mayer noted in her *Dallas Times Herald* column:

"Democrat Lloyd Bentsen hit a nerve when he berated the White House for using its long distance lines to call campaign workers in Texas on behalf of Republican candidates.

"Republican George Bush's office wanted to know who was responsible for the calls and learned they were inspired by GOP gubernatorial candidate Paul Eggers.

"Not satisfied to limit the telephone effort to Eggers, the composer of the White House message advised Texans that anything they could do for Eggers would also help Bush," said Miss Mayer.

There were repercussions, too, from a report shortly before President Nixon visited Texas that Bush might be his running mate in 1972 if he won the Senate race. That idea was planted by White House sources with David S. Broder, a highly respected columnist for the *Washington Post*, in an obvious effort to enhance Bush's election prospects. It backfired, however, and aroused great resentment among Agnew fans, who were appalled at the idea that he might be ditched in '72.

Bentsen fielded that rumor cleanly on the first bounce and threw it back with the brief statement that, "We are trying to elect a U. S. Senator to represent Texas for the next six years—not another speechmaker for the Republican Party."

The vice presidential report prompted Leslie Carpenter to write in his column:

"Some cheap political award should be given for the absolute originality of that desperate effort to influence the outcome of a single Senate contest.

"Take note of the immediate results:

"(1) It sent Agnew's enthusiastic admirers throughout the nation—most of whom have never heard of Bush—reeling.

"(2) It must have sent Agnew, who has put up with a lot of traveling everywhere, reeling.

"(3) It must have sent Texas's senior senator, Republican John Tower, reeling. Tower, first of all, is the man most responsible for electing a GOP Senate as chairman of the Senate Republican Campaign Committee. Tower, second, was one of the most industrious and effective Nixon promoters at the 1968 GOP National Convention—to whom a 'thank you' has never arrived in more than words. And Tower, third, is a Texan loftily outranking Bush within the GOP. Tower could well expect to be mentioned for the 1972 vice presidency before any other Texan.

"(4) It caused Texas voters to wonder how independent a senator they'd have in Bush—with him already heralded for the 1972 vice presidency if he spent two years as a senator on good behavior. He could hardly function as more than a White House errand boy if he expected the No. 2 spot on the national ticket to become a reality," said Carpenter.

The "Agnew issue" probably hurt Bush on both ends of the political spectrum. Agnew fans resented the idea of his being ditched and his visit to Texas on behalf of Bush antagonized many Negro voters, who dislike him intensely, prompting them to turn out in force and vote the Democratic ticket.

In Fort Worth, for instance, sound trucks toured Negro neighborhoods just before the election to spread the word that "a vote for George Bush is a vote for Spiro Agnew." Democratic candidates rolled up margins of about 9 to 1 in those areas.

The voter turnout really was the greatest imponderable factor as election day neared. Nearly everyone agreed that Bentsen would win if as many as 50 per cent of the state's 4,149,250 voters went to the polls. Crisp, clear weather throughout the state helped produce a total vote of 2,297,802, when inclement weather might have kept enough people home to reverse the results.

Bentsen had expressed confidence he could win with a turnout of 1,800,000 but said he would be "on thin ice" if only 1,600,000 voters cast ballots. His efforts to stimulate a big vote were aided immeasurably by his family, which did a magnificent campaigning job throughout the year.

Bentsen's wife, B. A. (for Beryl Ann), traveled the state almost constantly for 10 months, making a big hit everywhere she went. Their older son, Lloyd M. Bentsen III, 26, took a leave of absence from his job in a brokerage firm to serve as finance director for the campaign. Their younger son, Lan Chase Bentsen, 23, left his studies at the Harvard Business School to work in the campaign and proved to be such a popular speaker that he spent the last three weeks of the campaign on a rigorous speaking tour. Their daughter, Tina Ann, a student at Southwestern University, developed "a sore thumb from tacking up posters on weekends," Bentsen proudly told his audiences.

He also quipped every once in a while, in describing his family's total involvement in the campaign, that his wife was traveling in another part of the state "but I saw her just the other day—she looked great."

Bentsen himself worked so hard that his staff members and his family became concerned over his hectic pace. He and the family (except Lloyd III, who felt he should stay at home and sell tickets to the fund-raising dinner) took a week's vacation in late August for a fishing and hunting trip to Alaska. But, except for that, the Democratic nominee refused to take a full day off at any time during the campaign—insisting that as long as he had half a day once a week to play tennis he could maintain his 16-hour-a-day pace.

That inspired similar efforts from his staff and especially from his state campaign manager, John Mobley. He took off three days immediately after the primary but otherwise maintained unbelievable hours, seven days a week.

Mobley, a 40-year-old former legislator who had worked on Governor Connally's staff, was chosen to head the campaign largely as a result of the enthusiasm he displayed when Bentsen came to Austin during the Christmas holidays in 1969.

Christian and Joe Kilgore arranged a small, private luncheon at the Headliners Club for Bentsen, to discuss the possibility of his running against Yarborough. Among the guests were Wade Spilman, Governor Shivers, Nash Phillips, Gary Morrison, Robert C. McGinnis, George D. Byfield, James W. Wilson and Mobley.

While Shivers told Bentsen he didn't think he could win (which was what President Johnson had told him), Mobley was one of those who exuded optimism. He expressed the opinion that Yarborough was vulnerable and had never had a tough test.

A few days later, Bentsen called him and asked him to take over the monumental task of organizing a statewide campaign.

"When I first started calling people to ask them to serve as county coordinators," Mobley recalled, "a lot of them would say, 'Lloyd who?' "

The fact that Bentsen was not widely known undoubtedly helped lure Yarborough into a false sense of security. He apparently did not begin taking Bentsen seriously until it was too late.

And, all the while, Bentsen's organization and his own campaign techniques were improving.

Art Wiese of the *Houston Post* State Capitol Bureau noted in an article on Nov. 1:

"As a campaigner, Bentsen has improved mightily since his bruising primary fight with Yarborough. Once considered to have a stiff-necked, aristocratic image, he now makes speeches in his shirtsleeves, uses gestures well in his talks and projects better on television.

"Bentsen, pencil-thin and handsome in a craggy manner, still is not as engaging or boyishly enthusiastic as Bush but his serious, issue-oriented style stands up well in comparison.

"On a personal level, Bentsen seems intelligent, sincere and articulate—and most, most conservative. He prefers to call himself a moderate, however, and some of his staff members insist that, if elected, he would be a middle-of-the-road Democrat similar to Senate Majority Leader Mike Mansfield of Montana.

"Wherever he campaigns, Bentsen hits the same issues—crime, drug abuse, campus violence, pollution, gun control (which he opposes) and welfare reform (which he favors in some other form than that proposed by President Nixon) . . . .

"As the campaign closes, Bentsen finds himself the beneficiary of a fragile coalition of the Texas Democratic Party's left and right wings. He and his staff are not without worries in the final hours before election day. . . ."

Few people realized that one of the principal worries among his family and staff members was a series of threatening telephone calls which had been received. The first two came to the Bentsen home 10 days before the election. Twice that day, Mrs. Bentsen answered the telephone and was told by an anonymous caller: "Your husband is going to be killed before the election."

Bentsen was inclined to dismiss the calls as coming from a crank but Mobley insisted on reporting them to Department of Public Safety authorities. They said that 99 per cent of such calls, particularly during political campaigns, do come from cranks—but you can never be sure which ones will wind up among the other one per cent. They assigned plain-clothes men to guard Bentsen during the remainder of the campaign.

After reporters covering the Bentsen campaign spotted two Intelligence Agents and began asking questions, they were told of the threats but asked to minimize publicity on them. Bentsen shrugged off the threats with a comment that "everyone gets those." A DPS spokesman noted that other candidates, including Bush, had received protection at various times during the campaign.

The alarming incident furnished one more reason, however, for Mrs. Bentsen to be overjoyed when the long, arduous campaign finally ended. She obviously was most grateful that those 99-to-1 odds prevailed on both the evaluations by CBS of early election returns and by the DPS on the telephone calls.

And it may have seemed a bit ironic to recall that most people figured the odds were about 99 to 1 against her husband when he announced his candidacy 10 months earlier.

Chapter 17

THE OPEN DOOR

A bitterly cold north wind battered Dolph Briscoe's rambling Catarina ranch house one December night in 1961 while, inside, Eugene Locke and Ben Barnes spent much of the evening on their hands and knees, poring over maps spread on the floor.

Barnes thought it was a waste of time. But as a 23-year-old freshman legislator, he hardly felt himself in a position to challenge the ideas of one of the state's richest lawyers, a man whom John Connally had just appointed his state campaign manager.

"In fact, I didn't understand why in the world I was even there," said Barnes. "I had received a telegram in DeLeon the day before inviting me—and that caused quite a stir, by the way, because they don't get a lot of telegrams in DeLeon."

The meeting had been called to plan Connally's strategy in his 1962 race for governor. Barnes was greatly impressed by the presence of such prominent people as former Congressman Lloyd Bentsen, Robert Strauss, Ted Connell of Killeen, John Peace of San Antonio, Cecil Burney of Corpus Christi, Herb Petry and Frank Erwin.

Connally introduced Barnes as "the brightest young man" he had ever known. He praised his "political savvy" and predicted he would go far in politics.

"As it turned out," Barnes recalled, "I was the only one down there who knew anything about the Legislature or about the state issues. They were all talking about how Price Daniel probably wasn't going to run for reelection. I took a strong position and told 'em I'd guarantee them Daniel was going to run. Connally said, 'I've got his word he's not.' But I still said I was positive he would run.

"Locke decided he was going to run Connally's campaign not on the usual county-by-county basis but on a 'shopping' area basis," said Barnes. "He had me down on the floor helping him divide the state into shopping districts and we were arguing about whether the people in certain counties shopped in one town or another. He's a great guy but I thought that was ridiculous.

"That was the first time I'd ever met Erwin but I liked him immediately because he was very outspoken. About 3 o'clock in the morning, he told Locke it was a dumb idea.

"Connally already had gone to bed and so had just about everyone else. In fact, all the warm beds were taken when we finally went to bed and we had to sleep on the screened-in porch—and it was cold. We had just crawled into those cots when the hunters started getting up and making a lot of noise," he added.

Barnes had met Connally for the first time about a month earlier, at a Texas Manufacturers Association dinner in Fort Worth. About that same time, he accepted an invitation from Charles Woodson, publisher of the *Brownwood Bulletin,* to introduce Connally at a December luncheon in Brownwood.

"After that luncheon," said Barnes, "we got in a car and that was Connally's first real day of campaigning. We went over to Bangs and saw some Negro leaders and then went to Comanche. He had a couple of military aides with him and I finally told them to get some paper and start writing down names. I started rattling off names to them and those were the first ones that went into John Connally's political card file."

The card file, containing names, addresses and pertinent political information, is a necessity for any successful politician. It is essential in such routine matters as addressing Christmas cards and in permitting staff members to dictate replies to letters with the proper salutation, such as "Dear John" or "Dear Mr. Doe." Barnes began building his own card file a short while later and, by the time he became lieutenant governor in 1969, had more than 100,000 names in it.

He told Connally that afternoon in Brownwood he would help him during the 1962 campaign. That night, Barnes returned to Austin and met with Representative Byron Tunnell of Tyler, whom he already had helped launch a campaign for the speakership of the Texas House of Representatives—and whose political fortunes, along with those of Connally, were to play a major role in his own.

It was his campaigning for Tunnell, said Barnes, which first kindled his interest in trying to go higher than the House of Representatives—and convinced him that he could.

Speakers are elected by their fellow House members. During recent years, it has become customary for candidates to collect "pledge cards" from their colleagues as much as two or even four years in advance. As a result, except in rare instances, the winner is known long before each regular session convenes, in January of odd-numbered years, and the actual election on opening day is merely a formality.

"I became convinced while campaigning for Tunnell that I knew how to run a speaker's race," said Barnes. "When I learned how to get members' pledge cards, I decided I could become Speaker of the House."

He already had displayed some of the skill for backroom negotiations which has made many observers compare him with Lyndon Johnson. Tunnell was one of four candidates—along with Representatives Robert Hughes of Dallas, Will Ehrle of Childress and W. T. Oliver of Beaumont—in the speakership race in 1961. There seemed to be little fundamental difference in their political philosophies, Barnes decided, and he finally managed to get the four of them together in a room at Austin's Commodore Perry Hotel to settle the matter.

Barnes, then serving his first term in the House, had pledged his vote to Ehrle. The hotel room meeting started with a showdown of pledge cards which eliminated both Ehrle and Oliver early in the game. Tunnell and Hughes still had almost equal strength after that but neither relished the idea of an all-out, cut-throat campaign.

They finally drew straws to determine which would quit the race. Thus, a bit of chance and a lot of help from Barnes put Tunnell in the speaker's office when the 58th Legislature convened in January of 1963.

"The first night we campaigned," Barnes recalled, "we met a guy and got to talking to him and I finally convinced him that Tunnell was going to be the next speaker. I told him he had a chance to have the honor of being the first contributor—and he donated $100. Byron said he knew then we were going to win because he could see that I'd be able to talk those members into signing pledge cards.

"We spent all summer working on Tunnell's race. We had several special sessions, so that gave us a good opportunity. Tunnell would meet with 'em and give 'em a pitch, then go on and I'd put the 'hard sell' on them and get a card out of them," said Barnes. "That's where I really became fascinated with politics."

Tunnell quickly collected enough pledge cards for reelection in 1965 and Barnes began soliciting pledges of his own for January, 1967. But political lightning struck on Friday, Jan. 8, 1965, when Connally announced his appointment of Tunnell to the Texas Railroad Commission to fill the unexpired term of the late Lt. Gen. Ernest O. Thompson, whose failing health prompted him to resign after a distinguished career.

Tunnell telephoned Barnes at 7:30 a.m., two hours before Connally's announcement, to tell him about it. Barnes immediately established a command post in Austin's historic Driskill Hotel for a 36-hour blitzkrieg which was to make him, at the age of 26, Speaker of the House. One hundred two of his colleagues already had signed cards pledging to vote for him in 1967. All day and all night, he phoned them and other House members soliciting their votes for the next Tuesday. By Saturday afternoon, Barnes was assured of becoming the youngest speaker since 1870 and the second youngest in history.

Connally made his victory possible, of course, by appointing Tunnell to the Railroad Commission but received undue credit for Barnes's winning the necessary pledges. Actually, Connally's powers of personal persuasion with legislators never seemed to match those of

Barnes—who won his spurs in that league the hard way, as a door-to-door salesman of vacuum cleaners.

That was one of several jobs he held, before earning his business administration degree from The University of Texas, which helped shape his moderate political philosophy. He also baled hay, hoed peanuts, mined molybdenum in Colorado, drove a creamery truck, worked in a law office, raised cattle and worked as a punch card machine operator.

It seemed almost incredible that, less than a decade after he had slaved in such unglamorous jobs, Barnes had become one of the most powerful politicians in Texas and one being mentioned as a potential President of the United States.

Dennis Farney, in the May 14, 1969, issue of the *Wall Street Journal*, noted that "he's the hottest property in Texas politics and political observers wonder whether he's 'another LBJ.' "

"Some powerful Texas backers," wrote Farney, "see him as the man who potentially could recapture some of the state's recently lost influence in national political affairs."

He said Barnes already had become a rarity in politically turbulent Texas.

"Here, where the liberal and conservative wings of the dominant Democratic Party still wage bitter, unrelenting warfare, Mr. Barnes currently enjoys support from both groups," said Farney. "His natural power base is the conservative oil-business financial complex that supported ex-Gov. John Connally and Lyndon Johnson before him. Already, under the patronage of a Texas contractor and others, Mr. Barnes's financial worth has grown dramatically with little effort on his part.

"But despite these associations, Mr. Barnes has won substantial liberal support by solidly backing such programs as a state minimum wage and improved anti-pollution laws. Perhaps prematurely, he is regarded as the man who just might do the near-impossible: Unite the emerging Texas left with the old conservative wing.

"Last fall, the *Texas Observer*, a liberal journal published every two weeks, concluded that Mr. Barnes 'has become, perhaps in ways Lyndon Johnson never did, in Texas, the consummate consensus politician.' Declares a liberal state senator: 'I wouldn't be a bit surprised to see Ben Barnes someday as vice president or president. I think he's got Lyndon Johnson's characteristics and abilities better than Johnson has.'"

Barnes was born on April 17, 1938, in Gorman and raised on his father's farm at nearby Comyn, between DeLeon and Dublin. He became a football star at DeLeon High School but had to turn down several college football scholarship offers because of a back injury—which finally necessitated corrective surgery in February, 1969.

Barnes attended TCU for one semester before marrying his high school sweetheart, Martha, on Feb. 22, 1957. He later attended Tarleton State College and then transferred to The University of Texas, where he sometimes worked 50 hours a week as a punch card machine operator while carrying a full load of courses. At the same time, he sold vacuum cleaners at night and on weekends.

"It's a good thing he finally quit that," a friend remarked later. "If he hadn't, every house in Austin would have at least two vacuum cleaners by now."

Barnes found the experience as well as the money most valuable.

"I'll never forget the insults and abuse I took as a door-to-door salesman," he recalled. "And you can be sure of this: I'll never be rude to any salesman who knocks on my door. It was really a great experience because I learned a lot about human nature—and I developed a thick hide, too. And you've got to have that in politics.

"But it took a lot of shoe leather," he added. "The company I worked for figured you had to average about 30 calls to get one opportunity to demonstrate the cleaner. And for every three demonstrations, you could figure on making one sale. You've really got to be a great optimist to sell vacuum cleaners. But I managed to do all right at it."

Barnes was optimistic enough to borrow $500 from a bank to post as a deposit on his initial consignment of vacuum cleaners. After he paid that off quickly, he borrowed $1,000 to buy eight head of cattle to put on his father's farm. Thus, he realized early the value of being able to borrow money for investment opportunities—many of which come to the attention of almost anyone who associates regularly with the rich and the near-rich.

"His rise in the political world has been so spectacular," *Texas Parade* noted in January, 1969, "it has overshadowed the steady progress he has been making at the same time in business. . . .

" 'Politics has helped me gain a reputation,' said Barnes. 'That, plus the fact that I've always tried to pay my bills on time and build up a good credit rating, has enabled me to borrow some capital to invest—and every young man has to do that if he's going to be successful in business.'

"Barnes now owns interests in a Brownwood construction firm, an apartment house, two radio stations and three motels—having borrowed the money to invest in all those projects," noted the *Texas Parade* article. "His political opponents have gone so far as to hire private investigators in unsuccessful efforts to find any evidence that he has used political influence in furthering his business interests. All they have found is that he has displayed the same type of judgment, talent and hard work in the business field that he has in politics.

"His main business partner, Herman Bennett of Brownwood, has been urging him for some time to quit politics.

"'If you would devote as much time to business as you do to politics,' he keeps telling Barnes, 'you could make us both a lot of money.'"

Barnes met Bennett during his first campaign for the Legislature, in 1960. He walked up and introduced himself, in the Brownwood post office, to solicit Bennett's vote. The two quickly became friends and Bennett later sold Barnes—on credit—an interest in his Brownwood contracting firm. Barnes helped reorganize the company and make it more profitable, even though they passed up much potential business by refusing to bid on state contracts while Barnes was in public office.

But when one of Barnes's friends complained in 1964 of a housing shortage at Howard Payne College in Brownwood, he heard opportunity knocking; after looking over the situation, Barnes persuaded Bennett to join him in building a 36-unit apartment house there. Every unit was rented even before the building was completed and the project was enlarged a short while later.

Meanwhile, Barnes disclosed that his political expenses—such as travel for speaking engagements—were being paid primarily by "Ben Barnes Clubs." He said 168 residents of his four-county district were contributing $10 a month each toward this fund and that the money was used strictly for political purposes, not for personal expenses.

The same idea was used by Congressman Jim Wright of Fort Worth, who later recommended it to the Democratic National Committee. It was designed to alleviate the need for an ambitious officeholder to spend his own money paying his political travel expenses. Barnes felt it better to have such expenses paid by a great many people contributing $10 per month each than by a few people paying a great deal more.

During the early part of 1969, Barnes passed up at least five fantastic offers to quit politics and devote full time to business. One of these would have involved moving to New York, one to Denver and the other three to Dallas. Any one of the five undoubtedly would have required far less work, ingenuity and skill than organizing, financing and carrying out the type of statewide campaign usually necessary to win one of Texas's top political offices. But after receiving a record-breaking 2,037,587 votes in his first statewide race in 1968 and, at the age of 30 becoming the youngest lieutenant governor in Texas history, Barnes could hardly be expected to seriously consider getting out of politics.

Instead, he resumed a full schedule of speeches—frequently making as many as 10 or 12 a week—almost immediately when the Legislature's second special session ended on Sept. 9, 1969. Before that, during the interval between sessions, he went to Tokyo to address the Lions International convention early in July. Even that journey failed to attract as much attention, however, as a brief speech Barnes made at an appreciation dinner for Senator Yarborough in Dallas on Thursday night, Sept. 25, 1969.

Raymond D. Nasher of Dallas, honorary chairman of the event, announced several days earlier that Barnes had accepted an invitation to speak at the dinner. Barnes denied this. He said he had not been invited to speak at the dinner honoring his potential rival and that he had a long-standing, conflicting engagement to speak at another affair in Dallas the same night.

Senator Mauzy had invited him, however, to "drop by" the Yarborough dinner and shake hands if he had time, Barnes said. Speculation on whether or not he would appear added a dramatic element of suspense to the affair, with many observers watching for a tipoff that Barnes perhaps had decided not to run against the Senator.

Mauzy took elaborate precautions to make sure Barnes found time to attend. He got a deputy sheriff to drive him to the Marriott Motor Hotel, where the Lieutenant Governor spoke to another group, and then whisk them to the Dallas Memorial Auditorium, where 2,500 people—at $10 per head—had gathered to honor Yarborough.

Congressman Earle Cabell of Dallas was speaking when Barnes arrived—trailed by local newspaper, radio and television newsmen who had shadowed him all afternoon, anxious to find out if he would appear and speak—at the Yarborough dinner. A buzz of excitement, and then applause, swept through the crowd, interrupting Cabell's remarks.

When Barnes was called upon to speak a few moments later, he made it short and much sweeter than the sponsors might have expected.

"I want to thank Mr. Nasher," he began, "for letting me be publicity chairman for this event. Senator Yarborough, if I knew I would get this much publicity, I'd come to all your dinners."

Barnes then politely praised Yarborough for "daring to dream 'The Impossible Dream' that all the people can have an equal opportunity in life."

"I think this is what the Democratic Party stands for in Texas and in America," Barnes declared. "The Democratic Party has a very fine warrior in Senator Ralph Yarborough—and Texas has a very fine citizen, a very fine senator in Ralph Yarborough."

Thus did Barnes extricate himself, without surrendering any ground or potential campaign issues, from what could have been a sticky situation. And he did nothing to reveal his political intentions.

Many felt that the die had been cast, however, when Barnes endorsed a proposal, during the Legislature's first special session in August of 1969, to repeal the sales tax exemption on groceries.

This resulted from a deadlock between the House and Senate on placing beer and liquor under the sales tax. With Speaker Mutscher staunchly opposing any move to raise the tax on beer, Barnes finally asked him under what conditions he would consider raising it.

"I'm not going to be for it unless we put food under it, too," said Mutscher.

Senator Tom Creighton of Mineral Wells immediately asked if he would agree to putting the sales tax on beer and liquor if it were also applied to food. Mutscher said he would.

Creighton then phoned Governor Smith, who said he would be happy to endorse such a bill—which would raise enough money to solve the state's financial problems easily. But when the House-Senate conference committee, which was to present the measure as its "compromise" version of the tax bill, met with Smith, Barnes and Mutscher in an open session, Smith balked, saying he did not know anything about it.

He refused to endorse the bill other than to say he would sign it if it passed. That prompted Senator Strong, a member of the committee, to call the Governor "a liar."

Barnes drew an imaginary line on the floor of his office later that night, in mock reminiscence of the scene at the Alamo in 1836, and asked any of the 15 senators who wanted to repudiate their pledged support of the food tax proposal to step across it. None did. The "food tax" finally won Senate passage, 15-14, after a determined filibuster quarterbacked by Mauzy, but the talkathon won enough time to provoke a deluge of taxpayer objections. As a result, the House killed the measure, 147-0.

That put what some felt was the biggest scar of his career on Barnes's record, prompting speculation that it might even be large enough to keep him from running against Yarborough. Barnes expressed little concern over that, saying Yarborough would not be able to "breathe life into a bill that didn't pass."

Barnes admitted that he would be more concerned, in a race against Yarborough, over his own hawkish attitude on Vietnam and his support for the policies of both Johnson and Nixon on it—at a time when the public appeared to be swinging more toward the dovish inclinations of Yarborough. The Senator had begun denouncing the war, after earlier supporting Johnson's policies.

Meanwhile, many conservative Democrats were urging Barnes to run against Smith in order to keep the liberals from capturing control of the state party machinery. They felt this could be disastrous during the 1972 presidential nominating conventions. Smith never had displayed much interest in intra-party politics and they feared his reelection would permit the liberals to take over almost by default and "run the moderates out of the party."

Gov. Preston Smith, left, and Lt. Gov. Ben Barnes confer with each other while sitting on the rostrum, with other dignitaries, at a joint session of the Legislature.

While Johnson much preferred to have someone like Barnes in control of the party machinery, he reportedly felt that a young man of such unusual ability belonged in Washington because it offered the greatest opportunities for both public service and personal achievement. He purportedly told one of his friends that Barnes's prospects were so bright that if he went to the Senate in 1970 he "might be running the country in another 10 years."

Jon Ford of the *San Antonio Express-News* noted in his Oct. 19, 1969 column:

"The lights burned brightly in the penthouse atop former President Lyndon Johnson's family television station one early evening last week.

"Downstairs at the curb stood the stylish new $6,500 sedan of Lt. Gov. Ben Barnes, with his faithful million-mile traveling companion at the wheel.

"Inside the LBJ penthouse, it can be assumed, Barnes was beneficiary of some battle-tested political counsel not available to many rising young state officeholders these days....

"The timing of the latest visit is interesting, to say the least, since Barnes has made no secret of the fact he is in the painful process of making the most important decision of his life."

Barnes would have to decide within the next three months, Ford noted, whether to run for the U. S. Senate, for governor or for reelection.

"Barnes's dilemma—one which most politicians would give their right arms to be on the horns of—has been somewhat over-publicized," said Ford. "His 'trouble' is all his soundings keep producing 'win' blips on the situation board—no matter what the situation.

"The Lieutenant Governor is reasonably assured that he would have Gov. Preston Smith all to himself in the Democratic Primary if he wants to book that fight. Uvalde rancher Dolph Briscoe reportedly would not get into a Smith-Barnes primary contest. Barnes is increasingly convinced the 'second term tradition' would not save Smith in a real shoot-out.

"Polls show him running well against U. S. Sen. Ralph Yarborough. And as for splitting the Democratic Party by attacking the senior senator, Barnes is now about to decide the party would split anyway during the next presidential year if he were governor and Yarborough still senator, since both would be battling for control of the state's nominating convention delegates.

"If Barnes were offered either job unopposed, it now seems obvious he would not hesitate to declare for the Senate... Johnson, whose entire political career was geared to Washington, could hardly be expected to do less than applaud Barnes's adventurous, move-along spirit.

"Before the final decisions are made, it would not be surprising if

Yarborough did not hear once more that familiar suggestion that he run for governor himself.

"When the idea was last seriously proposed two years ago, Yarborough said he gave it serious thought. He dropped it, he said, because he could accomplish more nationally in the Senate where he has 12 years' seniority. At the same time, he observed, he could do more for Texas in a year as governor than two as senator," noted Ford.

There was speculation that Barnes might have more difficulty raising the money to finance a campaign in 1970 against Smith, since that would split the conservative forces, than against Yarborough. This would be partly offset, however, by the liberal support he would gain in a race against Smith—while running against Yarborough would alienate the liberals, perhaps permanently.

As he wrestled with his decision, Barnes did not seem to be unduly worried about raising the necessary campaign funds for either race although he admitted that financing is the first major hurdle in any campaign.

"There's a real art to raising money," he said. "It's a difficult art to master and I'm a long way from mastering it. But I do know that one of the main things you have to do is to sell potential contributors on your ability to provide leadership.

"It's not uncommon, in political fund-raising meetings, to have three or four people planted in the audience who will get up and say they are going to give $5,000 or maybe $1,000 or $500—just to get the ball rolling. When some people start giving in front of other people, all of them are inclined to give.

"You've got to get the people together and the candidate has to sell them," he declared. "Personally, I have a policy that I'm never present when they give their money. Oh, sometimes during a campaign someone will come up and stick a check in my pocket, but what I usually do is make my pitch, talk about the issues and what we have to do in our state, and then leave. Then my campaign manager or some of the other workers take it from there."

Barnes, like Smith and other successful politicians, insists that it is not difficult to get large contributions without becoming committed to the contributors personally.

"With a few exceptions, and there are some, most of the people who give you the most money you never hear from again until the next campaign," said Barnes. "Most of them really just want good government and a candidate who shares their political philosophy.

"I'm really an outspoken advocate and admirer of the so-called 'establishment,'" he added. "I had a fellow from San Antonio, Doug Sanders, who's in real estate and the construction business, who probably gave me a total of $5,000 during my 1968 campaign. He and his wife came up here for the inauguration and I shook his hand. Then, a little later, his son came to the office one day and I invited him in to have a cup of coffee with me. And when they had a luncheon for me at HemisFair, I invited him and he brought his younger boy with him. I got a nice letter from him about the time the regular session ended telling me what a great job he thought I'd done, and thanking me for what I'd done for San Antonio.

"Now, those have been my only contacts with him since the campaign. He's just interested in good government. We met in 1966, when he came by a reception for me and then went to lunch with several of us. We've gotten to be good friends since then but we hardly knew each other when he first started backing me. But he's never asked for a thing.

"I'd say that ninety per cent of the people who gave me money—I'm talking about the big contributors—I haven't heard from since the campaign. Oh, some people will give you $100 or $50 and then worry you to death, wanting you to get them football tickets or appointments or jobs for fifteen or twenty relatives. But usually, the bigger the people are, the less they're going to ask you for," said Barnes.

He cited Gus Wortham, the Houston insurance magnate, as another example of a man who had contributed "probably several thousand dollars" to his campaign but had never asked for anything.

"I know he had an insurance bill that he wanted passed pretty badly but it met with a lot of opposition and was killed," said Barnes. "He never did even contact me about it.

"George Brown has called me one time since I've been lieutenant governor. He just said he hoped I would help pass the bill to let the College Coordinating Board contract with the Baylor Medical School to train medical students because he didn't want to see the school lost. He said he had put over one million dollars of Brown Foundation money into it and knew they really had financial problems. But he would never call me on a contractors' bill or anything that affected his own business.

"Pat Rutherford gave me some money and also gave Preston some money during the 1968 campaign," said Barnes. "He called me during the regular session to ask if he could do anything to help on passing the one-year budget. He just said he thought it was a good approach.

"Now, there are always going to be people like Billie Sol Estes," Barnes added. "One fellow wanted to give me $5,000 but said if I was elected governor he wanted to be appointed to the University of Texas Board of Regents. I told him I was sorry, that I couldn't take his money because I wasn't going to make that kind of promise.

"You'll find maybe one out of a hundred who are like that," he said.

"But I really believe that most of the big contributors in politics are unselfish people."

Oil men generally are overrated as campaign contributors, said Barnes, and the lobbyists are the most overrated of all. "They don't give anything," he said.

The lobbyists, and particularly the trade association executives, did work hard for Smith in 1968, according to Barnes, "because he was the only candidate they knew."

"He had gone more places and shook more hands—that's how Smith won. He'd done it for eight years. Sure, that's a dying technique, to some extent, but it was still enough. He lost the cities but he carried the rural areas real strong. When you go out and see the people and shake their hands, they tell their neighbor to vote for you—they've seen you and they've touched you and they feel that they know you."

Nick Kralj (pronounced crawl), then Barnes's administrative assistant and travel aide, noted the importance of personal appearances in small towns.

"In some of the places we went to, it was the biggest thing that had ever happened," he said. "They remember it. But in the cities, it doesn't matter."

"That's right," said Barnes. "They don't appreciate it when you go to Houston; you have to get on TV there. But they sure appreciate it when you go to DeLeon."

Barnes admitted that Connally had tried to get him to run for governor in 1968 "but only after it was too late—after I had already announced for lieutenant governor."

"I've got to confess," he said, "that when I announced, I thought that would force Connally to run for governor again because I knew he couldn't find anyone else."

In addition to Ikard and Kilgore, said Barnes, Hal Woodward of Coleman, a former member of the Texas Highway Commission, was discussed as a possibility. He added that if either Locke or Briscoe had reached the runoff, he probably could have defeated Smith—and that Connally was "not aggressive enough when it came to keeping people out of races."

"Locke and Briscoe certainly should not both have been in that race," said Barnes. "And Connally could have kept Galloway Calhoun out of Crawford Martin's race for attorney general in 1966 and prevented that expensive runoff."

Calhoun, a Tyler attorney and former state senator, joined Governor Smith's staff early in 1969 and Smith appointed him in October to a district judgeship.

Since Barnes had supported Martin in 1966 and appeared on television with him, Calhoun could hardly be considered one of the Lieutenant Governor's admirers. As a matter of fact, some of those who were in that category suspected Calhoun of instigating much of the friction between Smith and Barnes.

But a large part of that friction stemmed from obvious differences in political philosophy, as Godfrey Sperling, Jr., noted in the Sept. 18, 1969, issue of the *Christian Science Monitor*.

"Mr. Barnes's main difference with the Governor is over how state government should be run," noted Sperling. "Governor Smith wants to keep Texas government much as it is, with the State Legislature meeting once every two years and with a governor being elected every two years. Mr. Barnes thinks that the Legislature should meet every year, that modern-day demands are too pressing for state government to come to grips with them in such a leisurely fashion. And he feels a governor must have a four-year term to be insured the kind of continuity necessary to govern effectively. . . .

"Mr. Barnes has just completed a year's term as president of the National Legislative Conference, made up of state legislative leaders of the 50 states. He is the youngest man to hold that office and also the first from the South or Southwest. . . .

"He is a member of the executive committee of the National Conference of State Legislative Leaders, past chairman of the Southern Conference of the Council of State Governments, and a member of President Johnson's Advisory Commission on Intergovernmental Relations. He also has had several important international assignments in government."

Despite such recognition, Barnes was considered by some to be extremely vulnerable in 1970—especially in view of his divorce and the many wild rumors which inevitably surrounded it. It seemed only natural for the Republican Party to make one of its massive miscalculations at this point and run against him an articulate and intelligent candidate who never before had sought political office, Byron Fullerton.

Fullerton, 47-year-old associate dean of the University of Texas Law School and a former assistant attorney general, said Republican leaders had to pledge $300,000 for his campaign before he agreed to run.

His campaign methods reinforced the widely-held suspicion that he had been persuaded to enter the race by friends of Senator Tower who wanted him to "cut on" Barnes as a precautionary measure for 1972. Fullerton staunchly denied this as he attacked Barnes on such matters as his personal finances, using his office as a "political stepping stone," advocating reduced penalties for possession of marijuana and supporting the ill-fated grocery tax.

Barnes ignored him and won the race by a margin of more than 2 to 1.

Dick West, editorial editor of the *Dallas Morning News*, had noted,

Lt. Gov. Ben Barnes impresses audiences with his sincerity and entertaining style —to such an extent that he is swamped constantly with speaking invitations.

on July 23, 1967, some of the Barnes qualities which have made such victories possible. They were demonstrated, he said, a few weeks earlier in Dallas at a reception for Barnes in connection with the State Bar of Texas convention, at the Sheraton Hotel, where the young politician displayed a sincere desire to meet people and they showed a desire to meet him.

"This affair at the Sheraton was supposed to begin at 5:30 and end at 7:30," wrote West. "At 9:15, Mr. Barnes was still there, surrounded by about 50 people who were waiting for a word with him."

One of Barnes's most remarkable assets probably is his willingness to "have a word" with anyone—friend or foe.

Ernest Stromberger, Austin correspondent for the *Dallas Times Herald,* noted on March 30, 1969, that Barnes had won new respect from liberals a few days earlier by fielding successfully some hot questions from the state's noisiest radicals at a University of Texas "sandwich seminar."

As an example, Stromberger cited a complaint from a member of that audience that "All you cats up at the capitol have clamped a lid on student radicals."

Barnes immediately shot back: "Well, I'll tell you: anytime you cats down here want to talk, come on up to the capitol. My door's open 18 hours a day."

Like most successful politicians, Barnes seems to have an uncanny knack for knowing—almost by instinct—when to open doors and when to close them. Once, during his first campaign, this probably saved his life.

Sleet had glazed the highways of West Central Texas that cold, dreary morning early in 1960. Despite a warning from a friend at a service station where he stopped for gasoline, Barnes tried to drive from DeLeon to Brownwood for a speech to a group of school teachers.

"I came over a hill between DeLeon and Comanche," he recalled, "and my car suddenly went into a skid. It turned sideways and kept going and I couldn't do anything to stop it. It was the most helpless feeling I've ever had. And then I saw a tree coming at me. The car skidded right into it, squarely in the middle on the driver's side. But by that time, I was jumping out the door on the other side."

Anyone who knows the irrepressible Barnes would take it for granted, without even asking, that he landed on his feet.

Chapter 18

DON'T PUSH, DON'T SHOVE

A 27-hour filibuster in the Texas Senate was nearing its fateful climax on Saturday night, August 23, 1969, when Representative Carl Parker of Port Arthur walked up to Senator Strong and began examining his unbuttoned coat. Parker, a witty, fun-loving liberal, grabbed the lapels of the flashy sports coat and pulled them outward, as if inspecting the lining.

"What are you doing?" demanded the shocked senator.

"I'm just looking," replied Parker, grinning, "for the thirty pieces of silver."

Even Strong had to laugh. That was one of the few laughs he and the other proponents managed to get out of the 61st Legislature's food tax fiasco, that unsuccessful attempt to put groceries under the retail sales tax. Mostly, it was a grim, almost grisly business—one which left in its wake a confusing scramble of political fortunes and a parade of mourning lobbyists.

Its birth resulted from the Legislature's ridiculous and mysterious conference committee system, with Smith, Barnes and Mutscher all serving as midwives. It was accompanied by a bomb scare that cleared nearly everyone out of the Capitol, an attempt by opponents to fly one-third of the senators to Mexico to break a quorum, a series of childish scuffles in the House of Representatives and a persuasive taxpayers' revolt. The latter was so convincing that even the five House members who voted for the bill in conference—supposedly as a "compromise"—ultimately joined their colleagues in killing it by that 147-0 vote which probably laid it to rest for many, many years.

That affair demonstrated many of the weaknesses in an antiquated legislative system designed in 1876, when the state budget had just been raised to $2,216,349 annually. For the biennium ending Aug. 31, 1973, the state budget will total about *seven billion* dollars—and yet the Legislature still is required to meet only once every two years. In view of what happened in 1969 and 1971, some people complain facetiously that even that may be too often.

Frustration fostered at least in part by the system itself led to formulation of the food tax plan—which Smith had eyed longingly as early as January—on Thursday night, August 21, 1969. Shortly after the Legislature convened, Smith recommended a revenue program, includ-

229

ing $321 million in new taxes, designed to finance the traditional two-year budget. He included a proposal to use part of the state's income from oil and gas properties for current spending, instead of putting it in the Permanent School (endowment) Fund, and Attorney General Martin ruled that unconstitutional. Smith also proposed the $10 "surcharge" on convictions for moving traffic violation fines—and he could not even find a sponsor for that in the House, where all tax measures must originate.

When it became obvious that the regular session, limited to 140 days, was not inclined to pass an adequate tax bill, Barnes and Mutscher teamed up on a one-year budget plan which would postpone new taxes until 1970. A special session to pass a budget for the second year of the biennium and new taxes to finance it would be necessary then. It was, basically, the same plan Connally had utilized in 1967 and 1968—which was one of the reasons Smith did not like it.

Barnes and Mutscher realized this and asked him repeatedly to tell them if he would veto the one-year bill, promising to abandon the idea if he said he would. Smith maintained his silence until June 20th—18 days after the regular session had adjourned and just two days before his deadline for acting on the measure. He vetoed the bill on June 21 but, although the state government had no budget beyond Aug. 31, did not call a special session until July 28.

That session, limited to 30 days, had only five more days to go when the Senate killed a tax measure, which had been hatched by the conference committee, 22-8. It would have raised the state sales tax rate from 3 per cent to 3.5 per cent and applied the tax to household and automobile repairs, raised the cigarette tax from 11 cents to 16 cents per package, increased the natural gas and franchise taxes and levied a tax of 10 cents each on mixed drinks served in private clubs.

The latter was an effort to get around the biggest obstacle encountered at that stage: the Senate's insistence upon putting beer and liquor under the sales tax and Mutscher's steadfast refusal to consider it. That's when Senator Creighton came up with the idea of repealing the food tax exemption and reducing the sales tax rate to 2.5 per cent.

During the filibuster, Creighton asked one newsman what sort of reaction he had heard to the proposal.

"You really want to know?" he was asked.

"Sure," said Creighton. "Good or bad."

"Well," said the newsman, "I heard a fellow say a few minutes ago that it's the worst bill that's ever been before the Texas Legislature. And that's the *nicest* thing I've heard about it."

Proponents contended that the food tax would not work an undue hardship on low income families, as critics claimed, but Barnes felt strongly enough about that to propose a system of rebates for them in case the bill should be passed. Barnes, anxious to get any tax bill passed, had told both Creighton and Senator Charles Wilson of Lufkin he would permit the first one who won pledges of support from 16 of the 31 senators to bring up his version of the tax measure. Wilson, a liberal who was determined to put a big percentage of the higher taxes on business firms (and preferably telephone companies) rather than individuals, quickly discovered that Creighton already had pirated away several of his key votes—including Strong's.

Until then, Strong had been one of the staunchest opponents of a higher sales tax. His defection was especially crippling to the sales tax opponents during the talkathon since he generally was conceded to know more about the rules, and how to use them effectively, than anyone else in the Senate.

But he felt that passing the bill was necessary if the state government was to spend the amount of money he thought it should spend.

"I believe Texas has been a very backward state until the last 10 years," Strong explained. "Our appropriations have increased 150 per cent since 1959, and we're still probably $500 million short on the money that's really needed for services to the people—for mental health, technical training, welfare and so forth.

"We've been able to double our appropriations in the last eight years only because the sales tax has provided an easy and expanding source of revenue," he declared. "It's easy to appropriate large quantities of money so long as the revenue is easy to obtain.

"Although the food tax is regressive," he admitted, "you also have to realize that the people against whom it's the most regressive are the ones who will enjoy the overwhelming part of the benefits from increased spending. If they pay 10 per cent of the food tax and receive 40 to 50 per cent of its benefits, it's really a good deal for them."

When the tax bill came before the Senate at 9:30 p.m. on Aug. 22, Senator Mauzy had no specific plans for fighting it. But he immediately called for a full reading of the voluminous measure by Secretary of the Senate Charles Schnabel, thus giving himself an hour and a half to plan strategy.

In counting the prospective votes, Mauzy noted the absence of Sen. V. E. (Red) Berry of San Antonio, a supporter of the bill who was ill in a hospital. With Berry absent, it appeared that the final vote would be 15-15 and, since Barnes would not vote to break the tie in that case, the food tax would die.

But proponents had arranged for Senator Bates, an opponent, to "pair" with Berry; in effect, that would nullify Bates's vote and make the score 15-14 for the tax.

So Mauzy decided to repeat a ploy the liberals had used a year earlier—mass disappearance to break a quorum. Barnes would be forced to adjourn if 10 liberals left and could not be found, and then one of the remaining sales tax opponents complained that 21 senators (the number needed for a quorum) were not present.

Mauzy arranged to charter three four-place planes and had them ready for a trip to Laredo. There, the senators could quickly drive across the border into Nuevo Laredo and be beyond the reach of state police, who could be ordered to bring them back. Mauzy talked seven of his colleagues into the trip: Senators Wilson, Bates, A. R. Schwartz of Galveston, Chet Brooks of Pasadena, Joe Bernal of San Antonio, Roy Harrington of Port Arthur and Don Kennard of Fort Worth. Several other senators said they would go if they were the tenth but he had to drop the idea when he couldn't find a ninth.

Senator Barbara Jordan of Houston, the first Negro to serve in the Texas Senate during the 20th Century (she was elected in 1966 and quickly won the overwhelming respect of her colleagues, newsmen and everyone else connected with the Legislature) had started the filibuster with a one-hour speech. Brooks took over next and held the floor until 4:30 a.m. Saturday, when Schwartz came to bat. Wilson relieved him at 10 a.m. and was followed, about 3:30 p.m., by Senator Mike Mc-Kool of Dallas. McKool yielded the floor at 8 p.m. to Kennard—who was destined to set a new Texas filibuster record on May 30, 1971, when he talked continuously for 29 hours and 22 minutes against a bill creating a four-year University of Texas branch at Dallas.

By the time Kennard took his place in that 1969 filibuster lineup, it seemed likely that the talkathon could last longer than the special session. But, shortly before 10 p.m., proponents caught two opponents—Senators Ronald Bridges of Corpus Christi and Joe Christie of El Paso—out of the Chamber at the same time. They quickly took a vote to impose the previous question and won a 14-13 majority to cut off debate.

Bridges and Christie returned in time for the 12:30 a.m. vote on the bill itself. The bill was passed, 15-14, since Bates was paired with Berry.

That sent it to the House but, by then, the filibuster had succeeded where few do. It had bought the time necessary for the public to realize what was happening and to express its opinions. By Monday, when the House convened, tons of mail and telegrams and countless telephone calls had swamped the representatives. Practically all the expressions came from voters who were outraged by the idea of forcing low-income families who spend most of their money on such necessities as food and shelter to pay a sales tax on groceries.

Mutscher, realizing that he was far short of the votes needed to pass the bill, won a 74-70 vote to recess the House until 3 p.m. Shortly be-

Senator Oscar Mauzy of Dallas, a leader of Senate liberals, spearheaded a successful filibuster against a proposal to apply the retail sales tax to groceries. The Senate passed the measure but created a public furor which killed it.

fore the appointed hour, Jim Garner, working at the Tourist Information Center in the Capitol, received an anonymous telephone call from
a woman who said a bomb would explode shortly in the Capitol.

State and city police and Austin firemen immediately converged on
the building and ordered everyone out. Smith and Barnes stayed in
their offices, as did most of the Capitol Press; a dozen or so representatives remained in the House Chamber. The House finally reconvened
at 4:30 p.m., after a thorough and fruitless bomb search which might
have been at least partly responsible for the frayed nerves exhibited
a few moments later.

Representative R. H. (Dick) Cory of Victoria, Mutscher's righthand
man in the House and leader of his tax conferees, was recognized for
what soon appeared to be a speech castigating the Senate for approving
the food tax. Representative Jim Nugent of Kerrville, meanwhile, tried
to monopolize the microphone just back of the press table in the middle
aisle, normally used for representatives to ask questions of the member
who has the floor. Representative Curtis Graves of Houston, a Negro
and a militant liberal, tried to wrestle the microphone away from Nugent and finally jumped up onto the press table, yelling that Cory was
supposed to be making a motion instead of a speech.

Three separate attempts at fisticuffs broke out within the next few
moments but the participants quickly proved themselves no more adept
at fighting than at taxing. When order finally was restored, the House
clobbered the tax bill, 147-0.

Representative Neil Caldwell of Alvin, a liberal and a talented artist
who spends much of his time sketching his colleagues, then was recognized to make a motion that the House conferees be instructed to re-
ject any future attempt to tax groceries.

"But first," he quipped, "I would like to call attention to the fact that
I wear glasses."

The grocery tax had not been considered in either house before the
conference committee—composed of five senators and five representatives, appointed by the presiding officers to "adjust differences" on the
tax bill—brought it up in a report that could not be changed, but only
accepted or rejected. There had been no public hearing on it and neither house had any opportunity to amend it.

That dredged up memories of Barnes's repeated efforts to restrict
conference committees to adjusting differences, as they are required
to do in Congress and in most other state legislatures. As Speaker of
the House, Barnes won House adoption of joint rules to do this but
Lieutenant Governor Smith killed them. As Lieutenant Governor,
Barnes got the Senate to adopt those rules—but Speaker Mutscher torpedoed them in the House.

The Second Special Session of the 61st Legislature, which lasted 14 days, finally passed a tax bill containing some provisions which had *not* been approved earlier by either house—but the Senate went through the formality of approving a resolution authorizing their inclusion in the conference committee report, as required by its rules. That at least gave the senators an opportunity to vote on the new material.

The $350 million revenue measure raised the state sales tax rate to 3.25 per cent, put beer and liquor under the sales tax (thus giving cities which had adopted the one per cent optional city sales tax a $10 million bonanza), raised the cigarette tax by 4.5 cents per package, increased the corporation franchise tax from $2.25 per $1,000 of assets to $2.75 and applied it to Texas sales by out-of-state firms, hiked the natural gas tax from 7 per cent of market value to 7.5 per cent and levied a 5-cent per drink tax on drinks in private clubs and on airlines.

Two years later, in 1971, the Legislature socked it to the taxpayers for another $700 million in new taxes. This time, it raised the state sales tax to 4 per cent, put another 3 cents per package on cigarettes, raised the motor vehicle sales tax from 3 per cent to 4 per cent, raised the corporation franchise tax another $1.25 per $1,000 of assets, and levied a 10 per cent tax on mixed drinks. The sale of mixed drinks had been legalized as a result of a constitutional amendment adopted by the voters in the November, 1970, general election.

Even this huge new tax package appeared to be only a stopgap measure and many feared the gap it stopped would be rather short, especially after Smith vetoed the second year expenditures in the two-year appropriations bill he apparently had wanted. In the greatest reversal since Roy Riegels's wrong-way run in the Rose Bowl, the Governor adopted the same reasoning he had rejected in 1969 and said he would call a special session to enact a budget for the second year of the biennium.

By that time, most people had learned to expect the unexpected from Governor Smith as well as from the Legislature. And they had become accustomed to the legislators' frequent attempts to get their salaries raised, then retaliating via the "fringe benefit" route every time a pay increase was rejected by the voters.

One of the main bones of contention between legislators and voters has been, for several years, the question of whether serving in the Legislature is a fulltime or a part-time job. Most voters seem to feel it is a part-time proposition, since the Legislature is required to meet for only 140 days every two years. In addition to their $4,800-a-year salaries, legislators get $12 per day for expenses while they are in session, plus travel expenses, a stake in one of the world's most liberal retirement programs and almost unbelievable expense allowances between sessions.

As one of their last official acts of the 1969 Regular Session, senators voted to raise their interim expense allowances—for staff help, travel, telephone, telegraph, postage and other expenses—from $1,000 per month to $1,700 per month between sessions. In 1971, they kicked the amount up to $2,000 per month.

House members boosted their allowances from $450 per month to $875 per month in 1969; then, in 1971, they increased that amount to $1,100 by putting their hometown secretaries on the state payroll, without having their salaries charged to individual members.

Sam Kinch noted in his *Fort Worth Star-Telegram* column on Sept. 14, 1969, that with such expense account increases the legislators "don't need any salary raises." The extra expense money, he declared, would provide "a big advantage in any campaign effort."

The legislators had just liberalized their own retirement benefits considerably—despite a warning from Rep. John Allen of Longview that passage of the retirement bill would help defeat the latest legislative pay-raise proposal being submitted to the voters. His warning went unheeded, however, and the Legislature raised its minimum monthly retirement benefit—for a member who had served only eight years—from $100 a month to $150 per month. The bill provided an additional 5 per cent of the monthly legislative salary at time of retirement for each year of service beyond eight years, enabling many legislators to draw retirement pensions much larger than their legislative salaries.

"Fringe benefits" came in for quite a bit of discussion during the 1969 Regular Session, especially after it was disclosed that Representative Heatly had several relatives who had been paid more than $140,000 for state employment during the previous six years. His brother, Dr. Maurice Heatly of San Marcos, was serving as a consultant to the Texas Youth Council—and the "Duke of Paducah" had just persuaded House and Senate budget conferees to raise his fee to $22,500 per year.

It also turned out that Heatly had been selling sand and gravel to the Texas Highway Department—and renting office space in his hometown to the Texas Employment Commission.

Smith, Barnes and Mutscher all issued statements defending the arrogant Appropriations Committee chairman who had won fame for slipping important provisions—many of them designed to reward his friends and punish his enemies—into state budget bills.

Smith said he saw nothing wrong with Heatly's selling sand and gravel to the state if he did so at a competitive price nor in his renting office space to the TEC "if the price was right and they needed the space."

"But I don't believe a public official should use his position to further enrich himself," said the Governor, "and I doubt anyone ever does."

That feeling did not seem to be shared by most of those attending the "Governor's Cup" football game between the Houston Oilers and

Senator A. M. Aikin, Jr., dean of the Texas Senate, checks the wording of a bill at his desk, looking it up in a book containing copies of all those recommended by committees. The soft-spoken Aikin wields great influence.

the Dallas Cowboys in Houston's Astrodome on Aug. 28, 1969. It was the largest crowd ever to watch an Oiler game in the Astrodome and, the moment Smith was introduced, it burst into a thunderous chorus of boos which drowned out the light, scattered applause.

It may be that many of the cat-calls were aimed at public officials in general instead of at Smith in particular. But individuals who are members of a group inevitably are going to be blamed for the actions of the group, regardless of its size and composition. Politicians suffer to some extent in this regard but most of them have a tendency to blame, unfairly, all members of "the press" for the actions of a few who may be irresponsible.

The truth of the matter, as usual, lies somewhere between the two extremes. Most people, whether they be legislators or newsmen or voters, are not all good or all bad—and neither are their actions. And it may well be that 49 per cent of any group hates to be judged by the acts of the majority.

Garth Jones, chief of the *Associated Press* Austin Bureau, took note of this in a column a few days after the 61st Legislature's Second Special Session ended:

"When the sound and fury of a legislative session subsides, it is interesting to note that the noise-makers usually are not among those credited with the real accomplishments of the session," said Jones.

"In both House and Senate a small group of quiet, efficient businessmen and lawyers take their law-making seriously and respect the responsibility handed them by voters.

"These legislators are not the ones who leap up on tables to attract the photographers' attention; who lose their tempers in public debate and cuss and rant and even try to settle legislative matters with their fists.

"These are not the ones who read long flowery speeches, which later are reprinted in political campaign literature, trying to blame everyone but themselves for legislative failures. These are not the leather-lunged filibusterers who roar like a lion when the spectators' gallery is crowded but lapse into a hoarse whisper when the pep squad disappears.

"No matter whether the speaker or the lieutenant governor or the governor or the House or the Senate dominates or sabotages an issue, it is this nucleus of good legislators that keeps state government operating in the best manner possible," said Jones.

"Sen. A. M. Aikin of Paris, dean of the Senate, is not only the most influential man in the Senate, possibly excluding the lieutenant governor, but the most respected. His voice is hard to hear 10 feet away but when he talks, the Senate listens.

Senator Barbara Jordan, the first Negro to serve in the Texas Senate during the 20th Century, is an eloquent speaker who quickly won respect from everyone.

"No one has ever heard him say a harsh word or insult against any-one. His calm, deliberate ways, yet always progressive, have played a major role in state financing and education legislation for many years.

"Rep. Tommy Shannon of Fort Worth plays a calm hand in the House appropriations debates, exerting powerful but unobtrusive in-fluence.

"Possibly the busiest legislator around is Rep. R. H. Cory of Victoria, who, despite a heart attack several years ago, takes the stairs two steps at a time because the elevators are too slow for his schedule. . . . Cory's drive and enthusiasm, particularly in the touchy tax negotiations, did not always please those in power but he is known for his ability to for-get personalities and concentrate solely on the task at hand. Cory has been increasingly successful as a liaison spokesman between the House and the Senate—experience he may put to use in a future Senate race.

"The Senate's champion peacemaker, negotiator and compromise-maker probably is Sen. Ralph Hall of Rockwall, who was a successful business executive before running for the Senate. With an eye on a fu-ture lieutenant governor's race, Hall has become increasingly influen-tial as a moderate who, as a senator from a rural area but with expe-rience and contacts with big city procedure, can talk for both areas," Jones declared.

"Senators Charles Herring of Austin and J. P. Word of Meridian are moderates whose abilities have played an important part in vital legis-lation without wide publicity.

"Sen. Oscar Mauzy of Dallas, efficient and mild-mannered, has earned recognition for his serious, logical arguments on legislation even in the midst of filibusters, which often are frivolous and devoid of any true legislative debate.

"Sen. Barbara Jordan of Houston, the first Negro in the Senate since Reconstruction Days, seldom speaks out but, when she does, she is known for her quiet eloquence.

"Maybe 15 or 20 House members seldom speak but play important roles in lawmaking because of their knowledge and experience in spe-cific matters of parliamentary procedures. Some of these are Repre-sentatives George Hinson of Mineola, Menton Murray of Harlingen, Rayford Price of Palestine, Bill Clayton of Springlake, DeWitt Hale of Corpus Christi, Jim Nugent of Kerrville, Cletus Davis of Houston, Delwin Jones of Lubbock, Charles Jungmichel of LaGrange, Felix McDonald of Edinburg and Carl Parker of Port Arthur," Jones con-cluded.

But you must take the bad with the good—and the inadequacies of the Texas Legislature probably never were demonstrated more dramatically than they were on Monday, Aug. 2, 1971. That's the day that a suit challenging the House of Representatives redistricting plan, adopted by the 62nd Legislature, came to trial before District Judge Herman Jones of Austin.

The redistricting bill was a classic example of gerrymandering—one that criss-crossed 23 county boundaries, in direct violation of constitutional directives, in order to put at a disadvantage as many foes of Speaker Mutscher as possible.

Those who caught the brunt of the redistricting discrimination were members of the "Dirty Thirty," a coalition led by liberals and Republicans who opposed Mutscher—and who, after the National Bankers Life stock scandal came to light, had the courage to challenge him.

Duncan Boeckman, the attorney for Republicans challenging the redistricting plan, dramatized his cause with devastating effect by calling as a witness Miss Laura Shoop of Austin, a 17-year-old high school senior.

Beside her was an easel holding a big state map depicting the redistricting plan pushed through the House by Mutscher.

As the *Dallas Times Herald's* Ernest Stromberger put it:

"Parts of the map looked like pieces of plate glass hit by a hammer, the zig-zag routes leaping across the middle of counties here, snipping off county corners there; a total of 23 county boundaries were criss-crossed by the erratic lines of the redistricters' pencils."

But it developed that Miss Shoop had been given a map of Texas, a pencil and census figures, and then was asked to divide the state into 150 House districts of nearly equal population, without crossing any county lines. She did.

"But it took me about 20 hours," she said.

Commented Stromberger:

"Here was a high school senior with only a fringe interest in politics, and she had done a better job in 20 hours than the House Redistricting Committee chairman, Rep. Delwin Jones of Lubbock, had managed in five months of hand-wringing, esoteric rhetoric, public hearings all across the state and elaborate trappings of exhaustive census research and calculations.

"In short, Miss Shoop had demonstrated that Jones had taken a very simple matter and, in keeping with Parkinson's Law, spent five months trying to expand it into something much larger than it actually was. Not only that, but Jones had done it unconstitutionally to boot. To make matters even worse, he and Mutscher had been bragging on themselves and praising their redistricting bill.

"The difference, of course, is politics. Miss Shoop was being objective, while Mutscher and Jones were admittedly designing their plan to eliminate Mutscher's opponents; they had to bend the constitution to suit their needs and they bent it too far. The fact that this abuse was so easily demonstrated is what made it so disturbing."

But perhaps the harshest criticism of the Legislature came not from the newspaper columnists but from Governor Smith, in his opening address to the second called session on Aug. 27, 1969. In one of the best speeches of his career, he tongue-lashed the lawmakers, declaring that some people "excuse their own failures by saying the Governor has not provided leadership."

"We have been treated to a spectacle of petty quarreling, jealousies between houses, obstinance and self-serving positions, demagogic rhetoric, childish personalities and undue interference from the lobby," he said. "It is my belief that the people of Texas are sick and tired of it. I want you to know that I am. . . .

"Some have dedicated themselves to placing the blame on the Governor," said Smith. "I say to those members—and they know who they are—'Don't push, don't shove; there will be blame enough for everyone.'"

Chapter 19

THREE TO GET READY . . .

B ehind the heavy steel, mesh wire lay treasure valued at several million dollars, recovered from a Spanish galleon sunk just off the Gulf Coast of Texas in 1553. State Land Commissioner Jerry Sadler, one of the most controversial figures in Texas history, stood guard over it and cast a wary eye at the motley crew which came to inspect it early on Tuesday morning, July 29, 1969.

Heading the parade was a three-member commission appointed by a district court to inventory the "loot." That was fine with Sadler, a snuff-dipping East Texan who had rather fight than do almost anything else. He gave a cordial welcome to Joe Kilgore, the chairman; Dr. W. W. Newcomb, director of the University of Texas Memorial Museum, and even to Representative Don Cavness of Austin, one of his most persistent critics.

About a dozen newspaper, radio and television reporters accompanied the commission members and Sadler had no objection to that. But when he spied Representatives Jake Johnson of San Antonio and Frances Farenthold of Corpus Christi, he flew into a rage almost as furious as the hurricane which purportedly wrecked that Spanish treasure armada and thus initiated this troublesome, 416-year-old hangover.

Sadler stopped Johnson, who had been heckling him for months and had even threatened to bring impeachment proceedings against him, at the door of the vault. Sadler snarled at Johnson, "I'm not going to let you in anywhere!"

"Why, Jerry," Johnson replied, "the Commission asked us to come over. You mean you're not going to let us - -"

Johnson's voice trailed off as Sadler thrust out his left hand and began squeezing Johnson's throat.

"Go on, now. Get out of here," Sadler growled.

"Are you trying to choke the representative?" asked Fort Worth radio newsman David Day, poking a microphone in Sadler's face.

Without a word, Sadler turned and grabbed Day's throat.

"Are you gonna choke *me* now?" asked Day.

He did not wait for an answer but angrily departed, as soon as he could.

The paunchy, crusty Sadler later said he considered the inventory procedure a court matter, not a public display of the treasure—and that he would let only "truthful" people come into the vault.

Thus did Sadler, a lawyer who became a millionaire by breaking a fabulous will, pop into the headlines again, as he had done periodically since 1938. That was the year he won election to the Texas Railroad Commission with a bitter campaign during which, he recalls, he was involved in 58 fist fights. He ran unsuccessfully for governor in the 1940 and 1946 Democratic primaries, then won election to the House of Representatives from his native Anderson County in 1954. He served there until 1960, when he was elected land commissioner.

Ten years later, Sadler was one of the few state officials who knew exactly where he was going. It was back to the farm for him, as a result of his defeat in the Democratic Primary by Representative Armstrong. But speculation already was beginning to mount on the political future of Armstrong, a personable, 37-year-old Austin lawyer who had served three terms in the House of Representatives.

He generally was considered the most valuable discovery made by the Democratic Party during the sunken treasure controversy.

While no one counted on anything as dramatic as another "choking" incident to alter the course of Texas politics, a great many politicians stood ready to stick their necks out.

The ebb and flow of political fortunes involving such people as Connally, Barnes, Briscoe, Bush, Yarborough, Tower, Bentsen, Hall and Smith continued to overshadow even the perennial, multimillion dollar question of new taxes. Some of those who did not have to deal with the tax problem undoubtedly had high hopes that some of those who did would wind up choking on it.

Some form of corporate income tax—or corporate "profits" tax, as its proponents preferred to call it—seemed almost inevitable. Its opponents insisted this would lead to a personal income tax; they claimed that broadening the sales tax base to include groceries and services, such as laundry and dry cleaning and repairs, and perhaps even those long-cherished political "touch-me-nots" of farm machinery and fertilizer, offered the only sensible solution to Texas's ever-growing demand for more state government spending.

Alvin A. Burger, shortly before his retirement as director of the privately-financed Texas Research League, estimated that the 10-year program of teachers' pay raises approved in 1969 would cost an additional $3.9 *billion* during the ensuing decade. He said it "would impose on every Legislature during the 1970s the need to provide substantial additional revenues." The bill authorized raises averaging about $800 per school year for each teacher in 1969, $1,000 in 1970 and 5 per cent annually thereafter, with special 10 per cent "cost of living" increases in 1974 and 1978.

The entire package was calculated to increase the average salary for all professional personnel in the public schools from $6,055 in 1969 to $11,433 in 1979.

Like much of the state government's spending, expenditures for public education are based on a formula authorized by the Legislature and then financed by automatic tax allocations—so the funds do not have to be specifically *authorized* by every Legislature but must be *provided*. Under this system, the number of students determines the public schools' total cost—and the money comes out of the State Treasury without going through legislative hands.

Jim Oliver, Governor Smith's budget director, noted in a June, 1969, interview with Stewart Davis of the *Dallas News* that about one-half of all state funds go into educational programs.

"Oliver claims one of the other reasons the lawmakers pass a tax bill nearly every time they meet 'is because we're so far behind,' " noted Davis. "Taxes have been levied by every Legislature except one since World War II."

Oliver said Texas, at that point, ranked 47th in the nation in the state-local tax burden but added, "I don't think we're 47th in the quality of services."

That, of course, was a matter of opinion which would be kicked around in future campaigns, probably for years to come, along with such problems as water and air pollution, care for the mentally ill, constitutional revision, annual sessions of the Legislature, four-year terms for state officials, automobile insurance rates, development of water resources, demands for still more new colleges and methods of correcting the poverty-stricken status of many Texans, particularly Latin Americans in the southern part of the state.

The root of all solutions to such problems appeared to be money. Although state government expenditures had tripled during the decade of the 1960s, no end to the increased demands appeared to be in sight.

Governor Connally, in his January, 1969, farewell address to the Legislature, noted:

"The requests for public funds sometimes seem unending. The appetite of government may appear insatiable. And yet the growth in demand for governmental services is the inevitable by-product of a vibrant and growing state. To give all that is asked is *extravagance*, but to provide less than substantiated need is *irresponsibility*."

Inevitably, the matter of striking the proper balance on both spending and equitable distribution of the ever-growing tax burden boils down purely and simply to the fascinating, complicated art of practical politics. And the essence of practical politics is to do what most of the people want done—or at least to convince them that you are trying to do so. This comes a lot easier, of course, if your heart is in the right place and you really try to do what you think is best for the majority of the people.

For generations, most Texans have thought that only the Democratic Party was interested in the welfare of the majority. But the Democrats, more than the Republicans, have done much in recent years to convince them that this is no longer the case.

Robert Baskin of the *Dallas Morning News* cited the drastically-changed complexion of the Democratic Party in his Sept. 24, 1969, column from Washington:

"It would appear that the traditional moderate-conservative Democrats of Texas, at long last, are getting wise to the modern National Democratic Party.

"The ultimate question, of course, is whether they can continue to live in it, particularly after the events of the Chicago National Convention in 1968.

"There is no question that the national party has abandoned the broad-based policies it had embraced in the days when there was a spirit of accommodation between the Southern conservatives and the Northern party leaders. The spirit of vindictiveness against the South, once the prerogative of the Reconstruction-type 'black Republicans,' was taken over almost entirely by the new breed of Democrats that has come into power in the North in recent years," said Baskin.

"Last week some of the dissatisfaction which conservative and moderate Democrats feel about the course the national party is following was voiced emphatically at a meeting in Washington of state chairmen and national committeemen.

"Texas National Committeeman Robert Strauss of Dallas complained that the party is leaning too far toward one point of view, specifically liberalism. His views were echoed by the Texas state chairman, Dr. Elmer Baum of Austin.

"It is difficult to understand some of the actions of the national chairman of the party, Sen. Fred Harris of Oklahoma. Harris has just set up a Democratic policy executive council and the conservative-moderate wing of the party has been omitted from its membership almost entirely.

"From Texas, Harris named two liberals, Congressman Jack Brooks of Beaumont and State Sen. Barbara Jordan of Houston, to the council. Apparently this was done without consultation with the ruling figures in the Texas Democratic Party, and Strauss was plainly unhappy about the selections.

"All of this should come as no surprise to Texas Democrats.

"The national party in the last few years has been going through a period of tremendous change. A good part of the old 'Solid South' has been written off in the process. The party now appears to want its principal identity to lie with the ethnic minorities, the wayward youth groups and the Northern latter-day abolitionists.

"The main point of all this may be how many times do you have to be hit over the head to learn you are out of place in the club?

"The humiliation John B. Connally and his delegation experienced at the Chicago convention should have been adequate evidence that the party they had known in the past was dead and buried.

"Yet the argument persists that the Democratic Party must be adhered to at the state level and the state party should attempt to adjust itself with the national party every four years for presidential elections. This is an obvious contradiction in political terms," said Baskin.

"But we have seen the spectacle of Connally, his head bloodied at the national convention, making an all-out pitch for the Democratic presidential nominee at the height of the campaign in Texas.

"While Strauss and Baum may be complaining now about how they are being treated by the national party, the rulers of the party feel they can count on them to get into line when the next national presidential campaign gets under way.

"Somewhere there must be a speck of pride left among these state Democratic leaders.

"At the same time, however, it is not clear how they can move in and change the tone of the national party. Nobody is really listening to them," Baskin concluded.

It wasn't long after that, however, until people in both parties did start listening. The Democrats got a new lease on life when Bob Strauss became their national treasurer and began a systematic program to carve down their huge deficit. And the Republicans had to look at their hole cards when Connally not only was named Secretary of the Treasury but quickly became Nixon's most important spokesman on nearly everything.

This led to speculation that Connally might replace Spiro Agnew on the 1972 Republican ticket but that possibility seemed unlikely. Connally's main value to Nixon appeared to lie in his being the "resident Democrat" in the Cabinet—not in his turning Republican.

There remained the intriguing possibility that Connally might suddenly resign, bemoaning failure to educate the Republicans, and become part of a Democratic Party ticket. But most of Connally's friends figured the Democrats were not smart enough to take advantage of that possibility.

Strauss and Connally had gained the attention of both Democrats and Republicans. That fact, plus the surprising amount of unity promoted by Lloyd Bentsen in the 1970 campaign, left Texas Republicans bewildered as well as frustrated.

A few weeks after the election, Nicholas C. Chriss of the *Los Angeles Times* Houston Bureau wrote that "The Republican Party in Texas is in disarray, disenchantment and deep financial trouble because of its disastrous setback in the last election.

"Dissension in party ranks has given impetus to a move to oust National Committeeman Peter O'Donnell of Dallas, the party's chief money raiser and one of President Nixon's longtime friends and advisers. . . .

"Many party regulars blame O'Donnell for the licking the state party took in 1970, the year that was supposed to mark transition of the Texas GOP into a full-fledged political party and Texas a two-party state. . . .

"The losses on Nov. 3 also brought renewed complaints of O'Donnell's high-handedness, and his reluctance to spread party leadership any further than his office door," Chriss wrote.

Perhaps the most shocking public statement issued in the wake of the campaign was one from Eggers, echoing what he had told a number of people privately during the campaign.

"God works in mysterious ways and the greatest thing that happened to me was not to win," declared the Republican nominee for governor. "Basically, I'm not a politician. I'd have given it all I had if I had won, but I didn't win and I'm better off for it."

That confession undoubtedly prompted a lot of Republicans, and especially those who made large campaign contributions, to have some second thoughts about their methods of candidate selection.

Meanwhile, the Democratic woods were full of prospective candidates for the 1972 races—and there did not appear to be an ounce of Eggers-type reluctance in a carload of them. Many of them were staunch believers, however, in the "domino theory" of politics and wanted to see what offices would become vacant by others' attempts to move up the ladder.

Senator Hall decided three weeks after the 1970 election that Barnes would run either for the U. S. Senate or for governor in 1972. Without waiting to find out which, he announced his candidacy for lieutenant governor.

William P. Hobby, Jr., executive editor of the *Houston Post*, also jumped into the lieutenant governor's race.

Briscoe continued running—but Barnes's decision to run for governor in 1972 prompted many of Briscoe's friends to suggest he run for the Senate against Tower. With Barnes and Briscoe drawing much of their support from the same sources, Briscoe was being urged not to run against Barnes; such a race, he was told, would be rough and ex-

Gordon McLendon, who made a fortune in radio and theaters, seriously considered another race for the U. S. Senate in 1972. He was defeated by Yarborough in 1964, after one of the most bitterly-fought campaigns in history.

pensive, it probably would eliminate the loser from the political picture and it would demolish the newly-found harmony within Democratic ranks.

Both Barnes and Briscoe realized, of course, that the fragile thread of unity would be destroyed if Yarborough decided to enter the 1972 governor's race, as he threatened to do. Yarborough still nurtured his lifelong ambition to be governor but some of his friends were trying to talk him into running against Tower.

Railroad Commissioner Jim C. Langdon, Attorney General Martin, and John Hill still were being mentioned as potential candidates for governor or the U. S. Senate. And many observers were wondering if another Lloyd Bentsen might come along from out of nowhere.

Gordon McLendon, after selling most of his radio stations to lessen his business responsibilities, was among those toying with the idea of running for the U. S. Senate or for governor. Barefoot Sanders, a Dallas lawyer and former aide to LBJ, also eyed the Senate race as a host of potential candidates studied possibilities.

With the Sharpstown Bank scandal continuing to unfold, no one could be sure of anything.

But against a background of uncertainty, conflicting ambitions, party strife, factional feuding, personality clashes and mammoth problems, most Texas political leaders—both Democrat and Republican—usually manage to maintain a comforting sense of humor.

Barnes and Bush demonstrated this at a luncheon in Houston's Shamrock-Hilton Hotel on Sept. 28, 1969, when Barnes succeeded Bush as chairman of the Texas Heart Fund. At the time, they generally were considered likely rivals for the U. S. Senate. They had great respect for each other and had, for some time, been better friends than some of their older colleagues in their respective parties cared to admit—or perhaps even knew.

After that luncheon, in fact, they spent about an hour together in the hotel's coffee shop—after politely declining an invitation to join Connally and Strauss at another table.

"We know you two have things to talk about and we have to plan each other's future—so we wouldn't want to bother you with that," Bush explained to Connally and Strauss as he and Barnes headed for the other side of the room.

At the luncheon, Bush had introduced Astronaut Frank Borman, the main speaker for the occasion.

Colonel Borman said he felt certain Bush was running for the U. S. Senate because "he arrived at a dinner honoring the astronauts the other night in typical Ben Barnes style—30 minutes late and with a big fanfare."

"What really made me realize that he was running was the fact that he was carrying his coat over his shoulder," said Borman, reminding the audience of a Bush campaign picture which had been used on countless billboards.

When Barnes spoke, he acknowledged that Bush had received fine applause when he was introduced but that Borman had been given a much greater ovation than anyone else.

"I hope you noted that, George," said Barnes. "I'm sure you will agree with me that this was most appropriate, and just another indication of the great esteem in which our astronauts are held, not only in this country but all over the world. They have received tremendous recognition and all of it was well deserved.

"Such recognition obviously would be a great asset to anyone in politics," he added, "and George, I think it is all you need to make your political portfolio complete. Therefore, I am happy to inform you that I have arranged for you to spend the next six years in astronaut training—and to be the command pilot on Apollo 23!"

Less than two months later, however, all signals appeared to be "go!" for Bush in the Senate race with the Barnes political countdown "holding."

On Monday night, Nov. 24, Barnes met in his office with some of his closest friends and advisers: Erwin, Larry Temple, Howard Rose, Christian, Julian Read, Nick Kralj, Robert Spellings, Richard West and Rep. Ralph Wayne of Plainview.

Some of them had felt originally that Barnes should seek reelection, only to have him convince them during the preceding months that he should strike while the iron was hot and go for a promotion. By the time they got together that night, however, he had decided he should seek reelection and they agreed with him almost unanimously. The suspense surrounding his decision had reached such proportions that they felt it should be announced quickly.

The next morning, Barnes telephoned Bush in Washington.

"George," he said, "it won't make you mad if I don't run for the Senate, will it?"

"It sure won't!" came the enthusiastic response.

Under the glare of television lights in the Senate Chamber that afternoon, Barnes said he was flattered by polls showing he could defeat either Yarborough or Smith—and insisted he could raise enough money for either race.

"However, such a decision for service cannot be based on personal ambition or on ability to win," he said. "Any responsible public figure must carefully make his own judgment as to how his leadership can best serve the current needs of this state."

Barnes's decision was one of the first in his career to draw a genuine, solid gold blessing from Governor Smith. As a matter of fact, some observers felt it more than mere coincidence that, a few moments after it was announced, Smith issued the Governor's traditional Thanksgiving Day proclamation.

The futile search for Democratic gubernatorial candidates intensified, especially after Smith butchered the pronunciation of Notre Dame Football Coach Ara Parseghian's name three times during a brief speech at the Texas Sports Hall of Fame luncheon in Dallas on Dec. 31, 1969. He also welcomed "all the Notre Dame visitors from Illinois."

Most Texans in the crowd of 1,200 were embarrassed but Smith was merely puzzled when Parseghian retaliated, in accepting the "Honorary Texan" certificate Smith presented him, by saying, "Thank you, Governor *Schmit.*"

A year later, Notre Dame came back to the Cotton Bowl and Smith found himself confronted once again with Coach Parseghian.

"You know," said Smith, "when you come back to Texas the second time, you're on a first-name basis. So I'm happy to introduce Ara."

"Thank you, Governor," said Parseghian, in response. "You've had a year now to learn my name—and you've learned to pronounce half of it!"

Smith ranks as the greatest beneficiary, at least in modern times, of the fact that Texans usually do not elect their public officials solely on speech-making ability. A candidate's eloquence can be a big asset today, however, just as it always has been. And it can still cover up a lot of shortcomings.

Gov. James E. Ferguson, who eventually was impeached, is said to have received a call from one of his managers during a campaign urgently recommending that he make a speech in Dallas.

"Look, Jim, you've just got to go to Dallas and make a speech," the man pleaded. "The opposition is telling lies on you over there."

"I'd like to," Ferguson reportedly replied, "but I've got to go to Houston."

"But Jim," said the manager, "they're telling lies about you in Dallas."

"Yeah," replied Ferguson, "but they're telling the truth about me in Houston."

JAMES H. BANKS

Even before graduating from high school, James H. Banks began to make his "By Jimmy Banks" byline popular with newspaper readers in Austin. He is now editor of the *Texas Star*, a weekly magazine supplement distributed by most of Texas's leading newspapers. For 16 years, he was a state capital correspondent for the *Dallas Morning News*, widely recognized for his prize-winning reporting in such varied fields as football, politics, crime and government.

He also served on the staffs of Governors Allan Shivers and Price Daniel, served as publicity director for Shivers's 1954 campaign for governor and as public relations director for U. S. Senator Lloyd Bentsen's successful campaign in 1970. He spent a year as director of public relations for the Texas State Teachers Association, editing its monthly magazine, and for two years edited a monthly magazine for the Texas Society of Architects. In addition, he has had more than 100 articles published in various magazines and is the Austin correspondent for *Sports Illustrated*.

Born Nov. 3, 1925, in Waco, Texas, Banks was raised in Austin, where he was an All-State tackle and co-captain of Austin High School's first state championship football team in 1942; as a part-time sportswriter for the now-defunct *Austin Daily Tribune*, he frequently covered the games in which he played. His University of Texas career was interrupted by World War II when he left school to earn a commission as a bombardier-navigator in the Army Air Corps. After the war ended, he returned to Austin to resume fulltime work on the *Austin American-Statesman* while carrying a full load of studies at The University of Texas. Despite the interruption for military service, he became sports editor of the *Austin Statesman* before his 21st birthday.

He is past president of the Austin Professional Chapter of Sigma Delta Chi (professional journalism fraternity), former vice president of the Headliners Club, former secretary of the Tarrytown Methodist Church Official Board and past co-president (having served with his wife in that capacity) of the Highland Park (Austin) Elementary School P-TA. He and his wife, the former Mary Virginia Bussey of Austin, have two daughters, Ginger and Janet.

ACKNOWLEDGMENTS

One of the nicest things about writing a book is the discovery that so many people are anxious to help in so many ways. Much of the material in this particular volume resulted from personal observation of the Texas political scene for more than 20 years, and from various newspaper articles, but most of it came from those who have played leading roles in this continuing drama and were kind enough to grant personal interviews. I am deeply grateful to all of them and especially to James Clay, who conceived the idea for this book and provided excellent guidance.

Alphabetically, the honor roll of others to whom the author acknowledges deep gratitude includes Lt. Gov. Ben Barnes; U. S. Senator Lloyd M. Bentsen, Jr.; Mrs. Terrell Blodgett of Austin, former University of Texas journalism teacher; Dolph Briscoe; Ambassador George Bush; George Christian, former White House Press Secretary who previously had served as press secretary for two Texas governors; the late John D. Cofer, who was a distinguished Austin attorney; Secretary of the Treasury John B. Connally; Charles E. Cooke, of the State Senate staff; Mike Cooper, of Gov. Preston Smith's staff; Jack Cox, who notched a new high-water mark for Texas Republicans; former Gov. Price Daniel; Mr. and Mrs. Charles K. Devall, publishers of the *Kilgore News Herald;* Sybil Dickinson, director of the Texas Secretary of State's Administrative Division; Fagan Dickson, for many years a leader among Texas liberals; Jack Dillard, who became a lawyer after achieving success in several other fields; Frank Driskill, a friend who is astute in both politics and publishing; the late Allen Duckworth, who was a great political editor for the *Dallas Morning News;* Dawson Duncan, former chief of the *Dallas Morning News* Austin Bureau; Roy Evans, president of the Texas State AFL-CIO; Wick Fowler, whose witticisms frequently camouflage his deep concern for the Texas political situation; Jerry Hall, Governor Smith's highly-respected press secretary; State Sen. Ralph Hall, a brilliant politician; Dorothy Hallman, chief clerk of the Texas House of Representatives, and her staff; Harry Hornby, Jr., publisher of the *Uvalde Leader-News*; former President Lyndon B. Johnson, the most fascinating of all politicians; W. Thomas Johnson, the former President's erstwhile executive assistant; Bill Malone, a great photographer; Attorney General Crawford C. Martin, an expert on state government; State Sen. Oscar Mauzy, the liberals' brightest hope in years; former State Sen. Jimmy Phillips, who would have made a great and exciting governor; James R. Sanders, director of the Legislative Reference Library, and his staff; Charles Schnabel, Secretary of the Senate, and his staff; former Gov. Allan Shivers, perhaps the greatest governor of all time; Gov. Preston Smith; U. S. Sen. John G. Tower, a miracle-maker, and Kenneth Towery, a great newspaper reporter who helped Senator Tower perform miracles before becoming Deputy Director of the U. S. Information Agency.

No book of this type could be considered authentic unless it drew heavily on the information contained in the *Texas Almanac and Industrial Guide,* published every two years by the A. H. Belo Corporation.

Newspaper files which proved extremely helpful in the preparation of this book included those of the *Dallas Morning News,* the *Dallas Times Herald,* the *Fort Worth Star-Telegram,* the *Austin American-Statesman,* the *Houston Post,* the *Houston Chronicle,* the *San Antonio Express* and the *Wall Street Journal.*

The biweekly *Texas Observer* proved helpful, as did the files of *Texas Parade* Magazine and *Saga* Magazine. Other publications, listed in the bibliography which follows, also were relied upon heavily in checking for historical accuracy.

And, while they had nothing to do with the preparation of this particular book, it would be a great injustice not to acknowledge the tremendous help received, years ago, from Lois Jarrell, Mary Hettie Marberry and Bertha Casey, all wonderful teachers; and from Curtis Bishop, Wilbur Evans, Pete Engelking, Gordon Fulcher, Weldon Hart, Felix McKnight and William T. Rives—great newspapermen and wonderful friends who were kind enough to share their vast knowledge with me.

But my deepest gratitude is reserved for my wife, Mary Virginia (Dit), and our daughters, Ginger and Janet, whose inspiration, patience and understanding really made this possible.

Jimmy Banks

BIBLIOGRAPHY

Governors of Texas, by Paul Bolton, The Corpus Christi Caller-Times, 1947.

The Handbook of Texas, Texas State Historical Association, 1952.

Mr. Sam, by C. Dwight Dorough, Random House, 1962.

My Name Is Tom Connally, by Senator Tom Connally as told to Alfred Steinberg, Thomas Y. Crowell Co., 1954.

Governing Texas, Documents and Readings, by Fred Gantt, Jr., Irving Owen Dawson and Luther G. Hagard, Jr., Thomas Y. Crowell Co., 1966.

Texas Presidential Politics in 1952 by O. Douglas Weeks, University of Texas Institute of Public Affairs, 1953.

Party and Factional Division in Texas, by James R. Soukup, Clifton McCleskey and Harry Holloway, University of Texas Press, 1964.

The Making of the President 1960, by Theodore H. White, Atheneum House, Inc., 1961.

The Chief Executive in Texas, by Fred Gantt, Jr., University of Texas Press, 1964.

Politics in America, 1945-1964, Congressional Quarterly Service, 1965.

Appendix

GOVERNORS OF TEXAS

Name and Term	Profession	Birthplace	Dates of Birth and Death
James Pinckney Henderson Feb. 19, 1846-Dec. 21, 1847	Lawyer, Soldier	Lincolnton, No. Carolina	Mar. 31, 1808- June 4, 1858

(Lt. Gov. Albert C. Horton served as Acting Governor from May 19, 1846, until July 1, 1847, while Henderson was commanding troops during the Mexican War.)

George T. Wood Dec. 21, 1847-Dec. 21, 1849	Soldier, Farmer	Cuthbert, Georgia	Mar. 12, 1795- Sept. 3, 1858
P. Hansborough Bell Dec. 21, 1849-Nov. 23, 1853	Soldier, Texas Ranger	Spotsylvania County, Va.	May 12, 1812- Mar. 8, 1898
James W. Henderson Nov. 23, 1853-Dec. 21, 1853			

(As lieutenant governor, Henderson became governor when Bell resigned to enter Congress.)

Elisha M. Pease Dec. 21, 1853-Dec. 21, 1857	Lawyer	Enfield, Conn.	Jan. 3, 1812- Aug. 26, 1883
Hardin R. Runnels Dec. 21, 1857-Dec. 21, 1859	Farmer	Mississippi	Aug. 30, 1820- Dec. 25, 1873
Sam Houston Dec. 21, 1859-Mar. 16, 1861	Soldier, Lawyer	Rockbridge County, Va.	Mar. 2, 1793- July 26, 1863

(Resigned when Texas seceded from the Union.)

Edward Clark Mar. 16, 1861-Nov. 7, 1861	Lawyer, Soldier	Georgia	April 1, 1815- May 4, 1880

(As lieutenant governor, Clark became governor when Houston resigned.)

Francis R. Lubbock Nov. 7, 1861-Nov. 5, 1863	Businessman, Soldier	Beaufort, So. Carolina	Oct. 16, 1815- June 22, 1905

(Resigned to enter Confederate Army.)

Pendleton Murrah Nov. 5, 1863-June 17, 1865	Lawyer	So. Carolina	Unknown- Aug. 4, 1865

(Administration terminated by fall of the Confederacy; Lt. Gov. Fletcher S. Stockdale performed some of the governor's duties when Murrah departed but President Andrew Johnson appointed Andrew J. Hamilton for immediate succession.)

Andrew J. Hamilton June 17, 1865-Aug. 9, 1866	Lawyer	Huntsville, Alabama	Jan. 28, 1815- April 11, 1875

(Provisional governor appointed by President Andrew Johnson.)

James W. Throckmorton Aug. 9, 1866-Aug. 8, 1867	Physician	Sparta, Tennessee	Feb. 1, 1825- April 21, 1894

GOVERNORS (Continued)

Name and Term	Profession	Birthplace	Dates of Birth and Death
Elisha M. Pease Aug. 8, 1867-Sept. 30, 1869	(see information above)		

(Pease was appointed under martial law; he resigned Sept. 30, 1869, and no successor was appointed until Jan. 8, 1870, when Republican Edmund J. Davis, elected on Nov. 30, 1869, took office.)

Name and Term	Profession	Birthplace	Dates of Birth and Death
Edmund J. Davis Jan. 8, 1870-Jan. 15, 1874	Lawyer	St. Augustine, Florida	Oct. 2, 1827- Feb. 7, 1883

(Only Republican who has served as Governor of Texas)

Name and Term	Profession	Birthplace	Dates of Birth and Death
Richard Coke Jan. 15, 1874-Dec. 1, 1876	Lawyer, Farmer	Williamsburg, Virginia	Mar. 13, 1829- May 14, 1896

(Resigned to enter U. S. Senate.)

Name and Term	Profession	Birthplace	Dates of Birth and Death
Richard B. Hubbard Dec. 1, 1876-Jan. 21, 1879	Lawyer	Walton Co., Georgia	Nov. 1, 1832- July 12, 1901

(As lieutenant governor, Hubbard became governor when Coke resigned.)

Name and Term	Profession	Birthplace	Dates of Birth and Death
Oran M. Roberts Jan. 21, 1879-Jan. 16, 1883	Lawyer, Teacher	Laurens Dist., So. Carolina	July 9, 1815- May 19, 1898
John Ireland Jan. 16, 1883-Jan. 18, 1887	Lawyer	Hart County, Kentucky	Jan. 1, 1827- Mar. 15, 1896
Lawrence Sullivan Ross Jan. 18, 1887-Jan. 20, 1891	Soldier, Farmer	Bentonsport, Iowa	Sept. 27, 1838- Jan. 4, 1898
James S. Hogg Jan. 20, 1891-Jan. 15, 1895	Lawyer, Editor	Rusk, Texas	Mar. 24, 1851- Mar. 3, 1907
Charles A. Culberson Jan. 15, 1895-Jan. 17, 1899	Lawyer	Dadeville, Alabama	June 10, 1855- Mar. 25, 1925
Joseph D. Sayers Jan. 17, 1899-Jan. 20, 1903	Lawyer	Grenada, Mississippi	Sept. 23, 1841- May 15, 1929
Samuel W. T. Lanham Jan. 20, 1903-Jan. 15, 1907	Lawyer	Spartanburg, So. Carolina	July 4, 1846- July 29, 1908
Thomas Mitchell Campbell Jan. 15, 1907-Jan. 17, 1911	Lawyer, Railroad exec.	Rusk, Texas	April 22, 1856- April 1, 1923
Oscar B. Colquitt Jan. 17, 1911-Jan. 19, 1915	Lawyer, Editor	Camilla, Georgia	Dec. 16, 1861- Mar. 8, 1940
James E. (Pa) Ferguson Jan. 19, 1915-Aug. 25, 1917	Banker, Lawyer	Salado, Texas	Aug. 31, 1871- Sept. 21, 1944

(Removed from office by impeachment.)

Name and Term	Profession	Birthplace	Dates of Birth and Death
William P. Hobby Aug. 25, 1917-Jan. 18, 1921	Publisher, Editor	Moscow, Texas	Mar. 26, 1878- June 7, 1964

(As lieutenant governor, Hobby became governor when Ferguson was impeached.)

Name and Term	Profession	Birthplace	Dates of Birth and Death
Pat M. Neff Jan. 18, 1921-Jan. 20, 1925	Lawyer	McGregor, Texas	Nov. 26, 1871- Jan. 19, 1952

GOVERNORS (Continued)

Name and Term	Profession	Birthplace	Dates of Birth and Death
Miriam A. (Ma) Ferguson Jan. 20, 1925-Jan. 17, 1927 Jan. 17, 1933-Jan. 15, 1935	Housewife	Bell County, Texas	June 13, 1875- June 25, 1961
Dan Moody Jan. 17, 1927-Jan. 20, 1931	Lawyer	Taylor, Texas	June 1, 1893- May 22, 1966
Ross S. Sterling Jan. 20, 1931-Jan. 17, 1933	Oil firm executive	Anahuac, Texas	Feb. 11, 1875- Mar. 25, 1949
Miriam A. (Ma) Ferguson		(see information above)	
James V. Allred Jan. 15, 1935-Jan. 17, 1939	Lawyer	Bowie, Texas	Mar. 29, 1899- Sept. 24, 1959
W. Lee (Pappy) O'Daniel Jan. 17, 1939-Aug. 4, 1941 (Resigned to enter U. S. Senate.)	Salesman	Malta, Ohio	Mar. 11, 1890- May 11, 1969
Coke R. Stevenson Aug. 4, 1941-Jan. 21, 1947 (As lieutenant governor, Stevenson became governor when O'Daniel resigned.)	Lawyer, Rancher	Mason Co., Texas	Mar. 20, 1888
Beauford H. Jester Jan. 21, 1947-July 11, 1949 (Died while in office.)	Lawyer	Corsicana, Texas	Jan. 12, 1893- July 11, 1949
Allan Shivers July 11, 1949-Jan. 15, 1957 (As lieutenant governor, Shivers became governor when Jester died.)	Lawyer	Lufkin, Texas	Oct. 5, 1907
Price Daniel Jan. 15, 1957-Jan. 15, 1963	Lawyer, Rancher	Dayton, Texas	Oct. 10, 1910
John B. Connally Jan. 15, 1963-Jan. 21, 1969	Lawyer, Rancher	Floresville, Texas	Feb. 27, 1917
Preston Smith Jan. 21, 1969-	Businessman	Corn Hill, Texas	Mar. 8, 1912

U. S. SENATORS FROM TEXAS†

Houston Succession

Name	Term
Sam Houston	Feb. 21, 1846-March 4, 1859
John Hemphill	March 4, 1859-July 11, 1861

(Louis T. Wigfall and W. S. Oldham served in the Confederate Senate from Nov. 16, 1861, until the fall of the Confederacy. On Aug. 21, 1866, the Texas Legislature elected David G. Burnet, who had served as first president of the Republic of Texas, and Oran M. Roberts, who later served as governor, to the U. S. Senate—anticipating immediate readmission to the Union—but they were not permitted to take their seats.)

Name	Term
*Morgan C. Hamilton	Feb. 22, 1870-March 3, 1877
Richard Coke	March 4, 1877-March 3, 1895
Horace Chilton	March 3, 1895-March 3, 1901
Joseph W. Bailey	March 3, 1901-Jan. 8, 1913
**R. M. Johnson	Jan. 8, 1913-Feb. 3, 1913
‡Morris Sheppard	Feb. 13, 1913-April 9, 1941
**Andrew J. Houston	June 2, 1941-June 26, 1941
W. Lee O'Daniel	Aug. 4, 1941-Jan. 3, 1949
Lyndon B. Johnson	Jan. 3, 1949-Jan. 20, 1961
**William A. Blakley	Jan. 20, 1961-June 15, 1961
*John G. Tower	June 15, 1961-

Rusk Succession

Name	Term
‡Thomas J. Rusk	Feb. 21, 1846-July 29, 1857
‡J. Pinckney Henderson	Nov. 9, 1857-June 4, 1858
**Matthias Ward	Sept. 29, 1858-Dec. 5, 1859

(Succession broken by secession from Union)

Name	Term
*James W. Flanagan	Feb. 22, 1870-March 3, 1875
Samuel B. Maxey	March 3, 1875-March 3, 1887
John H. Reagan	March 3, 1887-June 10, 1891
**Horace Chilton	Dec. 7, 1891-March 30, 1892
Roger Q. Mills	March 30, 1892-March 3, 1899
Charles A. Culberson	March 3, 1899-March 4, 1923
Earle B. Mayfield	March 4, 1923-March 4, 1929
Tom Connally	March 4, 1929-Jan. 3, 1953
Price Daniel	Jan. 3, 1953-Jan. 15, 1957
**William A. Blakley	Jan. 15, 1957-April 27, 1957
Ralph W. Yarborough	April 27, 1957-Jan. 3, 1971
Lloyd M. Bentsen, Jr.	Jan. 3, 1971-

*Republican members
**Appointed to fill vacancies
‡Died in office

†These lists, and those following of the Attorneys General, Secretaries of State, State Treasurers, Commissioners of the General Land Office, the Texas Railroad Commission and Comptrollers of Public Accounts were compiled by the *Texas Almanac and State Industrial Guide*, published and copyrighted by A. H. Belo Corp., Dallas, Texas, and are reprinted by permission.

ATTORNEYS GENERAL

Name	Term
Volney E. Howard	Feb. 21, 1846-May 7, 1846
John W. Harris	May 7, 1846-Oct. 31, 1849
Henry P. Brewster	Oct. 31, 1849-Jan. 15, 1850
A. J. Hamilton	Jan. 15, 1850-Aug. 5, 1850
Ebenezer Allen	Aug. 5, 1850-Aug. 2, 1852

Ebenezer Allen was the State's first elected Attorney General. Prior to his election in 1850, the Attorney General was appointed by the Governor.

Thomas J. Jennings	Aug. 2, 1852-Aug. 4, 1856
James Willie	Aug. 4, 1856-Aug. 2, 1858
Malcolm D. Graham	Aug. 2, 1858-Aug. 6, 1860
George M. Flournoy	Aug. 6, 1860-Jan. 15, 1862
N. G. Shelley	Feb. 3, 1862-Aug. 1, 1864
B. E. Tarver	Aug. 1, 1864-Dec. 11, 1865
William Alexander	Dec. 11, 1865-June 25, 1866
W. M. Walton	June 25, 1866-Aug. 27, 1867
William Alexander	Aug. 27, 1867-Nov. 5, 1867
Ezekiel B. Turner	Nov. 5, 1867-July 11, 1870
William Alexander	July 11, 1870-Jan. 27, 1874
George Clark	Jan. 27, 1874-April 25, 1876
H. H. Boone	April 25, 1876-Nov. 5, 1878
George McCormick	Nov. 5, 1878-Nov. 2, 1880
J. H. McLeary	Nov. 2, 1880-Nov. 7, 1882
John D. Templeton	Nov. 7, 1882-Nov. 2, 1886
*James S. Hogg	Nov. 2, 1886-Nov. 4, 1890
*Charles A. Culberson	Nov. 4, 1890-Nov. 6, 1894
M. M. Crane	Nov. 6, 1894-Nov. 8, 1898
Thomas S. Smith	Nov. 8, 1898-March 15, 1901
C. K. Bell	March 20, 1901-January, 1904
R. V. Davidson	January, 1904-Dec. 31, 1909
Jewel P. Lightfoot	Jan. 1, 1910-Aug. 31, 1912
James D. Walthall	Sept. 1, 1912-Jan. 1, 1913
B. F. Looney	Jan. 1, 1913-January, 1919
C. M. Cureton	January, 1919-December, 1921
W. A. Keeling	December, 1921-January, 1925
*Dan Moody	January, 1925-January, 1927
Claude Pollard	January, 1927-September, 1929
R. L. Bobbitt (appointed)	September, 1929-January, 1931
*James V. Allred	January, 1931-January, 1935
William McCraw	January, 1935-January, 1939
Gerald C. Mann	January, 1939-January, 1944
Grover Sellers	January, 1944-January, 1947
*Price Daniel	January, 1947-January, 1953
John Ben Shepperd	January, 1953-January 1, 1957
Will Wilson	January 1, 1957-January 15, 1963
Waggoner Carr	January 15, 1963-January 1, 1967
Crawford C. Martin	January 1, 1967-

*Later elected Governor of Texas

LIEUTENANT GOVERNORS

Name	Term
Albert Clinton Horton	1846-1847
John Alexander Greer	1847-1851
*James Wilson Henderson	1851-1853
David Catchings Dickson	1853-1855
*Hardin Richard Runnels	1855-1857
*Francis R. Lubbock	1857-1859
*Edward Clark	1859-1861
John McClannahan Crockett	1861-1863
Fletcher S. Stockdale	1863-1866
George Washington Jones	1866-1867
James Winwright Flanagan	1869-1870
*Richard Bennett Hubbard	1873-1876
Joseph D. Sayers	1878-1880
Leonidas J. Storey	1880-1882
Francis Marion Martin	1882-1884
Barnett Gibbs	1884-1886
Thomas Benton Wheeler	1886-1890
George Cassety Pendleton	1890-1892
Martin McNulty Crane	1892-1894
George Taylor Jester	1894-1898
James Nathan Browning	1898-1902
George D. Neal	1902-1906
Asbury Bascom Davidson	1906-1912
William Harding Mayes	1912-1914
*William P. Hobby	1914-1917
W. A. Johnson	1917-1920
Lynch Davidson	1920-1922
Thomas Whitfield Davidson	1922-1924
Barry Miller	1924-1931
Edgar Witt	1931-1935
Walter Frank Woodul	1935-1939
*Coke R. Stevenson	1939-1941
John Lee Smith	1943-1947
*Allan Shivers	1947-1949
Ben Ramsey	1951-1963
*Preston Smith	1963-1969
Ben Barnes	1969-

*Later became Governor of Texas.

SPEAKERS, TEXAS HOUSE OF REPRESENTATIVES

Name	*Term*
W. E. Crump	1846-1847
J. W. Henderson	1847-1849
C. G. Keenan	1849-1851
D. C. Dickson	1851-1853
H. R. Runnels	1853-1855
H. P. Bee	1855-1857
William S. Taylor	1857-1859
M. D. K. Taylor	1859-1861
N. H. Darnell	1861-1863
M. D. K. Taylor	1863-1866
N. M. Burford	1866-1870
Ira H. Evans	1870-1873
M. D. K. Taylor	1873-1874
Guy M. Bryan	1874-1876
T. R. Bonner	1876-1879
John H. Cochran	1879-1881
George R. Reeves	1881-1883
C. R. Gibson	1883-1885
L. L. Foster	1885-1887
George C. Pendleton	1887-1889
F. P. Alexander	1889-1891
R. T. Milner	1891-1893
John H. Cochran	1893-1895
T. S. Smith	1895-1897
L. T. Dashiell	1897-1899
J. S. Sherrill	1899-1901
R. E. Prince	1901-1903
Pat M. Neff	1903-1905
F. W. Seabury	1905-1907
Thomas B. Love	1907-1909
A. M. Kennedy	1909
John Marshall	1909-1911
Sam Rayburn	1911-1913
Chester H. Terrell	1913-1915
John W. Woods	1915-1917
F. O. Fuller	1917-1919
R. E. Thomason	1919-1921
Charles G. Thomas	1921-1923
R. E. Seagler	1923-1925
Lee Satterwhite	1925-1927
Robert Lee Bobbitt	1927-1929
W. S. Barron	1929-1931

SPEAKERS (Continued)

Name	*Term*
Fred Minor	1931-1933
Coke R. Stevenson	1933-1937
Robert W. Calvert	1937-1939
R. Emmett Morse	1939-1941
Homer Leonard	1941-1943
Price Daniel	1943-1945
Claud Gilmer	1945-1947
W. O. Reed	1947-1949
Durwood Manford	1949-1951
Reuben Senterfitt	1951-1955
Jim Lindsey	1955-1957
Waggoner Carr	1957-1961
James Turman	1961-1963
Byron Tunnell	1963-1965
Ben Barnes	1965-1969
G. F. "Gus" Mutscher	1969-

SECRETARIES OF STATE

Name	Term
Charles Mariner	Feb. 20, 1846-May 4, 1846
David G. Burnet	May 4, 1846-Jan. 1, 1848
Washington D. Miller	Jan. 1, 1848-Jan. 2, 1850
James Webb	Jan. 2, 1850-Nov. 14, 1851
Thomas H. Duval	Nov. 14, 1851-Dec. 22, 1853
Edward Clark	Dec. 22, 1853-December, 1857
T. S. Anderson	December, 1857-Dec. 27, 1859
E. W. Cave	Dec. 27, 1859-March 16, 1861
Bird Holland	March 16, 1861-November, 1861
Charles West	November, 1861-September, 1862
Robert J. Townes	September, 1862-May 2, 1865
Charles R. Pryor	May 2, 1865-August, 1865
James H. Bell	August, 1865-August, 1866
John A. Green	August, 1866-August, 1867
D. W. C. Phillips	August, 1867-January, 1870
J. P. Newcomb	January, 1870-Jan. 17, 1874
George Clark	Jan. 17, 1874-Jan. 27, 1874
A. W. DeBerry	Jan. 27, 1874-Dec. 1, 1876
Isham G. Searcy	Dec. 1, 1876-Jan. 23, 1879
J. D. Templeton	Jan. 23, 1879-Jan. 22, 1881
T. H. Bowman	Jan. 22, 1881-Jan. 18, 1883
J. W. Baines	Jan. 18, 1883-Jan. 21, 1887
John M. Moore	Jan. 21, 1887-Jan. 22, 1891
George W. Smith	Jan. 22, 1891-Jan. 17, 1895
Allison Mayfield	Jan. 17, 1895-Jan. 5, 1897
J. W. Madden	Jan. 5, 1897-Jan. 18, 1899
D. H. Hardy	Jan. 18, 1899-Jan. 19, 1901
John G. Tod	Jan. 19, 1901-January, 1903
J. R. Curl	January, 1903-April, 1905
O. K. Shannon	April, 1905-January, 1907
L. T. Dashiell	January, 1907-February, 1908
W. R. Davie	February, 1908-January, 1909
W. B. Townsend	January, 1909-January, 1911
C. C. McDonald	January, 1911-December, 1912
J. T. Bowman	December, 1912-January, 1913
John L. Wortham	January, 1913-June, 1913
F. C. Weinert	June, 1913-November, 1914
D. A. Gregg	November, 1914-January, 1915
John G. McKay	January, 1915-December, 1916
C. J. Bartlett	December, 1916-November, 1917
George F. Howard	November, 1917-November, 1920
C. D. Mims	November, 1920-January, 1921

SECRETARIES OF STATE (Continued)

Name	*Term*
S. L. Staples	January, 1921-August, 1924
J. D. Strickland	September, 1924-Jan. 1, 1925
Henry Hutchings	Jan. 1, 1925-Jan. 20, 1925
Mrs. Emma G. Meharg	Jan. 20, 1925-January, 1927
Mrs. Jane Y. McCallum	January, 1927-January, 1933
W. W. Heath	January, 1933-January, 1935
Gerald C. Mann	January, 1935-Aug. 31, 1935
R. B. Stanford	Aug. 31, 1935-August, 1936
B. P. Matocha	August, 1936-January, 1937
Edward Clark	January, 1937-January, 1939
Tom L. Beauchamp	January, 1939-October, 1939
M. O. Flowers	October, 1939-January, 1941
William J. Lawson	January, 1941-January, 1943
Sidney Latham	January, 1943-February, 1945
Claude Isbell	February, 1945-January, 1947
Paul H. Brown	January, 1947-Jan. 19, 1949
Ben Ramsey	Jan. 19, 1949-Feb. 9, 1950
John Ben Shepperd	Feb. 9, 1950-April 30, 1952
Jack Ross	April 30, 1952-Jan. 9, 1953
Howard A. Carney	Jan. 9, 1953-May 1, 1954
C. E. Fulgham	May 1, 1954-Jan. 21, 1955
Al Muldrow	Jan. 21, 1955-Nov. 1, 1955
Tom Reavley	Nov. 1, 1955-Jan. 15, 1957
Zollie Steakley	Jan. 16, 1957-Jan. 2, 1962
P. Frank Lake	Jan. 2, 1962-Jan. 15, 1963
Crawford C. Martin	Jan. 15, 1963-March 12, 1966
John L. Hill	March 12, 1966-Jan. 22, 1968
Roy Barrera	March 7, 1968-Jan. 23, 1969
Martin Dies, Jr.	Jan. 23, 1969-Sept. 1, 1971
Robert D. Bullock	Sept. 1, 1971-

STATE TREASURERS

Name	*Term*
James H. Raymond	Feb. 24, 1846-Aug. 2, 1858
C. H. Randolph	Aug. 2, 1858-Oct. 2, 1865
Samuel Harris	Oct. 2, 1865-June 25, 1866
W. M. Royston	June 25, 1866-Sept. 1, 1867
John Y. Allen	Sept. 1, 1867-January, 1869
*George W. Honey	January, 1869-January, 1874
A. J. Dorn	January, 1874-January, 1879
F. R. Lubbock	January, 1879-January, 1891
W. B. Wortham	January, 1891-January, 1899
John W. Robbins	January, 1899-January, 1907
Sam Sparks	January, 1907-January, 1912
J. M. Edwards	January, 1912-January, 1919
John W. Baker	January, 1919-January, 1921
G. N. Holton	July, 1921-Nov. 21, 1921
C. V. Terrell	Nov. 21, 1921-Aug. 15, 1924
S. L. Staples	Aug. 16, 1924-Jan. 15, 1925
W. Gregory Hatcher	Jan. 16, 1925-Jan. 1, 1931
Charley Lockhart	Jan. 1, 1931-Oct. 25, 1941
Jesse James	Oct. 25, 1941-

*Honey was removed from office for a short time in 1872 and B. Graham replaced him for that brief interval, beginning May 27, 1872.

COMMISSIONERS OF THE GENERAL LAND OFFICE

Name	Term
George W. Smyth	March 20, 1848-Aug. 4, 1851
Stephen Crosby	Aug. 4, 1851-March 1, 1858
Francis M. White	March 1, 1858-March 1, 1862
Stephen Crosby	March 1, 1862-Sept. 1, 1865
Francis M. White	Sept. 1, 1865-Aug. 7, 1866
Stephen Crosby	Aug. 7, 1866-Aug. 27, 1867
Joseph Spence	Aug. 27, 1867-Jan. 19, 1870
Jacob Kuechler	Jan. 19, 1870-Jan. 20, 1874
J. J. Groos	Jan. 20, 1874-June 15, 1878
W. C. Walsh	July 30, 1878-Jan. 10, 1887
R. M. Hall	Jan. 10, 1887-Jan. 16, 1891
W. L. McGaughey	Jan. 16, 1891-Jan. 26, 1895
A. J. Baker	Jan. 26, 1895-Jan. 16, 1899
George W. Finger	Jan. 16, 1899-May 4, 1899
Charles Rogan	May 11, 1899-January, 1903
John J. Terrell	Jan. 10, 1903-Jan. 11, 1909
J. T. Robison	January, 1909-Sept. 11, 1929
J. H. Walker	Sept. 11, 1929-January, 1937
William H. McDonald	January, 1937-January, 1939
Bascom Giles	January, 1939-Jan. 5, 1955
J. Earl Rudder	Jan. 5, 1955-Feb. 1, 1958
Bill Allcorn	Feb. 1, 1958-Jan. 1, 1961
Jerry Sadler	Jan. 1, 1961-Jan. 1, 1971
Robert L. Armstrong	Jan. 1, 1971-

TEXAS RAILROAD COMMISSION

(Three members, each elected for a 6-year term)

John H. Reagan, June 10, 1891-Jan. 20, 1903
L. L. Foster, June 10, 1891-April 30, 1895
W. P. McLean, June 10, 1891-Nov. 20, 1894
L. J. Storey (succeeding W. P. McLean), Nov. 21, 1894-March 28, 1909
N. A. Stedman (succeeding L. L. Foster), May 1, 1895-Jan. 4, 1897
Allison Mayfield (succeeding N. A. Stedman), Jan. 5, 1897-Jan. 23, 1923
O. B. Colquitt (succeeding John H. Reagan), Jan. 21, 1903-Jan. 17, 1911
William D. Williams (succeeding L. J. Storey), April 28, 1909-Oct. 1, 1916
John L. Wortham (succeeding O. B. Colquitt), Jan. 21, 1911-Jan. 1, 1913
Earle B. Mayfield (succeeding John L. Wortham), Jan. 2, 1913-Mar. 1, 1923
Charles H. Hurdleston (succeeding William D. Williams), Oct. 10, 1916-
    Dec. 31, 1918
Clarence E. Gilmore (succeeding Charles H. Hurdleston), Jan. 1, 1919-
    Jan. 1, 1929
N. A. Nabors (succeeding Allison Mayfield), March 1, 1923-Jan. 18, 1925
W. M. W. Splawn (succeeding Earle B. Mayfield), March 1, 1923-Aug. 1,
    1924
C. V. Terrell (succeeding W. M. W. Splawn), Aug. 15, 1924-Jan. 1, 1939
Lon A. Smith (succeeding W. A. Nabors), Jan. 19, 1925-Jan. 1, 1941
Pat M. Neff (succeeding Clarence E. Gilmore), Jan. 1, 1929-Jan. 1, 1933
Ernest O. Thompson (succeeding Pat M. Neff), Jan. 1, 1933-Jan. 8, 1965
G. A. Sadler (succeeding C. V. Terrell), Jan. 1, 1939-Jan. 1, 1943
Olin Culberson (succeeding Lon A. Smith), Jan. 1, 1941-June 22, 1961
Beauford Jester (succeeding G. A. Sadler), Jan. 1, 1943-Jan. 21, 1947
William J. Murray, Jr. (succeeding Beauford Jester), Jan. 21, 1947-April 10,
    1963
Jim C. Langdon, Jr. (succeeding William J. Murray, Jr.), May 28, 1963-
Ben Ramsey (succeeding Olin Culberson), Sept. 18, 1961-
Byron Tunnell (succeeding Ernest O. Thompson), Jan. 8, 1965-

COMPTROLLERS OF PUBLIC ACCOUNTS

Name	*Term*
James B. Shaw	Feb. 24, 1846-Aug. 2, 1858
Clement R. Johns	Aug. 2, 1858-Aug. 1, 1864
Willis L. Robards	Aug. 1, 1864-Oct. 12, 1865
Albert H. Latimer	Oct. 12, 1865-March 27, 1866
Robert H. Taylor	March 27, 1866-June 25, 1866
Willis L. Robards	June 25, 1866-Aug. 27, 1867
Morgan C. Hamilton	Aug. 27, 1867-Jan. 8, 1870
A. Bledsoe	Jan. 8, 1870-Jan. 20, 1874
Stephen H. Darden	Jan. 20, 1874-Nov. 2, 1880
W. M. Brown	Nov. 2, 1880-Jan. 16, 1883
W. J. Swain	Jan. 16, 1883-Jan. 18, 1887
John D. McCall	Jan. 18, 1887-Jan. 15, 1895
R. W. Finley	Jan. 15, 1895-Jan. 15, 1901
R. M. Love	Jan. 15, 1901-January, 1903
J. W. Stephen	January, 1903-January, 1911
W. P. Lane	January, 1911-January, 1915
H. B. Terrell	January, 1915-January, 1920
M. L. Wiginton	January, 1920-January, 1921
Lon A. Smith	January, 1921-January, 1925
S. H. Terrell	January, 1925-January, 1931
George H. Sheppard	January, 1931-Jan. 17, 1949
Robert S. Calvert	Jan. 17, 1949-

INDEX

271